AF628498

Sandra Johnston

Beyond Reasonable Doubt

European Studies in Culture and Policy

edited by

Prof. Máiréad Nic Craith
and
Prof. Ullrich Kockel
(Heriot-Watt University, Edinburgh)

Volume 13

LIT

Sandra Johnston

Beyond Reasonable Doubt

An Investigation of Doubt, Risk and Testimony
Through Performance Art Processes
in Relation to Systems of Legal Justice

LIT

Cover image: Nils Kenninck

Printed with support of The Golden Thread Gallery,
Belfast, Northern Ireland

This book is printed on acid-free paper.

Bibliographic information published by the Deutsche Nationalbibliothek
The Deutsche Nationalbibliothek lists this publication in the Deutsche Nationalbibliografie; detailed bibliographic data are available in the Internet at http://dnb.d-nb.de.

ISBN 978-3-643-90440-9

A catalogue record for this book is available from the British Library

Klosbachstr. 107
CH-8032 Zürich
Tel. +41 (0) 44-251 75 05
Fax +41 (0) 44-251 75 06
E-Mail: zuerich@lit-verlag.ch
http://www.lit-verlag.ch

LIT VERLAG Dr. W. Hopf
Berlin 2014
Fresnostr. 2
D-48159 Münster
Tel. +49 (0) 2 51-62 03 20
Fax +49 (0) 2 51-23 19 72
E-Mail: lit@lit-verlag.de
http://www.lit-verlag.de

Distribution:
In Germany: LIT Verlag Fresnostr. 2, D-48159 Münster
Tel. +49 (0) 2 51-620 32 22, Fax +49 (0) 2 51-922 60 99, E-mail: vertrieb@lit-verlag.de
In Austria: Medienlogistik Pichler-ÖBZ, e-mail: mlo@medien-logistik.at
In the UK: Global Book Marketing, e-mail: mo@centralbooks.com
In North America: International Specialized Book Services, e-mail: orders@isbs.com
e-books are available at www.litwebshop.de

ACKNOWLEDGEMENTS

Sandra Johnston's sincere thanks go to Margaret and Eric Johnston,

and Mia Lerm Hayes, Brandon Hamber, Willie Doherty, Alastair MacLennan, Dominic Thorpe, Brian Catling, Heike Roms, Shirley MacWilliam, Marilyn Arsem, Boris Nieslony, Slavka Sverakova, Hugh Mulholland, Aarhus Art Building, Helle Hansen, Pauline Cummins, Frances Mezzetti, Mary McIntyre, Susanne Bosch, Sally Taylor, Laura Graham, Fergus Byrne, Bbeyond, Peter Richards and all the staff at the Golden Thread Gallery.

Christa-Maria Lerm Hayes: to Hugh and Liam and Belfast artists – with love.

We would particularly like to thank the JOSEPH BEUYS-STIFTUNG, Basel, for their contribution that enabled us to realise this publication in this form; the Golden Thread Gallery, Belfast, Ulli Kockel and Máiréad Nic Craith for including this book in their series and Miriam de Búrca for editing.

Front Cover: Sandra Johnston, *REMEMBE::RED*, 2011, solo performance for TO BE PRESENT: LIVE NO TECH, commissioned by Anet van de Elzen and Mirjam Westen at MMKA Museum, Arnhem, Holland. Photo: courtesy Nils Kenninck.

CONTENTS

FOREWORD

Peter RICHARDS, Director, Golden Thread Gallery, Belfast

Toward the end of 2012 I had the great pleasure of working with Sandra Johnston on the realisation of her solo exhibition *The Shadow of a Doubt* at the Golden Thread Gallery in Belfast. Every year, we set out to work with an artist whose practice makes a significant contribution to the formation and understanding of the region's visual language, and offers an insight into approaches that have been employed to make sense of the often incomprehensible and contradictory versions of our recent history.

Johnston is perhaps best known for her performance art practice: exploring and challenging the strategies of ambiguity, narratives and counter narratives. In *The Shadow of a Doubt* she offered an insight into the breadth of the artistic processes and the variety of engagements with materials that she has explored to date. The resulting exhibition took the form of an enveloping installation, comprised of a number of individual yet sensitively interrelated works. The installation appeared as a collection of fragments in the form of found and adapted objects, text, videos, performance gestures and the filmed documentation of actions.

The exhibition's title was borrowed from a term in law that relates to an act of judgement, and offered the viewer a way into the competing dialogues located between the shifting material and loaded qualities of the installation. At the centre of the exhibition there were nine chairs that Johnston had acquired from a scrap yard after they had been salvaged from the Maze prison. Johnston referred to them "as extending the dialogue about the retracing pivotal moments of the 1980s through recollecting the mediatised versions of events paralleling them with memories of a protected home life" (press release). Present throughout the exhibition was a poignant sense of personal history wrestling with collective memories.

Here I have the great privilege of welcoming the *Beyond Reasonable Doubt* publication as it comprehensively sets out to record aspects of the contexts and themes, relating to Sandra Johnston's ongoing practice as an artist. Professor Christa-Maria Lerm Hayes an art historian, curator and critic, University of Ulster, within her substantive introductory essay insightfully offers a sense of the artistic, socio-political and psycho-historical contexts that have contributed to and been challenged by Sandra Johnston through her practice.

Sandra Johnston's study illuminates a multitude of entry points to her practice and sets the scene for critical discourses concerning contemporary art in Northern Ireland with regard to the nature of art and conflict, contested histories, mediation and trauma. Her contribution, and that of art in such contexts, concerns the central role of witnessing and gesture. She sets up a space for doubt, risk and ephemeral exchange where words have failed. It is all the more remarkable then that this book exists: this major study is the first monograph in relation to Northern Irish performance art, long internationally highly regarded, but very much under-researched and, while continuously present in Belfast public spaces, also under-exhibited.

Beyond Reasonable Doubt is a significant and timely contribution to understanding gesture, testimony and evidence in legal and artistic contexts, as well as the breadth of Sandra Johnston's art practice and contemporary art from Northern Ireland. In documenting the exhibition and adding the artist's study and academic writing to it, this publication offers the reader access to all aspects of Johnston's practice and her interrogations of its formative context.

Sandra Johnston: Doubt, Gesture, Love And The Paradoxes Of (Political) Art In Northern Ireland

Christa-Maria Lerm Hayes

This text seeks to introduce and complement Sandra Johnston's study by focussing on aspects of her practice and creating – mostly oblique – links to the investigation in front of us. It also occupies a privileged position (I am implicated you could say), as I have had the opportunity to accompany Johnston's writing process[1] and view repeatedly the exhibition that arose from her work on Northern Ireland and the relationships between (her) performance art practice and systems of legal justice. This exhibition at the Golden Thread Gallery, *The Shadow of a Doubt*, is represented in this book through installation shots and stills. Recourse is needed to the means and to contexts of Johnston's practice, to the meanings in and for art and Northern Ireland that are conjured and evoked – sensitively.

I will fail to do justice to Johnston's work. This is not only because I have viewed far too few of her performances, have worked in Belfast for too short – or too long – to reach understanding, or started and stopped writing far too often. The doubt that has guided Sandra Johnston in the creation of her work, however, needs to remain with us throughout. This is an important reminder – and Johnston's study takes in and through its humility a powerful position – because all too many certainties still pervade this part of the world. (Re-)reading Thomas McEvilley's "The Art of Doubting" is recommended to students, audiences, politicians here and elsewhere

1 It was a privilege to supervise Sandra Johnston's PhD together with Willie Doherty and Brandon Hamber. I thank them all. Over the three years, I usually did not keep notes of conversations, but here I have to use some information that arose from them. I kept detailed notes of the viva with Brian Catling, Heike Roms and Shirley MacWilliam (Johnston et al. 2012).

(McEvilley 1999: 3-30). It also explains simply and effectively why the university was ultimately the right home for Johnston in undertaking her study, as Karl Popper is quoted: "The scientific method means questioning everything" (McEvilley 1999: 4).

When Johnston's exhibition *The Shadow of a Doubt* took place at the end of 2012, the internationally mediatized flag protests provided a direct point of connection, a spectacle against which Johnston's work could be read and which the visitors of her performance and exhibition opening had to brave, in order to attend. Then our sense of loss was quite overpowering. Johnston and other highly respected artists had recently left the art college in Belfast, which had for difficult decades employed artists who were in the right place for the right reasons and attracted excellent students, who themselves became respected artists and teachers, not least Sandra Johnston. The University of Ulster could until then with some justification claim to have created and sustained "shared spaces" and a pre-eminent vehicle for social recuperation. Now it became evident – as it is in so many places – that we had not as yet succeeded (not even through moneys and reputation gained) to convince those in the region who are tasked with supporting art of its value, or even just to consider it beneficial for sustaining the edgy tourism magnet that Belfast had become. All that despite the fact that many books have been written, even in a popular science mode (Nussbaum 2010; Readings 1996), about the necessity of art and the humanities for a democratic society (and a functioning economy!). Public life in Northern Ireland, inadequately masking uncertainties deriving from an understandable lack of experience with democracy likes to appear certain, "normal" – and that for many translates into a disinterest in art, ideas – and democracy. I am not alone in confronting the difficulty of speaking with certainty about the necessity of doubt.[2]

It is quiet now, a lovely, sunny afternoon in Belfast – on 12th July 2013. As the helicopters are faintly heard across the city, there is understandable desperation for some in the arts (Jewesbury 2013), quiet resignation and a numb carrying on for others, much advance compliance, or even faint hope – in the knowledge, however, that both the task of acting and creating freely and constructively under the circumstances and the obstacles are dauntingly

---

2 See Nancy on the violence of truth, particularly (2012: 37, 28).

large. It is also a calm before the storm, as the building that has for so long been associated with Belfast's artistic excellence, the Co-op, or Orpheus building, of Northern Ireland's only art school in whose ballroom many a local fell in love, is about to be demolished. It will be replaced by an over-sized office block that will advertise through cheap red-brick cladding (functioning as spoliation) what one had no qualms of destroying. It will reveal and invalidate in the same breath the institution's wish to be a "red brick university". This will be a victor's architecture, untroubled by doubt and unaware of positions such as Jane Jacobs' dictum "new ideas need old buildings", (which the Heritage Lottery Fund has adopted as its motto).

My approach will have to be more varied than these paragraphs let appear, as it is easy to write a pamphlet, to express pain when something that we love – and we can take this love to be the common denominator – is being endangered, possibly destroyed. To remain in pamphlet or manifesto mode, however, would not do justice to Sandra Johnston's achievement. I need to take a leaf out of Johnston's, out of this book, and present several (not neatly distinguishable) voices, one being a "tranquilized spectrality" (I shall explore the term) of – in this case – descriptions of Johnston's exhibition. Beyond this, uncertainty also remains, as "It is not clear, at least to me, exactly how to change the register of the conversation when talk goes from a picture's structure, or even its politics, to its agency, its voice, its life" (Elkins, Naef 2011: 9). Boring or unsettling as this may sound, it is necessary to try to juxtapose accounts: the exhibition is worth knowing about and investigating in detail, and it is worth taking seriously that unbroken accounts are not for Johnston. Furthermore, trying to move in and out of cooler descriptive or academic prose may prevent me from replicating too much of what I am critiquing. I also wish to foreground and acknowledge emotion as a vital part of our ethical reasoning (Nussbaum 2008), be it in performance art or in the writing about it. It is necessary then also to explore how to write about it, which art-historical / theoretical traditions may suit. Lastly, it is at least intended to conjure love against all the odds, a complicated, non-triumphant hope that I wish to tease out of Johnston's practice and by extension Northern Irish performance art – if not the current situation at large (32 police officers were injured, some critically, last night).

Among the many merits of Sandra Johnston's study *Beyond Reasonable Doubt* is that she found a voice, or a multiplicity of voices that are capable with both appropriate assertiveness and poetry to pose the modes of contribution that (her) (performance) art can make to (our understanding of) legal processes, which seek to find truths in and for (post-)traumatic contexts, such as that of Northern Ireland. She did so with a humility, subtlety and precision that immeasurably aide the investigation and are born out of her practice and experience, in order to be returned to both: to practice as it manifested itself in her exhibition *Shadow of Doubt*, Golden Thread Gallery Belfast, and to the experience of her audiences, as well as the readers of this volume.

In this introduction, therefore, there is no need to double up. I wish to begin at the time of the exhibition (December 2012 / January 2013) and set the scene with what I hope to elaborate in more detail: some of the works (in the exhibition or outside), short remarks on some "political" artworks in Northern Ireland, as well as some art-historical and philosophical foundations: a rough genealogy of positions that for the purposes of social / democratic commitment obliquely focus on sensitivity and (artistic) autonomy and oppose the spectacle as much as possible.[3] Considerations of gesture will take me to Warburg, failure to Beckett and love to Joyce. What I am attempting to trace is itself subject to the paradoxes conveyed: they are most truthfully captured in and through their inabilities, their doubts.

BELFAST 2012/13

As Sandra Johnston installed her exhibition, the effects of the symbolic order (the domain particularly of art) on the lives of people is again demonstrated: the suggestion of flying the Union Jack from the City Hall in Belfast for only 17 days a year met with flag-waving "protests" that saw over those few days several dozen people injured and resulted in the destruction of offices of the moderate Unionist Alliance Party, as well as death threats to its politicians. It was not that they had suggested that the Irish Tricolour be flown on the other days, or on any day. The temporary absence of the flag caused offence. The protesters' rhetoric culminated in the pronouncement

[3] "To analyze the spectacle means talking its language to some degree – to the degree, in fact, that we are obliged to engage the methodology of the society to which the spectacle gives expression. For what the spectacle expresses is the total practice of one particular economic and social formation; it is, so to speak, that formation's agenda. It is also the historical moment by which we happen to be governed" (Debord 1967: I, 11).

that "Culture is the new theatre of war".[4] What – if any – avenue remains for artists to work in and on these conditions?

It seems like as viable strategy to me that, if culture is the new theatre of war, one may learn something about the symbolic order ("culture") and its regimes of performance and display ("theatre") on this field's terms. Have not Christo and Jeanne-Claude proven conclusively through their many projects of wrapping that occluding something may in fact strengthen the viewers' memory of it? Socially engaged artists such as Alfredo Jaar would seem to concur with Jim Allistair, stressing that culture really is the only arena in which one can today operate (Bishop 2006). However, it is unlikely that they mean the same. I am stating the obvious: images are contested and will always be part of their contexts. The question is how.

NORTHERN IRISH (POLITICAL) ART

According to the Arts Council-sanctioned narrative, Expressionist painting was the dominant artistic reaction to the Troubles (Long n.d.). Liam Kelly also asserts that artists responded to Bloody Sunday in 1972 by turning away from abstraction (if they did indeed practice it) and returned to figuration (Kelly 1996), presumably in order for their responses to be widely understood – if not directly and purposefully taken as supporting one side or the other. Expressionism's politics have been incisively discussed by Ernst Bloch and Georg Lukács in the late 1930s (Bloch et al. 1988), when initial Nazi approval for the movement needed to be understood. Its "apolitical" stance saw it heavily criticized by Lukács as open for co-option, while Bloch considered the stylistic means as meaningful, too, not just the overt content: they registered the disjointed nature of modernity via its emotional effects and thus it needed to be viewed as critical of the Nazis (who had misunderstood it, but then considered it to be "degenerate"). In the Northern Irish context, painters like Rita Duffy generally do not seem to have relied on a politics of form, but worked in ways that use relatively standard (political) iconography to convey emotional upheavals and generally unambiguous meaning directly, in order to "illustrate" symbolically arranged scenarios or events.

4 Jim Allister, TUV, during Belfast City Council debate 10th December 2012.

A pictorial strategy that appears to have learned from Bloch is Victor Sloan's. He has scratched marks into the negatives of images of political marches, bomb sites etc. Looking more closely, however, these marks do not universally register disturbance, they often overlay and may "censor" images, but they go with the drum beats: they are those of an accomplished artist more familiar with Hogarth's line of beauty than the probing and uncertainty of a Cy Twombly. The danger is that the symbolic order on view in the photographs' Northern Irish (political) motifs is aestheticized and thereby rendered harmless: an uncritical going along with the status quo. Only at another remove could the clash between the marks and the motifs be interpreted as an outcome of the desensitization that is a side effect of living with prolonged violence. But should we not hope that art might attempt an analysis, rather than just presenting symptoms? It is a difficult aspiration: to find artistic strategies in Northern Irish art that steer away from illustration, that take seriously the specific power of the image, while resisting its facile one-sided and triumphalist[5] employment.

If one chooses not to stop working as an artist under quite impossible conditions, such steadfastness can also become foolhardy. And this is not just because of one's own inevitable, human shortcomings (as an artist), but due to the fact that in this very context, where the (self-)destructive force of the power of images is again and again let loose, the academic field that seeks the image to be examined, mediated and (however deficiently) understood in its many facets, rationalized and somewhat curtailed in its still pervasive power, does not exist in this little part of Western Europe as a properly functioning part of the art "eco system". Art History with its 160 year-old academic history has, e.g. in Basel, where it arguably emerged, taken on the mantle of the "lead discipline"[6] in the humanities, enhancing through its image-critical work (*Bildwissenschaft*) the findings and credibility of all sciences and the law, which would otherwise employ images

5 Vikki Bell positions herself similarly: "This argument is developed in opposition to those who, looking for the signs of successful transition in Northern Ireland, point to the rise of commercial and 'cultural' interests as they are felt on the streets of the two major cities, Belfast and Derry. The process of 'normalization', here, becomes synonymous with the triumph of commercial capitalist enterprise" (Bell 2011: 326). See also Jewesbury (2005, 2013).

6 Symposium in honour of Gottfried Boehm, University of Basel and Schaulager, October 2012.

merely as un-reflected, naively conceived, supposedly unproblematic "evidence". Gottfried Boehm's and W.J.T. Mitchell's pictorial / iconic turn, proposed in the 1980s, claimed that the proliferation of images (accompanied by image fatigue particularly in heavily mediated places such as Northern Ireland) encouraged reception of images as proxy for living, as simulacrum, i.e. as distraction from the complex power of the multi-layered, ambiguous, even paradoxical image as which it can be employed in art. It is only now that one asks in English "What is an Image?" (Elkins, Naef 2011).

The excellent artistic work that has emerged in Northern Ireland during the Troubles and since (see Jewesbury 2005; Lerm Hayes, Walters 2011) thus requires interpretation and interpreters for its specific merits to be debated and understood, and in order to enable further complex, ambitious practice.[7] It seems vital to me to attempt this work of turning culture, the "new battleground", into a more complex space, where one may invite dissent, seek doubt, encourage agonistic encounters and ethical conversations in inclusive, ambiguous artistic modes of meaning-making. This may even over time – and obliquely pursued – create a happier, more diverse and rounded people, although all animals gathering around Orpheus' lyre is of course too idyllic an image to entertain.[8]

I need briefly to acknowledge the very unusual achievements of artists here, who have resorted to self-help, to writing about the contexts and theories pertaining to their areas of interest. Even despite an element of conflictedness – it would be preferable if others, too, were writing about the

7 According to Heinrich Dilly, speaking at CIHA Nuremberg July 2012, there are 24,000 people in Germany who have studied art history, half of whom work in the field. In relation to the population of Northern Ireland, there could (and should) thus be close to 250 art historians, cultural theorists, etc. There are about half a dozen who studied it elsewhere, or have come from art practice and write. One of the largest cohorts of PhDs with Practice in the UK, the PhD programme only compensates inadequately, even though a high percentage of artists in Northern Ireland are "artist philosophers". The doubt espoused in these pages goes nicely with a socially constructionist perspective, which can give us hints on what to do (Hannigan 2006: 78). The attested need for "Dramatisation" (the spectacle), however, presses exactly on the wound of what may prove counterproductive in and for visual art and is, therefore, in danger of preventing understanding and change.

8 A few public intellectuals and critics like Colin Graham, Daniel Jewesbury, Robert Porter, Slavka Sverakova and others have taken on this task. Paula Blair's work in relation to Sandra Johnston should be noted.

artists' works – the PhDs that have been more than worth-while, such as Sandra Johnston's, combine rigour and depth of commitment with humility and openness. Especially when the practice includes personal investment to the degree to which Johnston's work does, to interrogate and circumvent, where necessary, the elements of academic procedures that are experienced as stifling: I am in awe of the artist-philosophers who have achieved this.[9]

Northern Irish Performance Art

> Performance art practices in Northern Ireland since the 1970s, the idea emerges that physical presence in itself is a medium of protest [. . .] seemingly modest transgressions by MacLennan over several years could be seen as experiments with the parameters of tolerance. (Johnston 2013: epilogue)

Performance in and from Northern Ireland can be offered as that area of practice in which consistently over the last decades, ambitious, locally rooted and internationally visible artwork has been created (Talec 2012). It has featured occasionally, but not that prominently in the Golden Thread Gallery's series of guest-curated exhibitions forming *Collective Histories of Northern Irish Art*. One of its strengths is to have sought strategies in order not to be co-opted by one side or the other in the conflict. Alastair MacLennan's *Target*, 1977, literally a going back and forth across the interfaces, can be seen as exemplary.

Beckett

In order to point to the strengths of performance art in Northern Ireland, I would like to begin to investigate its strategies and achievements through brief consideration of Samuel Beckett.[10] Not only has Beckett been of importance to MacLennan, Johnston and others, he is likely to have developed his sense of art's complex stance towards politics and power – later honed in Nazi-occupied France – by his close familiarity with Northern Ireland's

9 As one of Johnston's supervisors, chair of various viva examinations and one-time leader of the programme, I need to record here the privilege that this work has meant for me.

10 The bigger Beckettian picture is planned to become a larger project in collaboration with Derval Tubridy at Goldsmiths, University of London.

tribal society in the early 20th century, thus providing in his work an analysis of the historical background of creativity in Northern Ireland today. I, therefore, offer Beckett as one of the founding moments of performance art in Northern Ireland – Joseph Beuys' presence here in 1974 being the other (Lerm Hayes, Walters 2011). Beckett's strategies and how they have been theorized also require a closer look in relation to Johnston's work.

Born in 1906 and coming from Dublin's protestant minority, Beckett was educated at Portora Royal College's boarding school, Enniskillen, Northern Ireland: fully belonging in neither place. Upon graduation, he taught at Belfast's Campbell College for a year, before he moved to Paris, worked for James Joyce, first wrote still in English, then in French. He turned towards the stage and later expanded his shorter and shorter plays-cum-performance works into the visual art field. When writing about Joyce's *Work in Progress* (*Finnegans Wake*), Beckett appears to have developed further what was earlier here connected with Bloch: the conviction that the art form and medium chosen must themselves be part of the interpretable means and meanings of the work: "Here form is content, content is form [... Joyce's] writing is not about something; it is that something itself." (Beach ed. 1929: 14)

Performance art in this sense – as it is aligned with visual art and not so much with traditional, naturalistic, non-Beckettian theatre – then does not in the first instance function as conveyor of a fixed narrative and unilateral meaning. Its focus is not, one could say, on what it can accomplish, but on what it fails to do and doubts. But it also does more than borrow the unintentional failures of Northern Irish political rituals and "performances". That would possibly result in farce or grotesque (to which we shall return). Instead, in Beckett and current local performance art, human failures, failures of the body over time and effects of embodied (traumatic) memories are evidenced, not played or acted out. Terry Eagleton, in his essay "Political Beckett?" focusses on what the politics of such a paring down and slowing down, of (ideally) de-spectacularized physical endurance work may be. Asserting (somewhat one-sidedly) that Beckett's work had been considered apolitical, Eagleton highlights that Beckett had risked all as a member of the *rèsistance,* that he had slept in ditches, knew hardship, hunger and fear. I.e. his anti-fascist politics could never be in doubt, but he chose not to pronounce smug certainties on account of this. Eagleton states:

> All one can salvage by way of consolidation is the fact that if reality is indeed indeterminate, then despair is not possible. An indeterminable universe must logically leave room for hope. If there are no absolutes, there can be no absolute assurance that Godot will not come or that the Nazis will triumph [...] if there is no sense of value in his universe, there would be no cause for so much shrieking and howling. Without some sense of value, we would not even be able to identify our plight as anything but normal. It is just that such value cannot be spoken outright for fear of its being ideologized, inflated to some sentimental humanism and so becoming part of the problem rather than the solution. Instead, value must manifest itself negatively, in the unswerving lucidity with which this writing confronts the unspeakable. (Eagleton 2006: 74)

It is Beckett's refusal to join triumphalism of any kind that enables the ethically superior position. Adorno's identification of Beckett's negative representation as the only thinkable strategy to connect art to the project of mourning the holocaust resonates here.[11] "Beckett's art maintains a [...] pact with failure in the teeth of Nazi triumphalism. [... He] knew that the sober, bleak-eyed realists serve the case of human emancipation more faithfully than the bright-eyed utopians" (Eagleton 2006: 74).

It is with this brief analysis of Beckett's politics and current Northern Irish public and artistic life in mind that we turn to Sandra Johnston's exhibition *The Shadow of Doubt.*

THE SHADOW OF DOUBT

Echoes of the British National Anthem accompany the viewer when entering the exhibition: we are embarking on a journey back in time, accompanied by two short texts, Cuttings 1 and Cuttings 2 (Johnston 2013: appendices). In these fragments, the artist poetically establishes connections between some of the works in the exhibition, gives insight into her thinking with regard to the connectedness of family history and memories to political and historical events, such as the hunger strikes of Republican prisoners at the Maze prison in 1981 and the 1982 bombings in London, where the IRA's casualties were not only soldiers, but also horses.

---

11 Didi-Huberman (2011) also insists, clearly in the wake of Deleuze and Guattari, that the merits of Kafka lie in the writings never engaging in triumphalism.

In Rank and File, 2012, a young woman, Queen Elizabeth as monarch in waiting, is seen on a large screen, parading on horse-back: a television experience from 1952, before Johnston was born. The monarch as intended anchor of certainty is presented in a context familiar to the artist. Familiarity and certainty are soon undone, however: the image is of low quality and in fact appears in double exposure. While one association may be televised Jubilees and Royal weddings, another would be the historical televisual "double take" when IRA members were interviewed and voiced-over by actors, who were eventually to speak their lines a-synchronously to the lip movements, so as to break empathy and de-humanize. Apart from a current television audience, those who are watching are also envisaged to be the absent (Republican) inmates of the Maze prison. The seating installed by Johnston in the gallery space are three groups of three welded-together plastic seats salvaged from the Maze prison. If the perspective of the televisual glitch is inverted, the viewers-cum-prisoners do not sit very solidly: these are cinema-like tilted seats, but they are orange and so don't serve one section of the population as very comforting "territory". Those who could sit comfortably, however, also won't, as the National Anthem is played, during which they would wish to stand. The chairs are welded together: a disciplining feature, so as to render them unsuitable as weapons. In fact, the groups lock the occupants in an arrangement reminiscent of interrogation (sharp neon light greets one when not looking at the screen) – or of the similarly disciplining and orange compulsive happiness of a McDonald's children's meal.

Johnston holds in suspense the multiply anchored identities and experiences with which most viewers in Northern Ireland / the North of Ireland will come equipped. Such assumptions are rendered conscious by being used for meaning-making, and they are minutely and multiply complicated, even shown to be paradoxical. The horse as an instrument of war and conveyor of status is likened by *Cuttings 2* to Sefton, originating from the Republic of Ireland and a target of the "Troubles" in London. The person who rode Sefton on the day of the bombing and nursed the horse back to health under media spotlight is revealed to have killed his family recently, 30 years later.

When the British National Anthem was played following cultural events, such as cinema screenings, they were to serve as an anchoring again in the certainty of power relations, i.e. reinstate exactly the notion that an artwork (any artwork) had likely worked to question. Adorno states: "Even in the most sublimated work of art there is a hidden 'it should be otherwise'" (Adorno 1962: 12). In hindsight, bringing the National Anthem back to an Arts Council-funded exhibition reveals that practice, which was formerly a condition of Arts Council funding, as counter-productive, as actively opposed to more democratic thinking, to the ways in which artworks (can) work, and thus opposed to hope. In its presence in the gallery this recent work measures the learning accomplished and acknowledges the considerable distance travelled. The work "homoeopathically" inserts the poison of old into a current context: one of analysis, remembering and possible healing.

For centuries, art has featured triumphant men on horseback. History painting and monumental sculpture are here (uncharacteristically) given attention – and found wanting: when not concentrating on coats and crisp packets at the end of the cinema night (of which *Cuttings 2* tells) a woman is seen on the back of a horse whose colour Johnston had not remembered.

As the monarch rides in a highly stylised, military and ritualistic formation, the horse does not obey. Another animal seems to throw all caution and training to the wind by nodding its head to the music. At the end, Elizabeth herself is seen as subject to the forces of nature: she needs to remove something from her eye and is seen to lift her gloved finger to do so. The minute attention that Johnston's art pays to her sources and that her exhibition instils in her viewers – without ever being didactic – reveals such glitches. And they demand to be explored.

This is formally acknowledged in the video's double exposure, but more than as a result of the viewers' double perspective, sitting or standing. Friend and foe are multiply intertwined, shown as human: Bobby Sands' favourite song was apparently *Jean Genie* by the British working class singer David Bowie. *Jean Genie* is a reference to (or mispronunciation of) Jean Genet's name, the writer, thief and homosexual who spent much of his writing life in prison. If there is anything it seems that both communities in Northern Ireland traditionally share it is homophobia – and still: Bobby Sands enjoyed Bowie's fascination with Genet and may indeed have identified with the prisoner and rogue Genet, who spelled sub-cultural cool.

Johnston was, with glittering swimsuit and gulping Coca-Cola, a child of the same times. Sand's starvation and dying, never discussed by the children in the Johnston household, is linked in the artist's memory with the dying of an inappropriately placed apple tree on the farm, whose fruit tasted bitter, just like the orange, the last thing Sands ate, had reportedly tasted for him (Cuttings 1).

Identification is a human instinct and is felt in corporeal experience. When trauma is added, through television or worse, e.g. kidnapping, identification with the "enemy" is also a human instinct, one necessary for survival. Such blurring of boundaries is clearly not appreciated and cannot be acknowledged under conditions of conflict. This contributes to numbing, surreal, ghostly experiences. Johnston's art acknowledges the possibilities, indeed likelihood of identification to transgress boundaries, to be human. It inserts doubt: still brave and exceedingly necessary.

As an accompanying piece in the Golden Thread Gallery's other large space, a video is projected onto a frame that holds a disintegrating sheep's fleece between two sheets of glass: Charlie Haughey, 2012. Camouflage patterns reaching the wall behind retain the military associations – clad literally in sheep's clothing. The video is of a man (a poet) on the Aran Islands planting trees in inhospitable soil outside the window (we remember reading about the apple tree). The radio in the background reports Charlie Haughey's death and broadcasts a vox pop about his contribution to Irish life. The love of a rogue is pervasive. Often this has been acknowledged to be a trait of post-colonial society.

Johnston complicates the story further, however, by screening the video onto the sheep's fleece. Corruption ("fleecing") marks one trajectory. Another one is the fact that Haughey had followed Thatcher in having his successful election campaign designed by Charles Saatchi's advertising agency in London. Irish West-Britishness is not often visible in Northern Ireland. The link between Saatchi as the largest collector of YBA art and Haughey as arguably the greatest benefactor of the arts in the Republic of Ireland add an institutionally critical element. Such intricacies are presented as the contradictions that are hallmarks of human life. Institutions fail, governments fail, just like individuals do. Johnston does not go as far as to see such failings as endearing or fatalistically as inevitable. Instead, there is the intrinsic hope that planting trees connotes. Even if they are not the apple trees that Martin Luther wished to plant on his dying day, we may perceive the gardening shown as replenishing, as compensation for the earlier demise of the Johnstons' tree of bitter apples.

These two main video installations in the exhibition enable the viewers to establish a narrative surrounding conflict that is multi-layered and human. It is (through *Cuttings 1* and *2*) in the first instance the artist's narrative, but it is crucially open for all viewers to establish their own connections in and to public life, The Queen, Haughey, horses, trees and anything that would appear in their "cuttings", their personal collections of newspaper clippings and family albums. Assembling photos and newspaper articles s is a creative work of and for memory. In an art-historical context it conjures the work of Aby Warburg (Warburg 1999) and much artistic practice in his wake (Schmidt, Rüttinger eds 2012). We will return to him. Let me first outline how the artist has framed her two main video installations in *Shadow of a Doubt,* focussing particularly on the quality of gesture that she seeks, before going into more analytical detail.

Entering the Golden Thread Gallery, Sandra Johnston first presents the viewer with a video of a performance staged for the camera, Settle, *2012, a new development in her work, which has more often than not refused documentation. One is greeted with a humorous, even slapstick moment: the artist is lowering her body to sit and, at the last moment, the chair is being pulled away. Crucially, she pulls away the chair herself – and she repeats the action over and over. There is no hope of comfort, even if the viewers will soon be offered a seat. The remarkable skill of the performance artist's alert and self-aware body is revealed at the very moment where she negates certainty: in the hand's accomplished removing of the chair, itself unstable: a folding chair. There could be no simpler, no clearer assertion of the need to remove the solidity of any location or basis for the body, especially as the performing body shows itself first to become more accomplished, trained – and then in the moment of optimal performance to lose that ability again, to become impoverished, to fail. The video loops, in order to connect the two "deficient" ends and let the viewer trace the movement's oscillating between accomplishment to failure and back. Such an oscillation also happens in the video piece that closes the exhibition,* 360° From the Heart, *2012, this time it is a movement forwards and backwards of the artist's body, while seated on the chair. She stretches and looks uncomfortable, nearly losing balance again.*

The origins of these works, Johnston says, are gestures remembered from previous performances: remembered by the body, as well as those observed in others. The pieces involving a chair come from witnessing her elderly mother's pain in getting up from a chair. The daughter – in what is both a gesture of defiance and loving mimicry – once refuses to rise and once refuses to sit.

Having established the connectedness between the larger, political picture and personal experience through the Cuttings and video installations, the work that occupies the half-way point in the exhibition between the larger rooms, takes the viewer into a domestic setting: the gallery space's openings are constructed to resemble domestic doorways, Untitled, 2012. Two screens, back to back, show another performance to camera, Hold In, 2012. Johnston is seen with arms wrapped around her naked trunk. The back is passive, fragile. It shares characteristics with the backs of the nearly translucent, orange, plastic chairs one has just left behind. The hands are active. One is briefly reminded of a pantomime routine that suggests love-making, but the hands turn the trunk, over and back, revealing folds of skin, a hungry, emaciated body trying to minimize its occupation of space. Again hunger strikes comes to mind – and even closer to home than the allusions to Bobby Sands: traces of years of anorexia, the result of two attacks that Sandra Johnston had suffered, in addition to threats that made her leave Belfast in 1995.

Her earliest night-time performances were attempts to blend into the surroundings to such an extent as to vanish: dressed as (presumably male) figures from Protestant murals in East Belfast, or naked among the bins and skips of alleyways and rural wasteland sites, she likened herself to both murderers and murder victims: detritus, invisible, overlooked (and not documented). Being visible would have meant to be a target, but the reverse logic of course fails, as such performances, in responding to the violence and numbness of society, expose it. Invisibility is traditionally socially required of women, where housework only shows when it has not been accomplished. In addition, a young, sensitive Protestant woman, confronted with hunger strikers on television at a formative age, starving may subliminally be an attempt to help, to minimize one's own "footprint" and let others live, whose complaint ultimately was with "settlement", i.e. Protestants' bodies occupying space on the island of Ireland. Disappearing is also enhancing safety, however, as can be heard in pleasant social conversation in Northern Ireland even today: a thin person is “a sniper’s nightmare”. Hence we can note here the need for the paradoxes in and of art, for both the presence and absence of performance of which Peggy Phelan has so incisively written as necessary and inevitable (Phelan 1993). This notion was here alluded to with reference to Christo and Jeanne Claude’s wrapping artworks and that Johnston’s performance demonstrates it in exemplary fashion.

Johnston’s work, shown on two screens, is redolent with such intricate connotations. The body can be thought of as inanimate, being manipulated by the hands, but it is also a work that asserts the body’s full-screen presence, its fragile, androgynous beauty. Reminiscent of Bruce Nauman’s body- and space-testing works from the 1960s and such canonical performances as Yoko Ono’s *Cut Piece*, 1965. The work also holds the memories of several of Johnston’s own live performances, such as one engaging with Marlene Dumas’ paintings, *Remembe::red*. It also shares with the work of Alastair MacLennan and other members of Bbeyond, the Northern Irish performance art collective, the quiet, enduring assertion of a body holding space: unremarkable, obstinate, brave, annoying, painful, human. It is what Northern Irish performance art is known for, has developed uniquely, and practices collectively.

SPECTACLE

Many performance artists have responded to war and violence with works that direct pain at the artist. Self-sacrifice is, according to Claire Bishop, a hallmark of socially engaged practice in the (now heavily criticised) “relational” mode. It has been found to have originated from particularly Protestant theological tenets, whereby the “good soul” gives itself up in the service of others (Bishop 2006: 182). Antje von Graevenitz (2013) has studied such practices, finding that the artists intend them to be sensitivity-inducing measures, but based on the findings of behaviourist Stanley Milgrim – that the vast majority of us have an extraordinary capacity to harm others when this is thought to be socially accepted and / or desired – the intended outcome or efficacy of Chris Burden’s *Shoot* or many of Marina Abramovic’s early performances remains doubtful.

There is a considerable body of literature on trauma, and performance (e.g. Duggan 2012; Meyer 2008; Guerin, Hallas eds. 2007; Murray 1997). Most of these writings concern theatre performance (except Meyer). Sandra Johnston has in this study also investigated Theatre of Witness, utilized as a peace and reconciliation initiative in Northern Ireland. Guerin and Hallas (2007) differentiate more than others and are indebted to W.J.T. Mitchell (the introduction's motto cites a pronouncement of his about images being like actors on the historical stage), but they still do not consider performance art, or the problems of the spectacle intrinsic in the theatre tradition, while distrust in (presumably spectacular) images is acknowledged.

Much international performance practice, particularly feminist performance, excels at telling stories of disadvantage and abuse. *Acting Out* is, indeed, the title of an anthology of feminist performance (Hart, Phelan eds 1993). Performance – as has been noted for visual art in the expressionist mode – often chooses as its register high drama, the spectacle (Guy Debord). It was established why this is not so in Beckett's or MacLennan's or Johnston's practices. Eschewing the spectacle is of course not possible, but in highlighting the embodied, material elements of the fleeting gesture, Johnston and others minimize (if that is the right word) the visual mode of transferring performance work from one body to the other, where it rests in the again embodied memory of viewers – with little or no images to aide us or re-spectacularize it:

> The spectacle is heir to all the weakness of the project of Western philosophy, which was an attempt to understand activity by means of the categories of vision. [...] far from realizing philosophy, the spectacle philosophizes reality, and turns the material life of everyone into a universe of speculation. (Debord 1967: 4)

Conceptual art and the simultaneously emerging performance practices in the 1960s were, of course, responses to the resulting and understandable wish to pare down, to dematerialize the contested image. Guerin and Hallas point more specifically to further paradoxical sources of this loss of image, as far as the representation of trauma is concerned: when New York's mayor Giuliani recommended not to take pictures of events on 9/11 both for the sake of national security and to honour the victims:

> In this double rationale for such iconoclastic policies, we find the very paradox at the heart of [...] the image: it potentially offers invaluable

> knowledge of the event and, at the same time, it fails to do justice to the human magnitude of the traumatic event. (Guerin, Hallas 2007: 6)

Johnston holds against both the disciplining manoeuvre and the "theatre of war" her presence in (durational) performance and, with the help of viewers, against commodification and spectacularization the "intentional or empathetic transference of content. Accordingly, in order that the idea of memory transfers generatively, the trace of the performer should in fact be erased" (Johnston 2013: epilogue). Through the eventual absence of the performance the "performer strategically offers upon the viewer, the task of holding the moment in memory against the grain of inevitable loss" (Johnston 2013: epilogue). And I would agree with Anna McMullan that this is a particular feature of the Beckettian tradition: she argues that "Beckett's drama produces new modes of intercorporeal embodiment out of the materials of subjection and vulnerability" (McMullan 2010: 9). I have experienced this in Sandra Johnston's performances.

It is then argued here that most of the theatrical and performance responses to trauma participate in the spectacle to a degree that ultimately has a disciplining effect and even disables not only critical thinking (as the spectacle does according to Debord), but also empathetic feeling, i.e. sensitivity. Sandra Johnston and Alastair MacLennan, but (among the artists investigated by von Graevenitz) also e.g. Bas Jan Ader, take a different approach – by virtue of the quality of gesture employed and the openness to doubt and failure – as we shall see. Let me briefly trace a genealogy of my thoughts in this regard.

SENSITIVITY, AUTONOMY, THE MINOR

In response to the violent excesses of the French Revolution and the ensuing debasement of its ideals, Friedrich Schiller formulated his ideas about aesthetic education and its importance for society's recuperation (Schiller 2002): only through the sensitivity that aesthetic experience can let grow in human beings is it possible for us to strive for a peaceful equilibrium (always strive for – never reach) and only in play, i.e. through the "unreal", "fictional" realm of art, can we be truly human. In recent times, Schiller's ideas have become highly influential for and through Jacques Rancière, who has argued that we are all capable of "making our own stories", i.e.

having and interpreting aesthetic experience in our own ways and let it productively alter the distribution of the sensible, i.e. have effect in the real world. That fiction is being re-thought in the context nearly goes without saying. Sandra Johnston's performances in gallery spaces make use of their fictionalizing function. Paula Blair has already noted in the context of Johnston's work that "we might begin to consider physcialization and fictionalization as legitimate forms of interpretation and analysis" (Blair 2012: 18).[12] Fictionalization is also part of the creation of history and accounts of events for legal purposes: "In keeping with trauma studies (and of course historiographical) insight 'the act of bearing witness is not the communication of a truth that is already known, but its actual production through this performative act'" (Guerin, Hallas 11).

In *The Emancipated Spectator* Rancière also has much to say against the spectacle and the efficacy of art through eschewing it while breaking the linear understanding of cause and effect and as a result insisting that paradoxes are necessary (Rancière 2009). Theodor Adorno thought, for example, that in Wagner's operas the audience was "accosted" and "attacked" (Phelan 1993: 195-196). In his essay on commitment he similarly favoured the indirect, oblique impact of art, particularly that of Samuel Beckett, in order to attempt to come to terms with historical trauma (Adorno 1962). As we have seen, Terry Eagleton, like Adorno – on whom he heavily relies – also focuses on Beckett's active and sustained engagement for the *résistance* as an important and incontrovertible basis, aiding the work's liberating effects through eschewing the triumphalism, i.e. the certainties of oppressors from any side. To engage in a "pact with failure", paying attention to the failing body, the small gestures and the slow decline of attention and strength in durational performance, rather than the spectacle's heightened expressiveness or even the drama of death (von Graevenitz' subject matter is artworks in whose execution artists nearly or actually died), is found to bear more credible engagement, relief and even hope – the only hope possible.

Deleuze and Guattari's notion of the power of the minor (through deter-

12 Paula Blair's PhD, Queen's University Belfast, includes investigations of Sandra Johnston's work from a media studies perspective. It is to be published.

ritorialization, political immediacy and collective enunciation)[13] appears to bear out these findings (Johnston makes use of this), as does for good measure Christian theology ("The last shall be the first", etc.). Current thinking on radical autonomy (Boomgaard 2006) owes much to Schiller, Adorno and Rancière, but adds to the mix the thought that the autonomous artwork's ideological associations with the bourgeois status quo have faded, when governments and corporations alike commission and buy "relational" work to occlude their abdication of responsibility for society. "It all seems so neat: art with a function, and artists included in the planning process. But this development robs art of much of its dissident potential" (Boomgaard 2006: 36). When lack of "participation" becomes a social sin, poetic "inactivity" (Frohne 2010) appears to bear new promises.

> Only an autonomous work that relates to its context, but which chooses its own time and place within that context, is capable of leaving the world of artificiality and of revealing something that lies beyond the limits of our expectations. [...] Because the artist chooses of his own free will to create an entirely personal world, he shows that it is possible to choose radically. (Boomgaard 2006: 37, 38)[14]

Adorno already noted in the early 1960s that

> today autonomous rather than committed works of art should be encouraged in Germany. Committed works all too readily credit themselves with every noble value, and then manipulate them at their ease. Under fascism, too, no atrocity was perpetrated without a moral veneer. (Adorno 1962: 11)[15]

---

13 For a transposition of the minor into visual art see Lerm Hayes (2012) and other contributions to the same volume.

14 "An autonomous work of art can, in this context, not only succeed in unmasking self-interest as the dominant principle, but can impart new authority to the symbolic freedom that was formerly the hallmark of autonomy. [...] Radical autonomy can play along with every process; the place, the public and the discourse are all factors that can be a part of it. But the radically autonomous work of art will always add something which transgresses the borders of the context and adds a value that cannot simply be classified as a pragmatic benefit." (Boomgaard 2006: 37-38)

15 "The uncalculating autonomy of works which avoid popularization and adaptation to the market involuntarily becomes an attack on them. The attack is not abstract, not a fixed attitude of all works of art to the world which will not forgive them for not bending totally to it. The distance these works maintain from empirical reality is in itself partly

Sandra Johnston inserts herself into such a genealogy by saying:

> from revolutions, to riots, and the growth of anti-capitalist movements among others. All of these events seem to indicate that the relationship between the performances of politics, legality and those of artists increasingly coincide in real space and real time in a multiplicity of activist forms [...]. It is not my position to say that activism and art activities are interchangeable: there are distinctions, and an important part of this research project has been to attempt to unravel why performance art remains not just on the margins of the culture industry, but is also persistently distanced from activist forms. One answer might lie in the framework developed by Deleuze and Guattari, where they term Kafka's writings as a 'minor literature'. Perhaps performance can best be understood as a 'minor' art form [...] capable of creating disturbances within the encompassing system. (Johnston 2013: introduction)

She was asked to work in difficult social circumstances, but what she offered were not the expected "sticking plasters" (which Claire Bishop would critique), occluding inadequate social provision in Gellerup. Johnston chose to give those who worked in grassroots organizations (community gardens, etc.) her time, admiration and support – privately. In her own work then, Rancière's tenets and those concerning radical autonomy hold true, in fact are confirmed in the reactions of "troubled" youths, who did not respond in the expected disruptive way, but showed themselves capable of having an aesthetic experience. Johnston's stance is quiet and disarming, but – one is almost tempted to say – authoritatively so, rather than courting self-sacrifice. The theological framework that seems to resonate most is liberation theology, as it has underpinned human rights movements globally, and in a non-denominational way. Johnston does turn the other cheek, even embraces the ever-present possibility of re-traumatization (Johnston et al. 2012) and so invites and conjures responsible, human reactions. In Gellerup these may or may not have been directly strengthened by her private engagements with locals over some months. Through her humility and because she does not preach or simplistically "educate", she compliments mature and thoughtful behaviour in her audiences.

---

mediated by that reality. [...] There is no material content, no formal category of an artistic creation, however mysteriously changed and unknown to itself, which did not originate in the empirical reality from which it breaks free." (Adorno 1962: 9)

In order to extend my genealogy further into performance art, even Helge Meyer, whose focus is work that foregrounds pain, concludes remarks about Eastern European performance by saying that, especially in authoritarian societies, the body of performance artists used as an image was immediately considered suspicious and subversive (Meyer 2008: 277). Its mere unspectacular presence appears to highlight the humanity, the real, unidealized person who is to be considered in her individuality – and can become an obstacle to the machinery of the spectacle.

The notion of radical autonomy, responding to the commodification of "relational" practices, reminds us that artistic strategies will have to vary according to the extent to which trauma is still present and previously used strategies have become commodified. Gene Ray (2011), whose work Sandra Johnston repeatedly uses, found that the development of performance art coincides with the Auschwitz Trials of the second half of the 1960s. Once holocaust memorials have been erected and satisfy the vanity of many a municipality, and once Israel's repressive politics are being justified with reference to holocaust memory, this memory may need a more spectacular vehicle in art: the *détournement* of shock.[16]

By the same token, Bakhtin's understanding of the grotesque, the disruptive qualities of the body, of laughter and the carnivalesque and Debord's notion of détournement (where one tries to disrupt the spectacle by means of spectacular images and language) can of course still be valid – at certain times and in certain places. When, as in the context in which Beckett wrote, triumphal, authoritarian language and spectacular images were or are employed to numb the public, to obfuscate the past and aspects of the present – one should possibly re-read Victor Klemperer's *LTI* in relation to Northern Ireland's "late bureaucratic phase" (Jewesbury 2005: 530) of the Troubles[17] – then retaining one's sensitivity to the nuances of speech and

---

16 What I am developing here as a necessary (temporal) oscillation of approaches is understood and posed as an open question by James Elkins: "If I write in one text about the nonlinguistic elements of the image, and then I write in another text about the historical discourses that have led me to want to claim that images have nonlinguistic properties, then what happened to me in between those two acts of writing? The answer cannot simply be that the conceptual has been captured by the historical, because the moment will very likely reverse itself." (Elkins, Naef 2011: 11)

17 Debord might also be called to comment: "The dictatorship of the bureaucratic economy cannot leave the exploited masses any significant margin of choice because it has had to

gesture appears as the more powerful strategy;[18] in conjunction of course with personal ethical engagement – and ideally with the benefit of the work of others, who mediate such an attitude to a wider public.

THE POLITESQUE

At the moment – and in Northern Ireland during the period in which Sandra Johnston has worked here – the grotesque, that which breaks the functionality of the system, can arguably be located not in art but in politics: as individuals often shun difference and seek comfort in the familiar, public institutions tend to be over-administered to appear effective and with an inward-facing, stubbornly authoritarian focus they expedite with utmost single-mindedness what to an observer cannot look like anything but self-sabotage. It is not so much flag protests or contentious parades and their expensive policing that renders the humanely functioning and further emerging of democracy impossible, but also the expenditure of vast sums for a doubled state apparatus, school and health system, as well as (and this is what concerns us here) bread and circuses (such as the World Police and Fire Games, the Titanic Festival, the Titanic Centre, Derry/Londonderry City of Culture, G8 etc.): an immense array of numbing spectacles and simulacra that, while well-intentioned, ultimately prevent memory and healing, in fact can give to many the impression of not having to live any pesky and (at least economically) threatened life in the here and now. Sandra Johnston has spoken of people in Northern Ireland for whom time stands still and has stood still for decades following a traumatic event or bereavement (other states of inactivity will still concern us), and she mentions Agamben's writings on holocaust survivors who could not tell their story (Johnston et al. 2012). A numbingly commodified simulacrum of a life may indeed have its advantages. Debord thought people were "drugged" by spectacles.[19] But

make all the choices itself, and because any choice made independently of it, even the most trivial – concerning food, say, or music – amounts to a declaration of war to the death on the bureaucracy." (III, 64)

18 George Didi-Huberman's book *How Images Take a Stance* should be translated (2011). The spectrum goes from the silent scream of Brecht's *Mother Courage* to, in the last instance, the irresponsible naivety of Chaplin's *Great Dictator*, where a Jewish girl defeats NAZI storm troopers (see Adorno 1962: 6).

19 "THE SPECTACLE, BEING the reigning social organization of a paralyzed history, of

for the artist other questions arise: how can one begin to speak, how is reality to be rediscovered? Certainly not through certainties, as Vikki Bell also states:

> The artworks, 'without the bigotry of conviction' as Seamus Deane put it, suggest that the task of dealing with the past is flawed wherever the past is conceived as a history that can be rendered present to be judged by subjects who are thereby placed beyond it. That is the illusion of a present 'no-time' that dovetails with the desires of commercial enterprise and neo-liberal conceptions of freedom. If this suggests an unceasing restlessness, the consolation is that this questioning does take a form, not as judgement or political decision but as artworks which by definition, remain open to reinterpretation and new understandings. (Bell 2011: 324)

But which register is appropriate and how to harness that restlessness? Departing from Bakhtin's use of the grotesque, the Ulmer Verein (which was first to investigate German Art History's role during the NAZI era) published an issue of their *Kritische Berichte* journal on the notion of *The Politesque* (2010). Ursula Frohne's essay's subject is the work of Korpys / Loeffler, who have created video works of "nothing happening", marginalia, e.g. body guards waiting for the arrival of a head of state's aeroplane. They are translating the "politesque" spectacle into an aesthetic of unspec-

---

a paralyzed memory, of an abandonment of any history founded in historical time, is in effect a false consciousness of time." (Debord 1967: VI, 158) "THE ORIGIN OF THE spectacle lies in the world's loss of unity, and its massive expansion in the modern period demonstrates how total this loss has been: the abstract nature of all individual work, as of production in general, finds perfect expression in the spectacle, whose very manner of being concrete is, precisely, abstraction." (I, 29) "THE SPECTACLE ERASES the dividing line between self and world, in that the self, under siege by the presence/absence of the world, is eventually overwhelmed; it likewise erases the dividing line between true and false, repressing all directly lived truth beneath the real presence of the falsehood maintained by the organization of appearances. The individual, though condemned to the passive acceptance of an alien everyday reality, is thus driven into a form of madness in which, by resorting to magical devices, he entertains the illusion that he is reacting to this fate. The recognition and consumption of commodities are at the core of this pseudo-response to a communication to which no response is possible. The need to imitate that the consumer experiences is indeed a truly infantile need, one determined by every aspect of his fundamental dispossession. In terms used by Gabel to describe quite another level of pathology, "the abnormal need for representation here compensates for a torturing feeling of being at the margin of existence." (IX, 219) tacular moments and thereby generate for the political, as well as for human action more generally, new creative spaces (Frohne 2010: 47). Frohne had referred both to Deleuze and Guattari's call for impoverishment, for the minor to find its own "desert", but also noted Giorgio Agamben's theological genealogy of economy and governance, where "inactivity" is seen as the essence of power. She reminds us that poetry is also based on such "inactivity", understood as space for the contemplation of one's own abilities, a space of self-empowerment.

Sandra Johnston has focussed in a video work documenting the Peoples' Tribunal against the Sri Lankan government on the audience's small gestures, on the marginalia, where Tamil expatriates sit quietly, journalists set up cameras: all awaiting the findings. While the verdict itself is heard in the work, complete with the hesitations that fail to mask emotion in the tribunal members' voices, one sees calm and relative inactivity: the inactivity of witnesses listening. This necessitates action afterwards: taking responsibility to transmit what one has witnessed. Johnston, together with Dominic Thorpe later created a performance on this tribunal, Due Process Part I, where they drew with charcoal. The Tamil survivors who were present later commented that the charcoal broke like bones.

GESTURES

- Breaking charcoal reminds Tamil survivors of breaking bones.
- Jane Ewart-Biggs gives painfully composed testimony on television about her murdered husband, only to sink into her chair, as soon as her delivery to camera is made.
- The Queen removes an insect from her eye.
- Mrs. Johnston gets up from her seat in pain.
- In Beckett's *Krapp's Last Tape*, Krapp remembers holding a rubber ball when his mother died.
- *Sandra Johnston stands motionless in the gallery with her head against a wire rope "fence", charcoal in each hand. She bends down, draws two lines as far as her arms can reach, falls to her knees, draws, falls on her front, draws, gets up, stands, repeats. The work is entitled Measure, 2012.*
- *In Johnston's video work Interview, 2011, we see a black screen on*

which, like credits for a film, white writing scrolls slowly: precise time measurements and short descriptions of gestures. The artist had filmed her father while she interviewed him about a bomb that he survived during the Troubles.

Through such gestures, most of them unpremeditated or involuntary, Johnston argues in her study, performance art can function as testimony. She has adopted an improvisation practice, which can, more than scripted performance, provide openness for such gestures to enter, and can also yield those that insert doubt and constitute an analysis of the situation, space and topic at hand. They are glitches in Deleuze and Guattari's sense – or epiphanies in Joyce's – through which more meaning, more emotional and psychological content is revealed than could be achieved through lengthy verbal reasoning. Johnston's practice could be regarded as an archive of such gestures. It is, however, not sufficient in the context of art (or law, or anthropology) just to collect and to let such minimal and fleeting gestures go unexamined.

> What is primarily valued in the art form are the diversions and innovations that occur spontaneously, taking both artist and audiences into a space of unstructured or premeditated encounter. The quality of these transactions is the opening of doubt and its introduction in a constructive space of communication. (Johnston 2013: introduction)

WARBURG

Aby Warburg (1866-1929) has provided a tool and an archive for the analysis of emotive gestures in images. He became known in the English-speaking world only when Giorgio Agamben wrote about his work, calling for the translation of the collected writings, which finally occurred in 1999. Warburg's "pathos formulae" traced agitation as evidenced in the frozen gestures of past ages and cultures, as they have been preserved for our investigation in artworks, for understanding their time and place. The tool that he developed and eventually applied through his atlas of memory (*Mnemosyne Atlas*) was so sharp that he came to think that someone was trying to kill his family and developed a depressive crisis. As a Jewish German in the Weimar Republic, he was it seems sensing what was ahead in his time, especially for potential scapegoats. He read images as seismographs of where a society was located on the continuum between enlightenment and irrationality, i.e. could tell how it would behave, what was to come.[20] Warburg could have said what Johnston is formulating here:

> What has perhaps interested me most [... is] what gestures can mean when asserted and reasserted through different contexts. The essential characteristics of suffering, whether the language is primarily verbal or gestural, continue to announce themselves onto all forms of human communication, the question is ongoing of how to turn the vital energy of pain and fear into constructive forces. Art is one of the few 'evidences' that show that this transformation is possible. (Johnston 2013: introduction)

Through our focus on gesture in the Warburgian tradition we find that the smallest gestural glitches, frozen or re-performed in (performance) art can function to reveal and acknowledge anger, revulsion and irrationality. Warburg had found a trace of medieval angst in Sandro Botichelli's *Primavera*, where a personification of wind blows vigorously, but has no effect on the apparently carelessly dancing maenads' dresses. Art bears contradictory emotions – and generally the contradictory elements of life – better than language can, and in possibly more meaningful ways than the spectacularized expressiveness of 1980s-style Neo-Expressionist outcries that form the canon of "troubles art" (Long n.d.). It is important to note that Declan Long in subsequent work about contemporary Northern Irish art (Long 2012),[21] while not focussing on performance art, used productively the notion of the spectral. In Derrida we can, indeed, locate (spectrally) notions

20 Didi-Huberman calls him prophetic (2010: 36).

21 "This is, then, a thesis about art and haunting. It is an argument *for* haunting, and for the contemporary art field as a specific sphere of haunting and hauntedness. The thesis proposes that the art of the post-Troubles period has imagined a 'public space' in which certain 'spectres', unwelcome elsewhere in the culture, might be accommodated or confronted" (Long 2012: 20). Jacques Derrida's comment that we must 'learn to live with ghosts' (1994: xvii-xviii) has become acutely relevant. This claim is, first of all, a call for fidelity in politics to those 'who *are not there* ... those who are no longer or who are not yet *present* and *living*' (Derrida, 1994: xviii): a commitment of anxious allegiance to the ghosts of our histories and our possible futures. And secondly, the insistence on 'living with ghosts' implies a requirement in 'Theory' that we address the 'spectral' element that haunts our knowledge of the world – what we might also think of as the 'blind spots' in our vision – and as such it necessitates attending to 'the non-contemporaneity with itself of the living present', and to 'that which secretly unhinges it' (Derrida, 1994: xviii).

that are – implicitly or explicitly – formed in Warburg's work, and here already developed and theorized in and for the sphere of visual art.

Warburg established (as Didi-Huberman explains)

> a phantom model of history [...], which finds its expression in compulsory return and ghostly 'afterlife' of forms [gestures]. Ultimately this phantom model is a [...] symptom-oriented model, in which the gestation of forms need to be analysed as an ensemble of tensions: e.g. between the wish to identify and the necessity of change, between cleansing and mixing, normal and pathological, order and chaos, that which is evident and un-thought. Warburg turned art history into a critical field as such – a space of knowing and of not knowing – for any historical intelligibility of his age. (Didi-Huberman 2010: 187)

In this spirit Johnston acknowledges that performance

> can be humble in its openness to the random, often leaving only traces of indefinite emotions. As with the museum of afterthoughts proposed, it creates the capacity to re-enter the briefly lived, to repossess those ambiguities and uncertainties that could not be contained. (Johnston 2013: epilogue)

Her museum of afterthoughts takes on qualities of Warburg's *Mnemosyne Atlas*, a document devoted to the afterlife or *Nachleben* of images and gestures and emotions in images, which Warburg had conceived of as "ghost stories" very much for grown-ups.

Bildwissenschaft as a Warburg-inspired field can come to the fore when considering performance art: Gottfried Boehm asserts a relationship between the image modelling a cognitive revelation (*deixis*) and the body: "The intelligent use of the body turns out not just to be a condition of the generation of images, but also and especially as their enduring basis: in the sense of an explanation based on premises or conditionality [...] *deixis* as the foundational meaning-generating capacity of the image" (Boehm et al. 2010: 39).[22] He has also focussed on the body's traces in art and the energy

[22] Translation by the author (C-M LH). "Der intelligente Gebrauch des Körpers erweist sich... nicht nur als Enstehungsbedingung der Bilder, sondern auch und vor allem als ihr dauernder Grund: im Sinne der Erklärung aus Prämissen bzw. Bedingtheiten [...] Deixis als die basale, sinngenerierende Kapazitaet des Bildes." Johnston formulates: "Therefore it is the sensorial activators and the 'failures' of memory that are often used

on which Johnston remarked earlier.[23]

Better than any semiotic certainties surrounding the meanings and efficacy of images, the field of Warburg with his *Mnemosyne Atlas* "ghost story", Didi-Huberman's insistence on Warburgian ghosts in and for Art History today (as a "science" without a name) and, on the other hand *Bildwissenschaft* (Boehm and Mitchell) who elaborate on the non-lingual meanings of images, their ontology as foundational to ideological conceptualization (Mitchell): all this opens up an area on which I cannot dwell on this occasion, but that stands to offer very fertile ground.[24] To attest ghostly presences in Northern Ireland and its art could not be more appropriate. When this trajectory encounters – connected through both Mitchell and Rancière as "hinges" – discourse about socially and politically engaged practices and accounts for radical autonomy as something very much underpinned by *Bildwissenschaft* ideas, most exciting meetings of minds and artworks can take place.

However, apart from acknowledging emotion (in itself useful enough, but possibly not as art, as we established earlier), the small gestures that Johnston has found, collected, memorized and re-performed are importantly opened up for analysis, as part of a historical psychology, an interpretation in anthropology, *Geistesgeschichte* and as a sensitive seismographic tool that can function as a warning sign – all in the Warburgian tradition (also known as the discipline without a name, or iconology). Warburg himself knew only too well how fundamentally unsettling the command of this

---

as the material of art invention. In effect, the agitation of tactile memory is a strategy utilised to provoke the attendant sensations attached to situations, as an alternative method of interpretation." (Johnston 2013: epilogue)

23 "Lassen sich nicht gewisse Bilder der Moderne als Seismogramme der Gebaerde beschreiben? Existiert nicht eine gestische Abstraktion? Roland Barthes hat dies in Bezug auf Cy Twombly versucht, wenn er das Linkische seiner 'Skripturen' betont, die zwischen Schrift und Zeichnung changieren [...] Die Kunst des Zeigens entfaltet Twombly gleichwohl zu ausserordentlichen Möglichkeiten [...]. Wir zum Entziffern der Spuren verlockt werden und es nicht können [...]. Was sich da zeigt, ist ohne 'Was', vage und unwiderruflich zugleich, voller untergründiger subsemantischer Energie [...]. Was sie enthüllt, wird niemals gesagt werden können. Gleichwohl mangelt es an nichts, denn es *zeigt* sich, was es ist." (Boehm et al. 2010: 29)

24 I would like to make the case again (as in so much of my teaching in Ireland over the last 16 years) that some Continental art history, Warburg and also Didi-Huberman, appear to be particularly well suited to (Northern) Irish art. (Lerm Hayes 1993).

tool can be. Like Johnston and some other Northern Irish artists, he persisted in looking into the abyss, proving his recuperation with a lecture on the symbol of fear, the snake, as it is not only the root of evil in biblical, mythological and historical narratives, but also qualifies as the symbol of pharmacology. Gestures of fear seem to heal if administered in small doses – and possibly over a long period of time. It is interesting to note that Orpheus, the mythological artist, is also thought to have been the originator of medicine.

HEALTH

Meyer remarks that through the complete devotion to present existence with all its negative and positive aspects, Alastair MacLennan succeeds in enduring extreme durational performances without suffering physical or psychical damage (Meyer 2008: 286). This approach is, still according to Meyer, an important condition of health, as health can also justifiably be understood as the ability to live with damage and disability, even to be capable of integrating death into life. It needs to be repeated that such subtleties are far removed from the spectacle with which official Northern Ireland tries to heal – or feign health. (As I hear on the radio about the fifth night of rioting in East Belfast following 12th July, I check the Titanic Centre website: despite fabulous weather, the 11am slot on Saturday is booked out. The two window slits on the Gehry/Liebeskind-esque façade of the Titanic Centre, in mimicking the Holocaust Museum in Berlin, appear to conflate the loss of the Titanic with the loss of life during the Troubles; as if to say that through spectacularly marking the one we will manage – away – the other. That is a mistaken hope.)

Johnston, by contrast, makes

> only modest claims for performance art, mainly on the grounds that it is a form that both creates and acknowledges dissonance in structures, ideas and situations. Yet, also performance has a capacity for empathy and healing: both are tools of the emotions, readily transferred from one body across to another, but usually only in instances of trust and concentrated engagement [...] A momentary but precise overturning of privilege and prejudice. (Johnston 2013: chapter 5)

Meyer's insistence on the present with its positive and negative aspects brings me to another vital moment in the constellation of health, critique / analysis and (non-fatalistic) acceptance.

LOVE AND DEMOCRACY

Considering the nature of images, I seem to have strayed inadvertently close to the idea, Félibien's theory, as recounted by Elkins and Naef (2011: 3), that images are traces of love, born of the absence of what is loved.

Love is for me inherent already in the prolonged, careful attention of both Johnston the artist and her audience to small gestures and tiny traces in the lived-in spaces around us in her performances. However, it would be facile to say simply that love heals when physical "love" can also so clearly and painfully be an instrument of power and violence, particularly in (post-) conflict societies. Even though the statistics do not appear to show that the pattern of increased violence against women that one often notes in post-conflict societies has been replicated in Northern Ireland after the cease-fires, there have been a number of incredibly brutal murders of women and there remains a very high level of domestic violence (always notoriously underreported).[25] The instances of race hate crime have clearly increased. Northern Ireland does not "do" difference terribly well.[26] We need to differentiate and can profitably, I think, use Martha Nussbaum's study of how emotions are part of our ethical reasoning and can (need to) become part of a democratization process.[27]

---

25 Over the years Johnston created four performance works in memory of Margaret Wright, a victim of the Red Hand Commando.

26 … as a colleague of mine memorably formulated. – Warburg has subjected to his scrutiny images showing the brutal murder of Orpheus. Albrecht Dürer's version in particular includes a note identifying Orpheus, who had after all nearly succeeded in having his wife returned to him from the underworld, as someone erotically interested in young boys. (Warburg 1999). For Warburg's emerging reception in Ireland see North (2012).

27 Of course love is also to be captured by the term solidarity. It has a clearly democratizing role. See e.g. Katalin Keserü in (Lerm Hayes, Walters eds 2011). Daniel Jewesbury (2005) rightly highlighted that the speciality of Northern Irish art – and the efficacy of its responses to the Troubles – lay in its self-organized network, in solidarity. It is also difficult to overlook that this is still strong in a younger generation setting up new studio co-operatives, but that the camaraderie so famed is certainly in crisis.

Nussbaum has found that many thinkers have idealized love and given it a role in cultivating a perspective of equality. Walt Whitman, for example, extended his loving gaze and democratizing zeal to men and women, blacks and whites and also across boundaries of sexual orientation.

> The best way to defeat the power and depth of sex is to render it superficial, commercial and unpoetic; the best way to defeat the gaze of the female is to pretend that she is just a thing to be bought and sold [...]. But the poet threatens these structures of denial, and is precisely for that reason a being to be feared and shunned. It is precisely for this reason that the poet is required as the public voice of democracy. 'He judges not as the judge judges, but as the sun falling round a helpless thing' [(Whitman)], seeing its helplessness sharply but with the illumination of love. (Nussbaum 2008: 671)

Whitman's and Nussbaum's analyses thus echo that of Warburg. To put it too bluntly: the more subtle the artist's / poet's / iconologist's analysis the more necessary for democracy, and the more threatening. "In one way, resignation without optimism would be far easier. To recognize that change is possible is, for Whitman, to assume the burden of working for change the whole of one's life" (Nussbaum 2008: 676). This commitment, grown over decades, can certainly still be felt in Northern Irish (performance) art.

There remains, however, a problem with love seen in Whitman's way: Nussbaum argues that the idealism of Whitman and others (I would add Schiller to this list), what she calls the ascent of love, can also work in a counter-productive manner: it is bound to create tensions, anger and fear when real life love inevitably does not live up to the ideal. It is in overcoming this conundrum that Nussbaum's, Johnston's and my own path converge: in reading James Joyce.

JOYCE

Johnston, living in working class East Belfast during troubling times, read Joyce (from *Finnegans Wake*) at her open window, on a threshold between public and private space – as a quiet, subtle, and I would argue effective, act of defiance against the certainties all around her. Johnston accompanied Joyce's text with marginalia: snippets gathered from street conversations outside, i.e. she followed precisely Joyce's procedure in his early epiphanies. I had in my book and exhibition *Joyce in Art* (Lerm Hayes 2004) found that socially committed artists since the 1960s had seen in Joyce the most congenial source – and were reacting to his writings not directly or illustratively, but responded to his conceptual attitude in faithfully unfaithful ways (as he had treated his sources). This approach, transposed to the visual realm, I identified as the combination of autonomy (focus on linguistic prowess) with engagement: insistence on the everyday, humanity and our personal failings.[28] The necessary obliqueness of responses that I noted then tallies well with Schiller, Adorno, Ranicère and the genealogy of radical autonomy advanced here earlier.

Nussbaum argues that Joyce, particularly in the juxtaposition of the Ithaca and Penelope episodes in *Ulysses*, affirms love in a non-idealistic way. Ithaca establishes the minutiae of mundane life in encyclopaedic format, taking scientific and / or religious wisdom (the format is that of a catechism) to its breaking point, where certainty becomes humorously suffused with doubt.

> To those hooked on the drama of Dante's spiritual journey, Bloom's return to his 'Beatrice' will seem vulgar. To those hooked on Platonic or Spinozistic contemplation, the preoccupation of these minds with 'mud hair and dirt' will seem perverse. To those who react with disgust to bodily functions and their products, it will seem like one of the most disgusting books in the world. But since the text draws the reader's attention and heart to these elements of daily life and does so with tenderness, the first 'take', which laughs at the absurd juxtapositions, soon leads on to a second set of thoughts, in which one wonders whether Bloom's simple kindness [. . .], his small speech against racial intolerance, his silly poem to Molly, his kiss on her bottom, are not the material of whatever is real in life [. . .] Through humour the text seduces us to this thought. (Nussbaum 2008: 691)

More details remain with the reader than she ever wanted to know (or

28 At an International Joyce Symposium in Rome 1998, I presented a paper on Joyce and Warburg as near contemporaries. A defence against the often levelled allegation that artists only engage with Joyce in order to jump on the canonical bandwagon can be found in: Lerm Hayes (2007), as well as in my "Convergence: Literary Art Exhibitions" (meta-) exhibition, which was theorized though Deleuze and Guattari and sited purposefully in Belfast (Golden Thread Gallery, 2011).

may ever notice outside of art) about domestic objects, materials, the universe and Joyce's characters – and we come to appreciate and analyse the small gestures, the tiny traces and snippets of revealing information that should now probably no longer be called epiphanies (Joyce abandoned the term), as that suggests ascent, drama, spectacle. They can possibly be captured with Warburg as pathos formulae: emotive gestures frozen in memory, visual art or language.

It is interesting to note that "Joyce described the episode's [Ithaca's] atmosphere as that of a 'tranquilising spectrality' [... and that Bloom] has need of the 'tranquilising spectrality' of the contemplative perspective" (Nussbaum 2008: 698). Thinking may stem the flood of commodification for a while, too: artworks "assimilate themselves sedulously to the brute existence against which they protest" (Adorno 1962: 1). Adorno adds: "Today the curmudgeons whom no bombs could demolish have allied themselves with the philistines who rage against the alleged incomprehensibility of the [then] new art. The underlying impulse of these attack is petty bourgeois hatred of sex" (Adorno 1962: 11).

> [Joyce's] novel's sexual explicitness and its insistent sexual focus can now be seen to have political significance. For, first of all, they are a linchpin on the project of restoring the reader to acceptance and love of the body, with all its surprises [...] a focus on the body's universal needs is an essential step on the way to the repudiation of localism, therefore of ethnic hatred. [...] the novel suggests [...] that the root of hatred is not erotic need [...], rather, the refusal to accept erotic neediness and unpredictability as a fact of human life. Saying yes to sexuality is saying yes to all in life that defies control – to passivity and surprise, to being one part of a very chancy world. [...] this yes to humanity, Joyce suggests, is the essential basis for a sane political life, a life democratic. (Nussbaum 2008: 709)

With Warburg and Boehm we can locate such a notion in images. What Boehm calls iconic evidence in visual images is something that will always eschew explanation or judgement by means of language. It retains a transparency, something undetermined and is characterized, if logically to be conceived at all, by connections, "conjunctions" he calls them, which result in continuity:

> They enable. They are familiar or at least known to us from acts of intuitive insight, in which previously unconnected parts of the world reveal themselves as belonging to one another, matching. We know such experiences [...] from love and friendship, not least from the spheres of intellectual productivity, of scientists and artists. (Boehm et al. 2008: 22)

When one then collects such image / gesture / object conjunctions one arrives not just at striking similarities between the motivations of Warburg's *Mnemosyne Atlas* and Johnston's museum of afterthoughts, but also with Joyce's "museyroom" in *Finnegans Wake*, a repository of world history through traces that also functions as a nucleus of the entirety of the *Wake*, this embodied night-book.

It is here, I would like to suggest, that certain features that pervade Sandra Johnston's work converge: the slow and tender, accepting and loving attention to small and even disgusting (abject) everyday detail in the world of gestures and objects. The disarming humility of her gestures provides both evidence and analysis of processes of witnessing as presented in her study. All are conjunctions, combining a Geleuzian / Guattarian tendency towards the minor, a Beckettian pact with failure, a Warburgian analytical eye for gestures that reveal emotional states and a Joycean, paradoxically but stringently hopeful acceptance of the very flawed world – with social and political, with human and democratic engagement. This is at once unspectacular by necessity, undetermined and resoundingly, credibly clear.

ORPHEUS

Could this be posited as a legacy of Belfast's Orpheus building and of who and what we are now missing in our small, but possibly representative art community: that we ask how we conceive of the artwork now, what we want art to do, or what we are to do in art under the present social, political and institutional circumstances?

Antje von Graevenitz (2013) followed Maurice Blanchot in suggesting that since it was Orpheus' "aesthetic gaze" that killed his wife for a second time, the "teaching situations" of Abramovic, Burden and others set out to break that gaze. This was so that performing artists – at its most extreme: artists endangering themselves in pursuit of their work – would make us as viewers consider them as real people. We would thus be compelled to help them. Some of Sandra Johnston's early work shares that approach and it was certainly powerful and successful, even though, or partly because, it was also bitterly disappointed.

Work based on *détournement* is an important kind of art at certain times (before – if there is a before – recuperation and renewed *détournement* beckon in a never-ending cycle), but I hope to have suggested here that it has limits. This is certainly not the only way of approaching artistic practice or the need to expedite witnessing and healing. Johnston's work shows that there are alternatives, differentiating ones, difficult ones. I am aware that this is a position in art theory between the seemingly irreconcilable poles personified by Claire Bishop and Grant Kester. While this needs to be detailed elsewhere, I think there are "lines of flight" to be found (in Beckett and other points in this chapter) and further to be explored.[29]

Johnston persevered. The gaze of Orpheus, loving and empathic, is also distancing. Von Graevenitz concludes that those who gaze like Orpheus take responsibility for the artwork, not for the dying artist (Graevenitz 2013: 151, 51). Rather than suggesting that this is irresponsible behaviour, it highlights that the immediate physical survival (of the artist and others) requires first to be secured by various means, the most important one of which is how we act in real life (Beckett was here the example). It is then through (Beckettian, Joycean, Warburgian) attention to the range of emotions conveyed through "ghostly" gestures that the valuable work of the kind of practice that was here in the foreground is done. We (artist and viewer) witness and share in the artwork and in the analysis, the meaning-making. Only obliquely, through Orpheus' gaze will we have a tool to write our own story (Rancière). Only through the practice of artists like Sandra Johnston, and through jointly continuing the paradoxical, ghostly, (im)possible work of pressing on that meaning-making capacity of the image and extending it into doubt-infused writing: only in these ways – if at all – will a reflected and democratic life,[30] healthy doubt, accepting love, will art prevail.

---

[29] For exciting discussions I thank Martin Krenn, who is undertaking such a re-thinking project on politically efficacious art practice, as well as the participants of the Colloquium – and of course, again, Sandra Johnston.

[30] Hans-Georg Gadamer, who has been influential for *Bildwissenschaft*, begins his 1977 study *Die Aktualität des Schönen* with the remark that it was in the Socratic tradition that (to our knowledge) art itself was first placed before any legitimization claim. Martha

REFERENCES

Adorno, T.W. (1962), "Commitment" http://ada.evergreen.edu/arunc/texts/frankfurt/commitment/commitment.pdf. Accessed July 2013. Also in Bloch et al. (1988): 177-195.

Beach, S. (ed) (1929), *Our Exagmination round his Factification of Work in Progress*. London: Faber & Faber.

Bell, V. (2011), "Contemporary Art and Transitional Justice in Northern Ireland: The Consolation of Form", *Journal of Visual Culture*, 10: 324-353.

Bishop, C. (2006), "The Social Turn: Collaboration and Its Discontents", *Artforum* (February): 178-183, also at: http://www.gc.cuny.edu/CUNY_GC/media/CUNY-Graduate-Center/PDF/Art%20History/Claire%20Bishop/Social-Turn.pdf. Accessed July 2013.

Blair, P. (2010), "Reframings: Art and the Moving Image", *mej: Media Education Journal*, vol. 51 (Summer): 13-18.

Bloch, E., Lukacs, G., Brecht, B., Benjamin, W., Adorno, T. (1988), *Aesthetics and Politics*, Jameson, F. (afterword), Taylor, R. (transl. editor). London, New York: Verso.

Boehm, G., Mersmann, B., Spies, C. (eds) (2008), *Movens Bild: Zwischen Evidenz und Affekt*. Munich: Wilhelm Fink.

Boomgaard, J. (2006), "Radical Autonomy: Art in the Era of Process Management", *Open* Nr. 10 / (In)tolerance: 30-38, http://www.skor.nl/_files/Files/OPEN10_P30-39(1).pdf. Accessed July 2013.

Debord, G. (1967), *The Society of the Spectacle*, http://www.bopsecrets.org/images/sos.pdf. Accessed July 2013.

Didi-Huberman, G. (2010), *Das Nachleben der Bilder*. Berlin: Suhrkamp.

Didi-Huberman, G. (2011), *Wenn die Bilder Position beziehen: Das Auge der Geschichte I*. Munich: Wilhelm Fink.

Duggan, P. (2012), *Trauma-Tragedy: Symptoms of Contemporary Performance*. Manchester, New York: Manchester UP.

Eagleton, T. (2006), "Political Beckett?" *New Left Review* 40 (July/August): 67-74.

Elkins, J., Naef, M. (eds) (2011), *What is an Image?* Stone Art Theory Institutes Vol 2. University Park: Pennsylvania State UP.

Debord, G. (1967), *The Society of the Spectacle*, http://www.cddc.vt.edu/sionline/si/tsots00.html. Accessed July 2013.

Frohne, U. (2010), "Paradoxa des Politischen", *Kritische Berichte: Das Politeske / The Politesque*, 1: 33-48.

Nussbaum (alongside many others) has highlighted the importance of Socratic questioning for democracy. There could be many further connections explored between art, its history and theory and their politics (in Northern Ireland).

Gadamer, H-G. (1977, 2012), *Die Aktualität des Schönen*. Stuttgart: Reclam.

Graevenitz, A. von (2013), "Das Dilemma des Betrachters: Sterben in der Performancekunst des 20. Jahrhunderts", Seubold, G., Schmaus, T. (eds), *Ästhetik des Todes: Tod und Sterben in der Kunst der Moderne*. Bonn: DenkMal: 135-154.

Guerin, F., Hallas, R. (eds) (2007), *The Image and the Witness: Trauma, Memory and Visual Culture*. London: Wallflower.

Hannigan, J. (2006), *Environmental Sociology: second edition*. London, New York: Routledge.

Hart, L., Phelan, P. (eds) (1993), *Acting Out: Feminist Performances*. Ann Arbour: U of Michigan P.

Jewesbury, D. (2005), "'I Wouldn't Have Started From Here' or the end of 'the History of Northern Irish Art'", *Third Text*, 76, vol. 19, no. 5 (September): 525-534.

Jewesbury, D. (2013), "On Waterloo Bridge", *Fugitive Papers* http://www.fugitivepapers.org/daniel-jewesbury. Accessed July 2013.

Johnston, S., Roms, H., Catling, B., MacWilliams, S. (2012), PhD viva voce conversation 18th June 2012. Unpublished notes taken by C-M LH. Belfast.

Johnston, S. (2013), *Beyond Reasonable Doubt: An Investigation of Doubt, Risk and Testimony Through Performance Art Processes in Relation to Systems of Legal Justice*. Münster et al.: LIT.

Kelly, L. (1996), *Thinking Long: Contemporary Art in the North of Ireland.* Kinsale: Gandon Editions.

Lerm Hayes, C-M. (2012), "Considering the Minor in the Literary and Photographic Works of Rodney Graham and Tacita Dean", *Minor Photography: Connecting Deleuze and Guattari to Photography Theory,* Bleyen, M. (ed), Lieven Gevaert Series, vol. 13, Leuven: Leuven UP: 85-102.

Lerm Hayes, C-M. (1994), "Das Jüdische Erbe in Aby Warburg's Leben und Werk", *Menora 5: Yearbook for German-Jewish History 1994*, Schoeps, J.H. (ed), Salomon Ludwig Steinheim Institute of German-Jewish History. Munich, Zurich: Serie Piper: 141-169.

Lerm Hayes, C-M. (2004), *Joyce in Art*, Senn, F. (introduction), Elkins, J. (envoi), Bonk, E. (design). Dublin: Lilliput.

Lerm Hayes, C-M. (2007), "'The Joyce Effect': Joyce in the Visual Arts", *A Companion to James Joyce.* Brown, R. (ed). Malden, Oxford: Blackwell: 318-340.

Long, D. (2012), Ghost-Haunted Land: Contemporary Art and Post-Troubles Northern Ireland. Unpublished PhD thesis, Dublin: NCAD.

Long, D. (n.d.), *Visual Art and the Conflict in Northern Ireland*. A Troubles Archive Essay. Belfast: The Arts Council of Northern Ireland.

McEvilley, T. (1999), *Sculpture in the Age of Doubt*. New York: Allworth.

McMullan, A. (2010), *Performing Embodiment in Samuel Beckett's Drama*. New York, London: Routledge.

Meyer, H. (2008), *Schmerz als Bild: Leiden und Selbstverletzung in der Performance Art*. Bielefeld: Transcript.

Murray, T. (1997), *Drama Trauma: specters of race and sexuality in performance, video, and art*. Routledge: London, New York.

Nancy, J-L. (2003, 2012), *Am Grund der Bilder.* Zurich: diaphanes.

North, K. (2012), "The Man Who Looked Back: Jeremy Millar & Aby Warburg", *Artefact: Journal of the Irish Association of Art Historians*, 6: 23-34.

Nussbaum, M.C. (2010), *Not for Profit: why democracy needs the humanities.* Princetorn, Oxford: Princeton UP.

Nussbaum, M.C. (2008), *Upheavals of Thought: the intelligence of emotions.* Cambridge: Cambridge UP.

Phelan, P. (1993), *Unmarked: the politics of performance*. London, New York: Routledge.

Ray, G. (2011), "Mourning and Cosmopolitics: With and Beyond Beuys", Lerm Hayes, C-M., Walters, V. (eds), *Beuysian Legacies in Ireland and Beyond: Art, Culture and Politics*. Münster et al.: LIT: 22-48.

Rancière, J. (2009), *The Emancipated Spectator*. New York, London: Verso.

Readings, B. (1996), *The University in Ruins*. Cambridge, Mas., London: Harvard UP.

Schiller, F. (2002), *Letters on the Aesthetic Education of Man*. First published 1794. http://www.searchengine.org.uk/ebooks/55/76.pdf. Accessed July 2013.

Schmidt, E., Rüttinger, I. (eds) (2012), *Lieber Aby Warburg, was tun mit Bildern?: Vom Umgang mit fotografischem Material / Dear Aby Warburg, what can be done with images?: Dealing with photographic material*. Exh. Cat. Museum für Gegenwartskunst Siegen.

Talec, K. (2012), *Performance Art in Northern Ireland: Re-thinking the links between art, politics and the aesthetics*. Unpublished BA thesis, Belfast: University of Ulster.

Warburg, A. (1999), "Dürer and Italian Antiquity (1905)", *The Renewal of Pagan Antiquity*, Foerster, K.W. (intro.), Britt, D. (transl.). Texts & Documents. Los Angeles: The Getty Research Institute: 552-560.

IMAGES

A substantial body of artworks was created in conjunction with this study. This is entitled *Beyond Reasonable Doubt* and responded over time to the questions raised by the investigation. It consisted of ten solo and collaborative performance works and three installations created over a three-year period.

The culminating exhibition that developed from *Beyond Reasonable Doubt*, but could not include all of its manifestations, is entitled *The Shadow of A Doubt*. It took place at The Golden Thread Gallery in Belfast between December 2012 and January 2013. Installation shots are given here alongside video stills and details from a ten-hour durational performance that took place on the day of the opening.

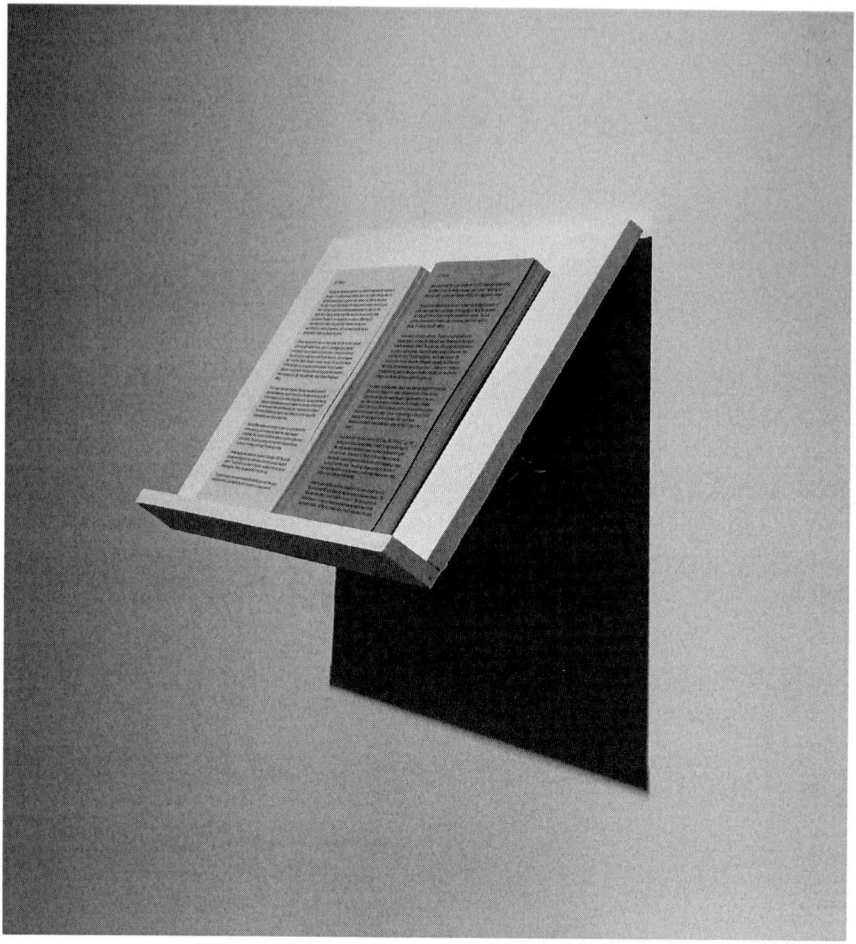

Cuttings 1 and *Cuttings 2*, 2012, two text works on card available for the audience to take copies.

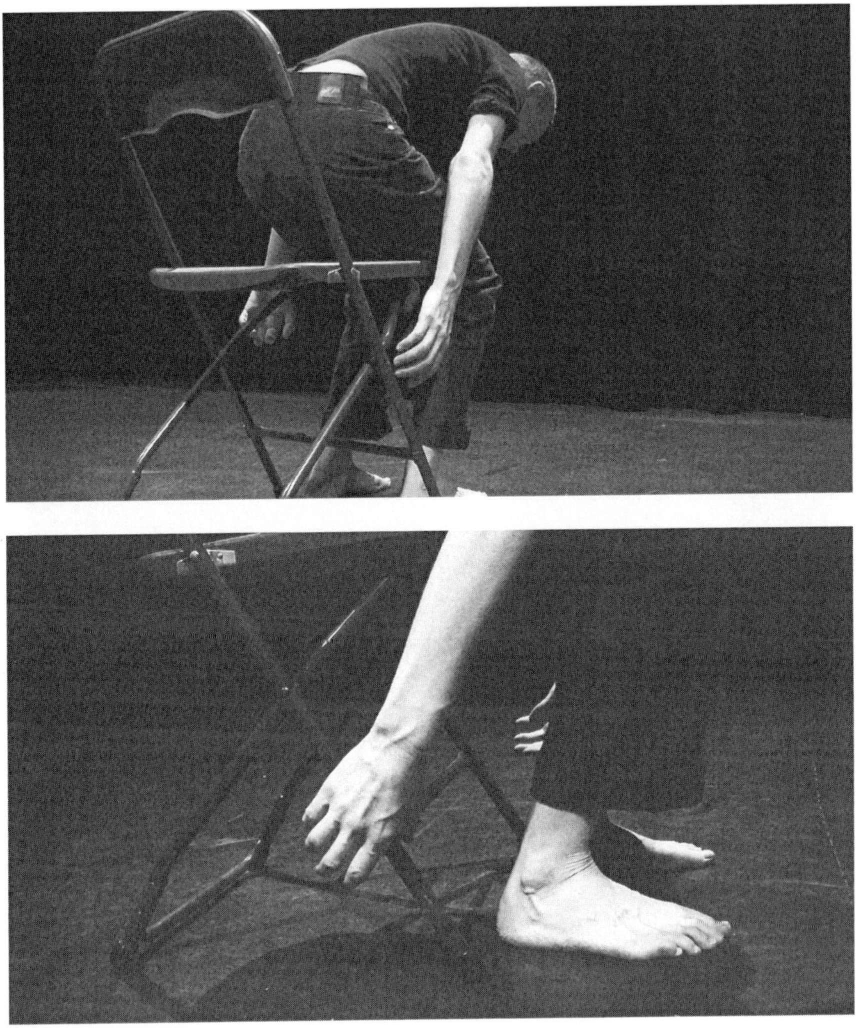

Settle, 2012, single screen video work documenting a performance with folding chair.

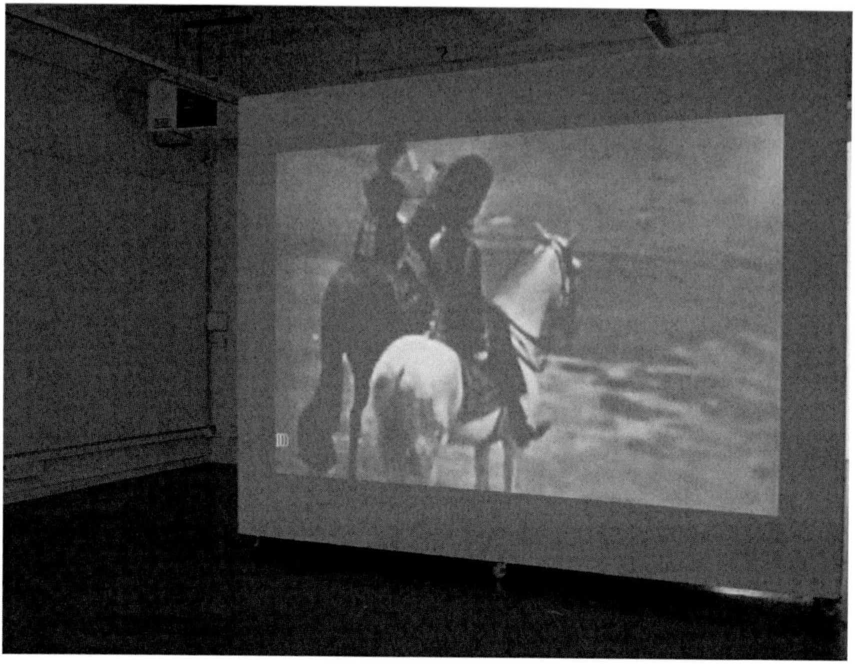

Rank and File, 2012, installation consisting of a single screen video work and found objects. The projected film footage documents the British Queen undertaking her first state duties in 1952. The installation involved nine plastic chairs salvaged from the Maze prison, mounted in steel frames and bolted to the gallery floor.

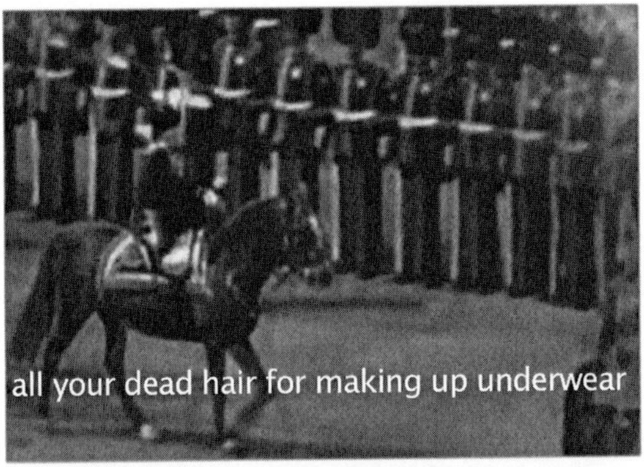

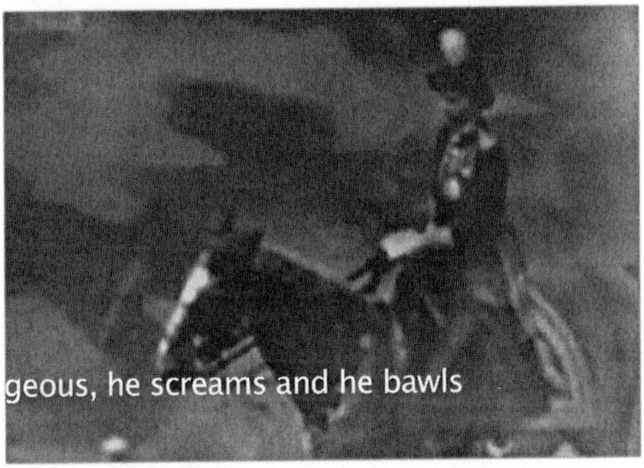

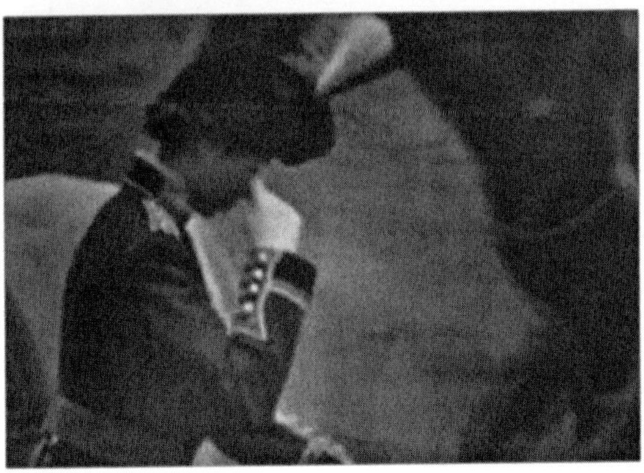

Rank and File, 2012, continued

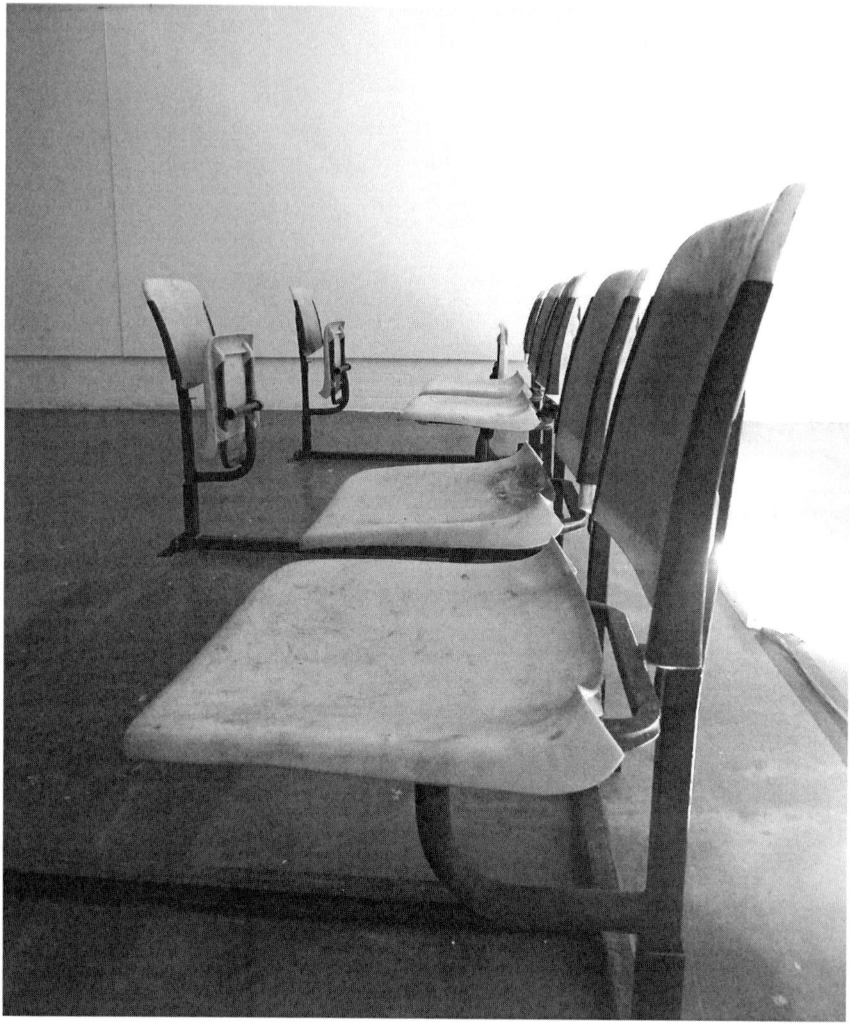

Rank and File, 2012, continued

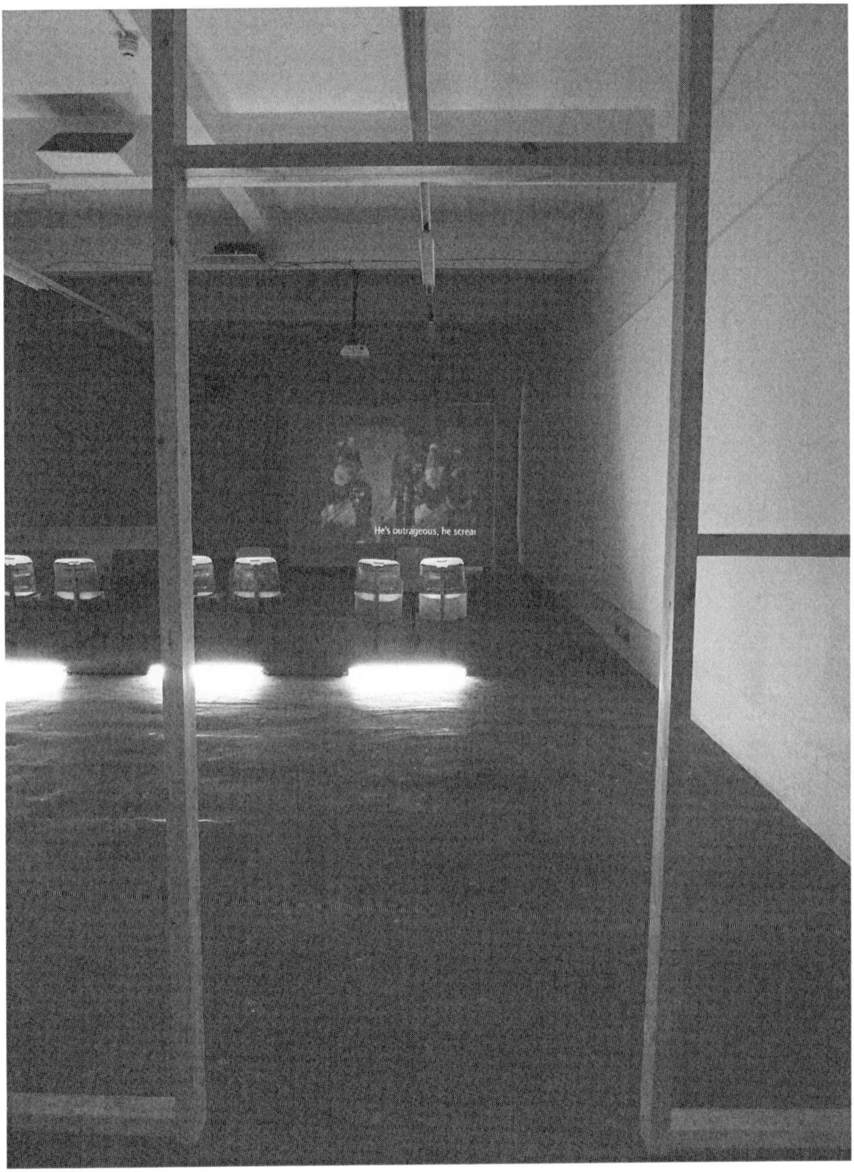

Rank and File, 2012, continued

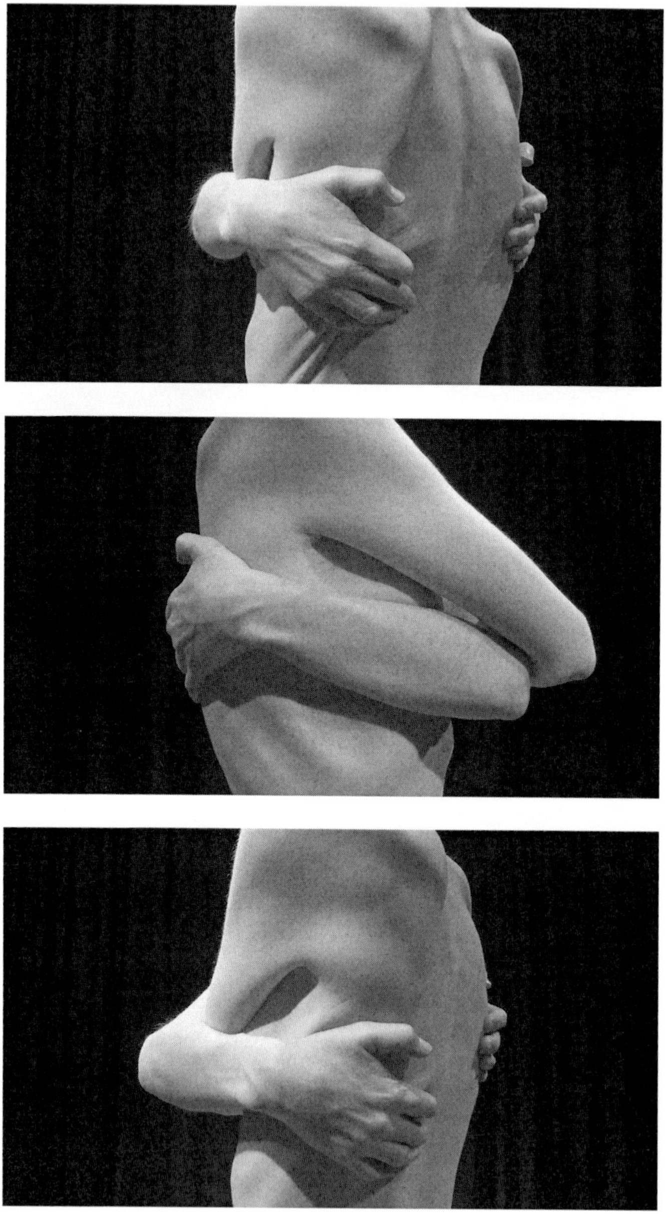

Hold In, 2012, two-part video shown on two standing monitors: torso filmed simultaneously from front and back of body.

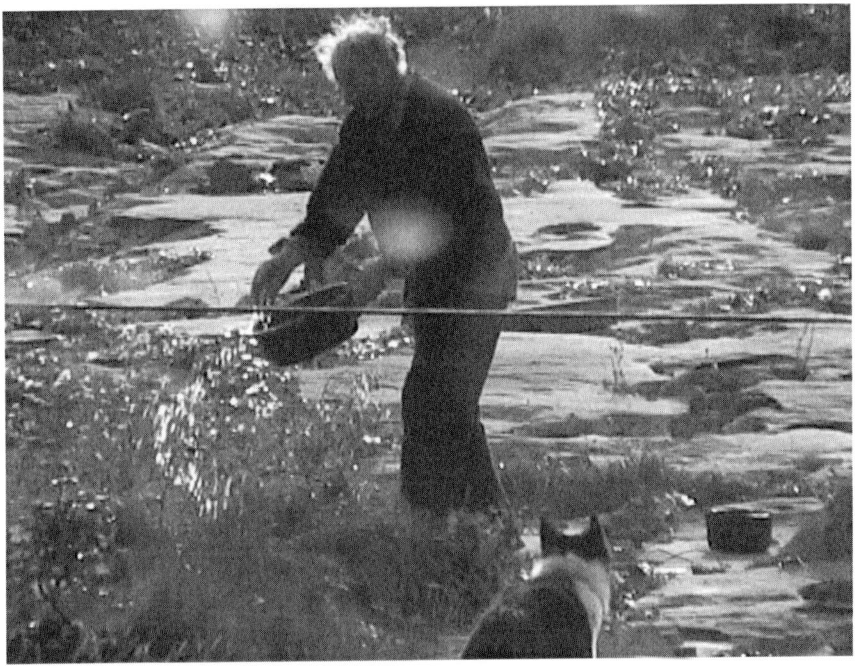

Charlie Haughey, 2012, single screen projection onto a double-sided glass frame containing a sheep's fleece. Filmed on Inis Oirr in 2006 in response to the broadcast on Irish radio of Charles Haughey's death.

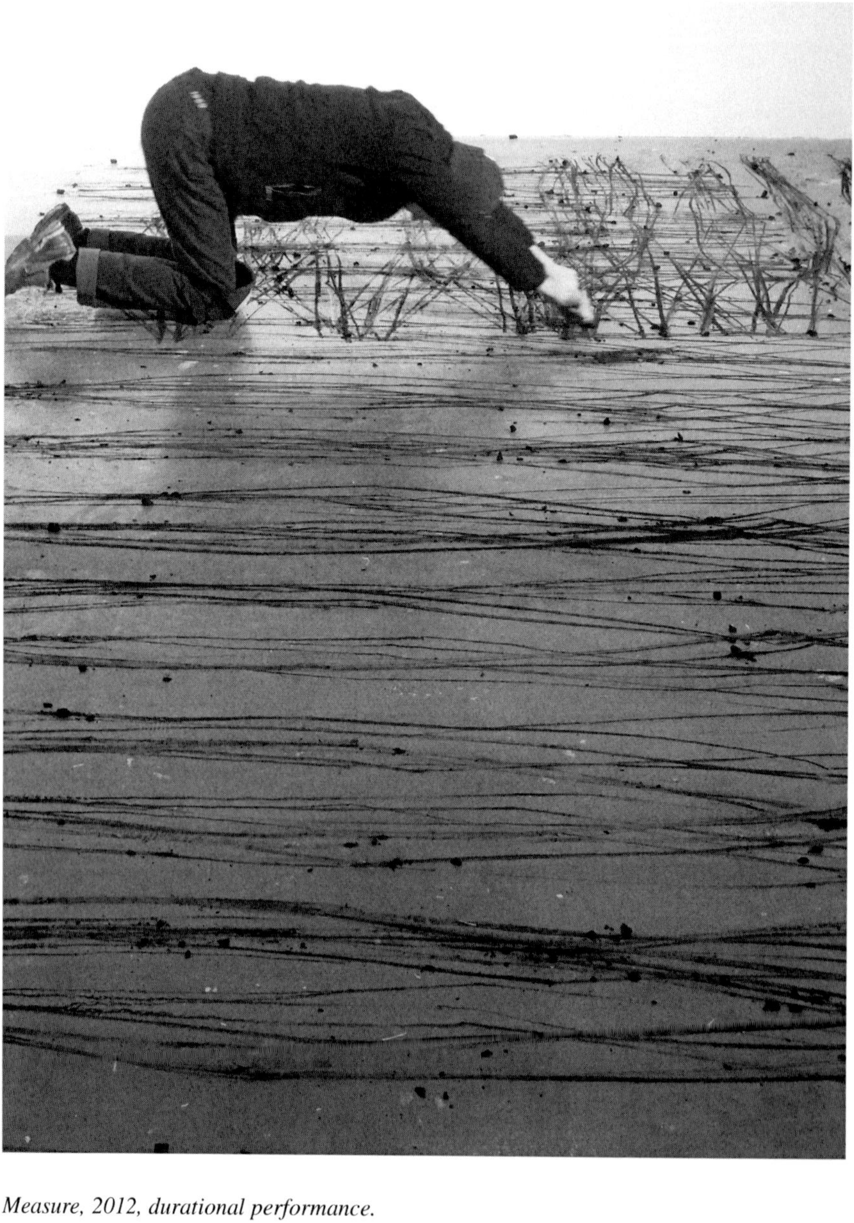

Measure, 2012, durational performance.

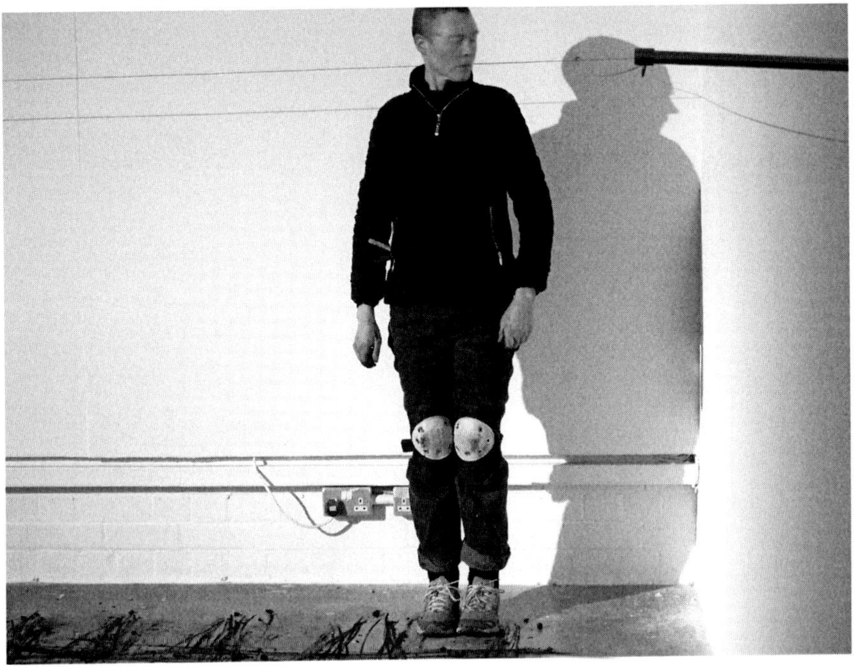

Measure, 2012, ten-hour durational drawing action, developed in a room installed with steel cables fixed at the level of the artist's neck, which regulated movement at each stage of the performance.

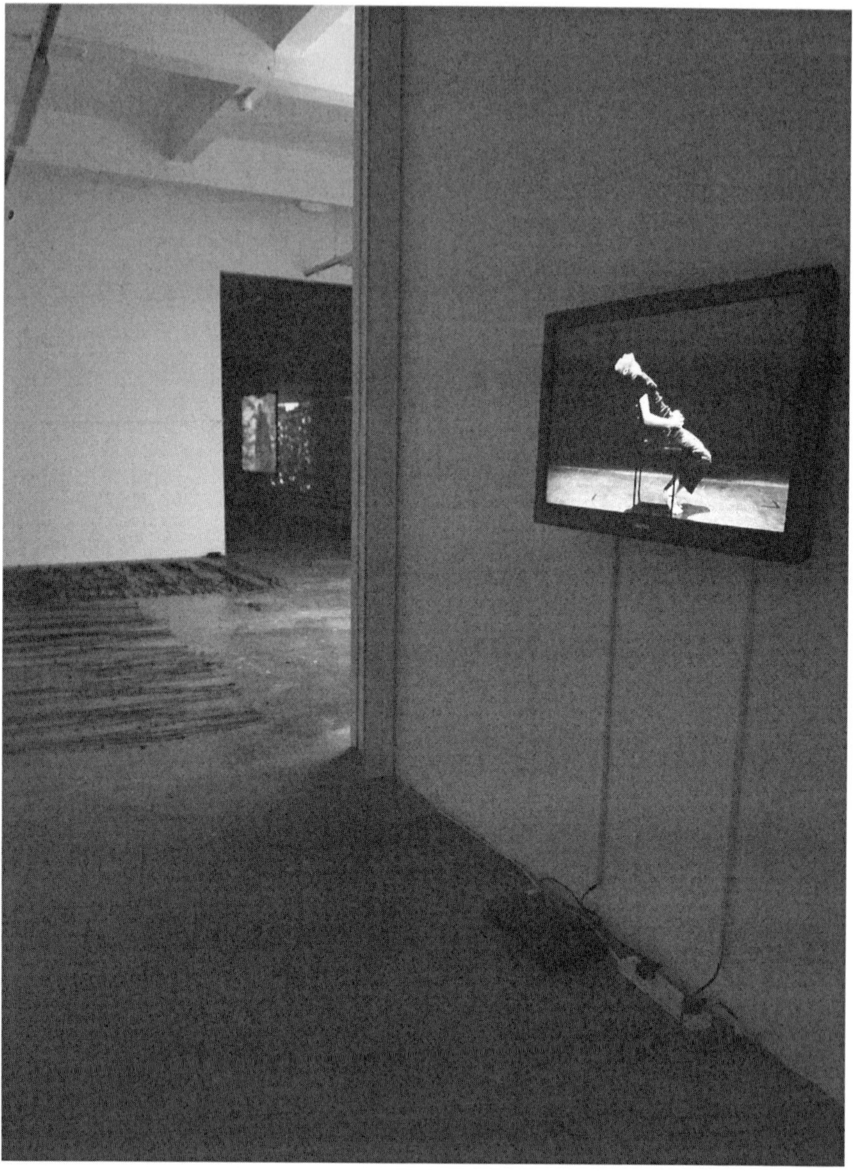

360° From the Heart, 2012, single screen video, installation shot.

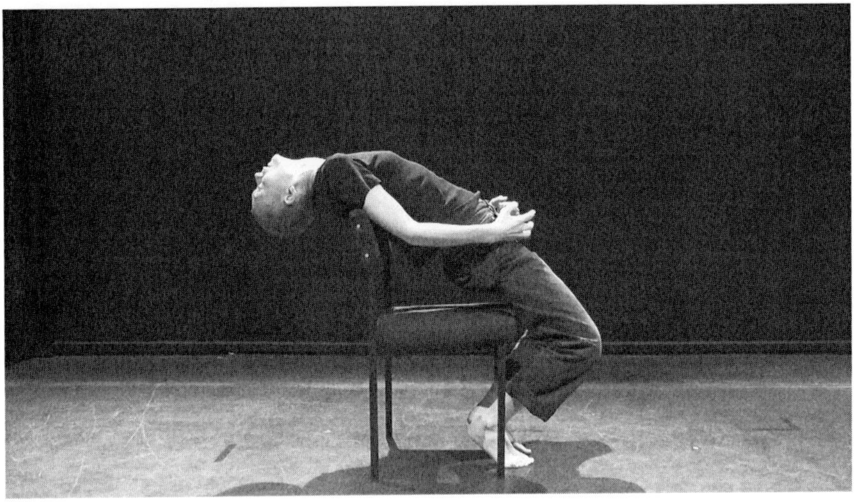

360° From the Heart, 2012, single screen video work.

INTRODUCTION: BEYOND REASONABLE DOUBT

> We always expect certain results from the truth: that it will transform the unknown into the known; that it will clear up a mystery; that it will prove or disprove a hypothesis. It is here that the judge – who demands of both witnesses and accused that they swear to tell "the truth, the whole truth, and nothing but the truth" – meets the theologian, the scientist, the philosopher, and the moralist. All share the expectation that the truth will help them to know an object that has heretofore been either partly or totally unknown. (Achour 2002: 123)

This study, entitled *Beyond Reasonable Doubt*, is an enquiry into legal processes, which began by considering how 'truth' is constructed by various practitioners in their relevant disciplines, from the staged aspects of legal situations to processes of evidencing, and ultimately how law is performed and its rulings mediated back into society. The investigation draws on literature and practice in the areas of performance art, its theory, anthropology, as well as studies on trauma, theatre, peace and reconciliation, culture, politics and the law. It is hoped that it will also contribute to debates in and between these fields. The core questions raised are pertinent to the peace process in Northern Ireland and elsewhere, but it was especially felt that it was appropriate and timely to make work about the performances of justice within a political climate of reactivated inquiries, bringing back into public awareness events from the Troubles. Additionally, since part of the legacy of the Troubles continues to be socially divisive (regarding concepts of justice, amnesty and forgiveness), it is an ongoing issue within Northern Ireland how this society continues to construct a collective basis of truth-making.

Essentially, the investigation proposes that the diverse evidence of human rights violations is primarily carried and conveyed through gestures: from the enacted staging of terrorist spectacles, the interpretive performances of legal testimony and the embodied gestures of protestors, to the responses of survivors sometimes existing on the cusp of invisibility and silence. This spectrum of embodied evidence forms the core of the study, which was led by subjective experimentation through performance and installation artworks (see here the documentation of the exhibition *The Shadow of A Doubt*) and writing, as well as an analysis of relevant texts and literature. The writing is, in part, of a performative or documentary nature. At other times it is academic, i.e. it theorizes and contextualizes viewpoints throughout the written text. These methods of diverse questioning reflect a search for structures that can address human rights violations through interpretive and empathetic forms of embodied movement. This is in contrast with the dominance of verbal and textual forms of evidencing, such as those legitimised in legal processes. The research shows that performance art as a medium can accentuate and enrich the territory of sensory and compassionate interpretation of events through interjecting doubt and risk as active elements within communication. This does not replicate or replace the traditional methods of gathering evidence, but can be understood as a parallel activation of aspects of content otherwise elusive to rational documenting processes.

The most relevant issues that emerged from considering the framework of legal process in comparison to that of performance art were those of: witnessing, violation, testimony, evidence and judgement. Therefore, the investigation has been structured in direct correspondence to these central aspects, addressing in turn the act of witnessing events, representations of violations, testimony of violations, and processes of evidence, leading to ideas of judgement. In establishing this alignment of legal process as the underlying structure, I am asking the question: how does performance art relate to the performances of human rights violations? I have proposed this question, because of the overwhelming number of performance artworks that I have observed in twenty years, which I consider to be fundamentally acts of protest, or moments of profound testimony. These actions are motivated, I believe, by a desire for empowerment, both on behalf of the artist and also in an expanded sense a making available internalised 'evidence' directed outwards towards witnesses. The potency of the collective situation creates a reciprocal cycle between the people giving testimony and those bearing witness, who in effect facilitate the process of improvisation. The audience functions as a litmus test for the 'authenticity' of the actions that are created in front of them, and, in response, the artist feels a weight of responsibility for the 'truthfulness' of the content and method of how it is conveyed.

In this way, the investigation proposes that, during performance improvisation, artists work in progressive stages of separation from an underlying structure. What is primarily valued in the art form are the diversions and innovations that occur spontaneously, taking both artist and audiences into a space of unstructured or unpremeditated encounter. The quality of these transactions is the opening of doubt and its introduction in a constructive space of communication. Similarly, all social processes require inexplicable or irrational moments of risk-taking, in order to produce change in entrenched patterns of social interaction between groups and their environments. Within improvisation, eruptive and, indeed, disruptive opportunities are actively sought by practitioners and are understood to be necessary for the production of an effective space of readjustment and reflection.

The underlying concerns of the study were, over the course of the research, adjusted and refocused in response to concurrent political events. Several areas of enquiry were explored, such as judicial procedures through both legal and quasi-legal forms, consideration of reconciliation processes and issues of mediatization. This spectrum of enquiry has created new perspectives on performance art with regard to questioning what the nature is of the political and social communication encapsulated in temporal acts. Additionally, it complicates the often unquestioned notion that legal processes are comprehensive, authoritive and rational, whereas improvisation practices are inaccessible, irrational and unverified. Therefore, through comparative reframing, the investigation shows that improvisation is not disconnected from other social processes, but can be strategised and traced in ways that illuminate the equally flawed ephemeral and embodied processes at the core of legal practices.

The tracing of these kinds of observations are occasionally identified in the following chapters through insertions of texts in italics. These separated sections of text have been written in a more personal and speculative style, in response to diverse experiences of locating source material, whether from the internet or directly from publicly staged situations, such as performances, lectures, a tribunal session, a peace march or visiting a Holocaust archive. As a general rule, while referring to canonical performance artworks when appropriate, I have tried to prioritise the works of contemporary performers whose practices I believe are significant and serve to emphasise the fragile nature of certain strands of performance work, which generally elude being evidenced through orthodox photographic documentation. Therefore, the act of writing is utilised as a form of self-reflection, in that to write the descriptions I had to in some respects re-embody what I had witnessed, and also acknowledge some of the blind spots that occur in direct encounters.

In developing this investigation, I have been searching for ways to propose agency into the place of apathy and cynicism, seeking to find the human impetus behind public disclosures and in doing so I have become increasingly aware of the relevance of ideas from different disciplines. The primary fields and disciplines that have informed the work in both theory and practice through reading are media representations of war, discussed in the work of: Andrew Hoskins, Ben O'Loughlin and John Taylor, and in particular with regard to Northern Ireland: Bill Rolston, David Miller and Brian McIlroy. Holocaust studies, especially issues of memory and witnessing: Cathy Caruth, Dora Apel, Andreas Huyssen and Ulrich Baer. In relation to trauma and memory I used the work of Francis Guerin, Roger Hallas, Katharine Hodgkin and Susannah Radstone; in the field of conflict studies and psychology: Brandon Hamber, Alan Young, Stanley Cohen, Fiona Ross and Elaine Scarry; and in anthropological studies: Michael Taussig, Victor Turner and Paul Stoller. Performance theory is represented by: Peggy Phelan, Adrian Heathfield, Richard Schechner, Philip Auslander, Kristine Stiles, Amelia Jones and Brian Massumi; socially orientated art practices by Claire Bishop, Shannon Jackson, Gregory Scholette, Grant Kester and Christa-Maria Lerm Hayes; and political theory in relation to culture by Gene Ray, Boris Groys, Paul Virilio, Jacques Rancière, Zygmunt Bauman, Walter Benjamin, Gilles Deleuze, Felix Guattari and Judith Butler.

The investigation was affected by the global events of 2010-2011: from revolutions, to riots, and the growth of anti-capitalist movements among others. All of these events seem to indicate that the relationships between the performances of politics, legality and those of artists increasingly coincide in real space and real time in a multiplicity of activist forms. These diverse performances of collective activism are accelerating globally and flourish apparently in response to the failures of neo-liberal society. However, it is not my position to say that activism and art activities are interchangeable; there are distinctions, and an important part of this investigation has been to attempt to unravel why performance art remains not just on the margins of the culture industry, but is also persistently distanced from activist forms. One answer might lie in the framework developed by Deleuze and Guattari, where they term Kafka's writings as a 'minor literature'[31]. Perhaps performance can best be understood as a 'minor' art form, i.e. in utilising some parts of the dominant languages, the 'minor' is capable of creating disturbances within the encompassing system. These ideas are explored in this study in relation to the development of performance art in different contexts and especially regarding its growth in Northern Ireland since the 1970s. Observing how in this society performance art has became increasingly visible in public space, the medium has demonstrated a capacity to remould itself (as it inherently can) to adapt and critique the dominant processes of regeneration.

Despite the inherent instability within any conception of truth to arrive at a point of judgement beyond conjecture and doubt, there seemingly remains a compulsive drive to formulate some understanding of past events, especially when these have been violent in nature. In this regard, issues surrounding the gathering and dissemination of intangible heritage resonate with those raised by evidencing performance art, in that both acknowledge the brittle and time-loaded quality of extracting something of the 'truth' engrained within embodied acts. This study argues that creative art forms are not gauges of truth, but potent elements in the broader social trajectory of movement towards consensus about the reality of what has happened in the past. Therefore, the 'truth' exists in a trajectory and can only be approached and extracted at different points during the society's movement away from violence: a watershed of hidden, stigmatised issues slowly unravelling, clearing the space for further inquiry within the fields of the witnessing, memory, performance and the trauma thresholds of survivors of violence.

In the last few years what has come to be frequently termed in the media as a 'crisis of democracy' indicates a certain loss of trust and respect in the key organisations of state, government, church, financial institutions,

31 Deleuze and Guattari (1986). See also O'Sullivan (2006).

policing and media. In this climate of adjusting values, culture holds an interesting position as a platform of 'free speech', its status, and that of other alternative voices such as activist organisations, have gradually increased in comparative credibility. Whether framed through the actions of artists, community groups or activist structures, an idea has emerged from this investigation that compassionate communication forms are humble (human scale) as opposed to monumental structures or gestures, can proliferate organically in the manner of 'rhizomatic' (Deleuze & Guattari 1988) systems and are more wide spread and effective than is generally publicly acknowledged. Researching has encouraged me to reappraise the many almost forgotten, fragmentary, singular gestures that have been created by artists under circumstances of social oppression. There is no canon that supports these intrinsically delicate works, which have come into existence almost imperceptibly from the multitude of controlled and censored gestures out of which they emanate. There are many aspects and attitudes of human resistance and my respect continually deepens for the persistent efforts of individual and collective endeavours to create openness and humaneness in the face of conflict.

With the privilege of hindsight, I now see that this study has been about searching through different kinds of voids, silences, disappearances, the spaces around objects or between bodies, the animate and inanimate, the spectral, simulated, sacred, mundane, between separations and encounters, blindness and the gaze. What has become apparent from this searching is the social and individual compulsion to capture sensory evidence, and the need to mediate loss through acts of embodiment. Beneath the processes of law and the diverse evidences of history lies this residue of the numerous human performances of remembrance.

WITNESSING

> The term [Beyond Reasonable Doubt] connotes that evidence establishes a particular point to a moral certainty and that it is beyond dispute that any reasonable alternative is possible. It does not mean that no doubt exists as to the accused's guilt, but only that no reasonable doubt is possible from the evidence presented.
>
> *Beyond a reasonable doubt* is the highest standard of proof that must be met in any trial. In civil litigation, the standard of proof is either proof by a *Preponderance of the Evidence* or proof by *Clear and Convincing Evidence.* These are lower burdens of proof. A preponderance of the evidence simply means that one side has more evidence in its favour than the other, even by the smallest degree. Clear and Convincing Proof is evidence that establishes a high probability that the fact sought to be proved is true. The main reason that the high proof standard of reasonable doubt is used in criminal trials is that such proceedings can result in the deprivation of a defendant's liberty or even in his or her death.[32]

'Beyond a reasonable doubt' is a common legal phrase that addresses the task of the various participants within a jury system, and the standard above which their collective judgement must pass in order to be validated by law. The phrase positions in the mind's eye the inherently abstract quality of decision making, developed from retrospective consideration of words, actions, locations and timings all of which are reproduced through diverse sources of documentation, performance and simulation. Within this system, members of the jury act as witnesses not of events, but of the 'facts' that survive events, the traces and reconstructions that produce the potential of a new understanding of what has occurred.

Some complexities around issues of witnessing can be focused through the following account made on 19th March 1988, by the journalist Mary Holland, reporting on the events at Milltown Cemetery, Belfast. Holland

[32] Legal dictionary, http://legal-dictionary.thefreedictionary/reasonable+Doubt. Accessed April 2012.

described the traumatic experience of witnessing the execution of two Corporals in the British army. She asked the newspaper's readers to consider:

> How did we let it happen? He passed within a few feet of myself and dozens of other journalists. He didn't cry out, just looked at us with terrified eyes as though we were all enemies in a foreign country who wouldn't have understood what language he was speaking if he called out for help [...] Later, it seemed like hours but was in fact minutes, I found myself in a bookmaker's shop phoning for an ambulance. Someone in the shop said to me, "If anyone had tried to stop it they'd have been killed too." Now several days later I wonder. Probably we couldn't have stopped their deaths but we might, if we'd made a concerted effort, have halted the frenzy of the crowd, giving some of them the moments they needed to become individual human beings again, responsible for their own actions... Nobody, at least as far as I could see, tried [...] Whenever in the future I see that green in a girl's dress or on a summer beach I will have to ask why I did not make some gesture to show the young man in the green sweater that he was not utterly alone in a hostile country. (McKittrick 2000: 1121-1122)

Holland articulates the inestimable distance that formed between her as a person present at the site of Milltown cemetery and two other presences that passed her by. In their condemned state, the soldiers David Howes and Derek Wood had almost ceased to register as human. Holland had become one of the many in the crowd, immersed in witnessing, yet struck passive in the crucial moment of conflict. Others in the crowd responded with a fury fuelled by a sequence of retaliatory killings over the proceeding days, creating a momentum of immediate reaction, retribution, and execution. The complexity of the event begins to open up multiple overlaps of sectarian reprisals and contextual motivations.

Taking the same event reframed through media cameras, how can we quantify the impact of the public broadcast of the killings? If these images from what became known as The Corporal Killings are juxtaposed with the events of two days previous, 16th March 1988, the Milltown Cemetery Massacre perpetrated by a UDA combatant Michael Stone, then the two events begin to illuminate some issues of mediatization. These two atrocities can be analysed in consideration of the effects of their public broadcast, and what the footage demonstrates in regard to the spectacle of terrorism.

Some acts of paramilitary violence were captured in defiance, even retaliation against the media; a demonstration of this occurred during The Corporal Killings, when the reaction of one man was recorded as he raised a fist against the media from the taxi holding the two soldiers. Other terrorist events such as Stone's attack at Milltown were intentionally 'staged' for the media, to create notoriety and a visibility deployed as a reprisal.

How do we read the body language of people involved in what later becomes recognised as significant historical moments? The intervention of the media gives the viewer a privileged overview. There would seem to be most of the component parts of information available that could create sufficient evidence in the viewer's mind to establish a sense of certainty about an event. Yet, several strands of evidence are missing: the cameras are pointed from fixed positions, there are blind spots, distractions and inadequacies in the visibility available through the technology. Then beyond logistic considerations, there are misconceptions of motives: most observers, including some of the judges who heard the resulting trials, accepted that those who initially surrounded the Corporal's car were acting in defence of other mourners from what they feared were Loyalist assassins. Further to this, there are the embodied aspects of evidence, such as the smell of the victims, the touch, the words, sounds and utterances, all of which become essentially inaccessible. The emotive testimony of Mary Holland gives some indications of this kind of textured evocation of the situation: the visceral quality of watching in a state of shocked awareness. The broadcast footage on the other hand relays a different kind of analytical intensity, what is viewed is shocking partly because of the distancing – the dehumanising aspects of a hierarchical overview, and the severance this entails from assimilating the 'information' in any sensorial forms. The narrative sequence as replayed in broadcasts holds a prevailing inevitability, exacerbated by the overlays of commentary that directs interpretation.

As a result of the multiplicity of ways in which events can be examined, there is real difficulty in attributing one stable position, name or role upon those who experience events. Often positions are malleable and charged with other prevailing social dynamics. A statement by Stanley Cohen demonstrates this difficulty with regard to the situation of school bullying as an archetypal situation for understanding the bystander effect. Due to the way such situations incorporate and/or merge the roles of perpetrator, victim or bystander, he states that:

> The violence literally gets inside you – even though you are the observer, watching an image relayed by another observer (the photographer) of other observers watching a victim being humiliated or beaten. [...] Only psychoanalysis has dealt with the shifting dynamics in the bully-victim-bystander relationship. Bystanders may become like victims – not necessarily identifying with them, but becoming passive, helpless, frightened and frozen. Or they may become like bullies – taking vicarious and voyeuristic pleasure, egging them on or even aiding them by screening off playground incidents from the teachers' view or creating diversions.(Cohen 2001: 74)

These issues can extend further into the ethical implications of this passivity, as in the example of Mary Holland's description; even in directly witnessing proceedings, the mind can be full of conflicting information, and infiltrated by a sense of guilt at an inability to respond to the situation. This self-reproach establishes another form of blindness: a separation between herself and a recognition of the humanity of the two Corporals. Holland found herself unable to 'identify' with the physical language that the Corporals embodied in that moment, and she substitutes that incomprehension with an abstract marker – the colour green, replacing the moment of profound passivity with a gauge in her consciousness denoting that failing. The art theoretician Peggy Phelan articulates aspects of this substitution in proposing that when science proved human vision to be fundamentally flawed, it facilitated a deepening understanding of the unconscious mind. Phelan describes in *Unmarked* the inherent unreliability of human vision stating that:

> Unable to perceive the full range of colour inherent in light, the human eye is physiologically falsifying. This notion of the eye's inability to see fully may well have prompted the subsequent description of consciousness' inability to absorb fully psychic data. Just as physiologists posited the idea of an "after-image"– a shadow of an image which remains on the retina for a brief second after the image has actually vanished from the visual field (a memory that makes the perception of cinematic continuity possible) – so too did psychoanalysts posit that a "trace" of a psychic event remains in the unconscious, Freud's mystic writing pad. In other

> words, the after-image participates in a kind of "optic unconscious" (the phrase is Walter Benjamin's) – a realm in which what is not visibly available to the eye constitutes and defines what is – in the same way as the unconscious frames ongoing conscious events. Just as we understand that things in the past determine how we experience the present, so too can it be said that the visible is defined by the invisible. (Phelan 1993: 14)

With regard to issues of visible evidence, performance art can sometimes function as an alternative form to displace the ocular dominance of other cultural and media representations. A key feature of performance art as a medium is the deliberate hybridization and/or subversion between aspects of the spoken, uttered and physically enacted forms. Dissonance is created between how forms of language converge or are dislocated, and by extension the space that this opens up around and within the performing body. Therefore, the sensorial aspects of communication that are emitted from performance artists frequently alternates between the 'authority' of stated presences, into an evocation of fragile but perceptible absences.

John Durham Peters has examined the concept of witnessing as it has evolved through religious and legal traditions, particularly with regard to the testimonies of Holocaust survivors. For Peters, witnessing is an act involving two possibilities: that of passive seeing, or the active form of telling. In his formulation, the witness is charged with being active through the knowledge of what they have seen. This shift away from the idea of passivity, or peripheral positioning, opens the possibility that the witness can be configured as central. Peters states that,

> In passive witnessing an accidental audience observes the events of the world, [while] in active witnessing one is privileged possessor and producer of knowledge in an extraordinary, often forensic, setting in which speech and truth are policed in multiple ways. What one has seen authorizes what one says; an active witness first must have been a passive one. (Polchin 2007: 210)

Frequently in contemporary writing on performance art there is prevalence among practitioners and theoreticians to use the word 'witness' interchangeable with the word 'audience'. This indicates an acknowledgement of the non-theatrical quality of the artworks discussed, pertaining to the intended actuality or 'authenticity' of live events. Traditionally, performance art has been defined by these qualities of non-artifice, non-acting, although this is a division that is contested persuasively by Philip Auslander (1999), since there have always been strands of performance art that are highly theatrical and reproducible, yet, in the tradition of fine art-related performance art, the ethos of ideas of real time and actuality are persistent values.[33] Regarding this, the legal terminology of witnessing, testimony and evidencing is important when put in conjunction with performance, because of the implications of these terms in relation to the irrevocable nature of events. What is spoken or given in court evidence carries the weight of the irreversible. This involves not only the ritual of the Bible oath, but also the process in itself, which records categorically the changes in the proceedings. In effect, court cases document the performance of violations to a level beyond ephemeral acts, they are structured re-enactments that can be fractured and reassembled in a number of combinations, in relation to the flow of evidence. But always there is the necessity of arriving at a point of judgement, which is usually considered to be irrevocable.

ACTIVE WITNESSING AND TESTIMONY

The act of giving testimony to atrocity has come to be understood as an extended, life long process that goes through protracted changes. The work of Dori Laub discusses the profound absence of the Holocaust witness, how historical and psychological processes conspired to deprive those who were traumatised by the Holocaust of the opportunity to come to terms with it internally: they lacked the ability to bear witness to their own destruction. In part, Laub suggests, this was because of an inner inscribed shame, or fear of the Nazi-propagated 'truth', where the Jewish survivors had absorbed and ingested a sense of being subhuman, which meant that they could not bear witness to their own destruction. However, Laub then proceeds to describe the process of gathering video testimony for the Fortunoff Video Archive for Holocaust Testimonies, as the moment of potential for creating an act of witnessing. Laub calls this process 'historical retroaction' (Caruth 1995: 70) wherein those things that could not be spoken of, or more accurately heard and received during the time of the Holocaust, have only after

33 For discussions of actuality in performance see for example Phelan (1993) and Schechner (1988).

the 1960s evolved as performative based practices of drawing out memory. The activation (through psychoanalytic treatment and/or giving archive testimony) of the 'internal witness' (Caruth 1995: 69) inside each survivor is an action of reaching into the survival mechanisms of the narrative that the survivor built internally to explain horrific circumstances. Laub describes how in the interview process:

> [T]o a certain extent, the interviewer-listener takes on the responsibility for bearing witness that previously the narrator felt he bore alone, and therefore could not carry out. It is the encounter and the coming together between the survivor and the listener, which makes possible something like a repossession of the act of witnessing. This joint responsibility is the source of the re-emerging truth. (Caruth 1995: 69)

Another perspective of active witnessing, that of the intermediary, is developed in Andrew Hoskins and Ben O'Loughlin's book War and Media: The Emergence of Diffused War (Hoskins & O'Loughlin 2010), where they analyse the complexities of the multiple perspectives involved in global newsgathering. With regard to the mediated material made by NGOs such as Amnesty International, they argue that, 'Media becomes weaponized, not as a weapon of terror but as a weapon of care' (Hoskins & O'Loughlin 79). In an interview, Theo Murphy of Amnesty International describes the process of giving testimony on behalf of the disadvantaged:

> [F]or Amnesty, the authenticity comes from the process of establishing empathy through direct contact with, in this case, the refugees. It may be a bit farfetched but I even think there is something of the researcher taking on the suffering he/she witnesses and when they speak about what is happening in Darfur they are able to transmit that; or better yet feel legitimate in speaking so emotively about what is happening as it has in a minor way happened to them or at least they have in some way shared in the experience. (Hoskins & O'Loughlin 78)

In this instance the NGO reporter takes on the authority to speak for others, whereas various human rights organisations such as Witness consider the act of transmitting testimony as a 'participatory panopticon' (Hoskins & O'Loughlin 79), where the NGOs act as enablers for communities to document their own circumstances, by giving them the technological means of production and providing a support mechanism for the dissemination of the recordings.

These diverse documentary forms of authored testimony have implications for how audiences then encounter and interpret artworks, and whether or not the 'evidences' of art are perceived as authentic or fictitious. This ethical ambiguity is often used strategically by artists, to unhinge formulaic readings of complex issues by interjecting, for example, the perspectives of people otherwise disregarded, or non-linear narrative structures among other forms. Art practices that produce testimony through the methods of documentary photography and filmmaking are touched on, but only in examples of artworks that subvert the visual and ethical conventions of traditional documentary methods, such as those by Steve McQueen, Willie Doherty and Artur Zmijewski. Concerning the issue of authenticity of responses, although a performance artwork may indicate that it has been informed or is responding to 'real' events, the medium of improvisation is inherently oblique. Therefore it constitutes an abstraction away from the proof of evidence. However, performance as a medium has the potential to accentuate and enrich the territory of sensorial and empathetic interpretation of events. This does not replicate or replace the traditional methods of gathering evidence, but can perhaps be understood as a parallel activation of aspects of content otherwise elusive to rational documenting processes.

Methods of reality television (Holmes & Jermyn 2004) such as crime scene reconstructions and appeals also raise questions of presence and the mutability of human appearances. This is an important issue, taking as an example the media news reports of the Joanna Yeates' murder investigation from December 2010. In these reports, the victim was repeatedly represented within a framework of loving family relationships, her 'ordinariness' reapplied in successive news bulletins. Yeates' initial introduction into media was as a 'missing person', and in the first few days of enquiry, her status could be described as liminal, suspended between possibilities of being alive or dead. When a body was discovered, it took some hours before it was confirmed to be the body of Joanna Yeates. In this moment, she appeared to be more real to the British public; she became a presence through the confirmation of her death. An increasingly detailed account of the events leading up to her murder was released over subsequent days, adding layers of association, statements from parents, press analysis of her movements, indications of lifestyle, all gradually evoking a constructed sense of personality. The most persistent aspect of this production of presence occurred through the use of CCTV footage, accumulated piece-by-piece and repeated sequentially. These unclear pictures created an indistinct spectre of Yeates moving through supermarkets, across the corner of a street. Retrieved movements created a timeframe within which she conceivably arrived at her home. Additionally, the *Crimewatch* TV programme (2011) produced a reconstruction of her last-known movements, supplementing the visual inexactness of the CCTV pictures with the enhanced images of an actress moving through the same situations.

These media methods for building presences from deaths make apparent some complexities in our acceptance of what is authentic or real, which has implications for all forms of evidencing ephemeral occurrences. The example of CCTV footage is a useful model concerning our understanding of the veracity of evidence, because it incites a sense of effortless familiarity, where isolated split seconds of mundane footage become hyper-volatile prompters of constructed emotion. It is a hybrid form of captured motion that appears to reveal facts, because it facilitates a segmented halting vision between the still and moving picture. The problematic here lies in the compelling cultural adoption of these forms of excavating from 'the real', since the forms are not inherently stable, but audiences' reactions to them have become prescribed and accepting. Comparatively, in watching video documentation of live performance actions there are also core problems with the emphasis on metronomic running time created by a camera, which compresses the sense of time and space, distorting perceptions of the quality of time experienced in watching something occurring live.

In contemporary theatre there are numerous examples of companies using various formulations of technologies integrated with live action, in order to alter perceptions of time and the ways in which audiences become engaged or even implicated in staged events.[34] An example of this is the media art collective, Blast Theory (2011), who have often produced work using actors and online gaming technology. In 1998 they staged a work entitled *Kidnap*, where they carried out a realistic kidnapping of two mem-

34 See for example Shannon Jackson's description of productions by The Builders Association and Rimini Protokoll in Jackson (2011: 144-181).

bers of the general public, and screened their imprisonment via the Internet. Online audiences could interact by manipulating a surveillance camera inside the safe house and communicating directly with the kidnappers. The work pivots on the fascination that people would volunteer themselves to 'win' this opportunity, and that therefore somewhere within the horror of kidnapping lies a degree of suspended fantasy. In fact, Blast Theory actually used cinemas to promote the trailer advertisements for this project, and from this campaign approximately one hundred people volunteered, which would seem to reinforce the link in the work between cinema representations and the glamorization of violence. Among the proliferation of reality television programmes since the 1990s, such tactics have been used to create entertainment from circumstances that ordinarily would be condemned as immoral. In the adoption of these tactics there is a guarded evasiveness around ethical conduct, however the situations are made possible by the legal agreement of the participants who accept responsibility for their voluntary participation. The echoing of terrorist strategy as theatrical intervention exposes a somewhat cynical contemporary rendering of affecting engagement, and the use of technology, either through internet interaction or television viewing, provides an emotional distance and sufficient disengagement for such events to be produced. However, other theatre practitioners, such as Theatre of Witness, develop their projects in carefully constructed processes that facilitate empathetic forms of witnessing between audiences and performers.

With regard to the aftermath of documenting events as public acts of witnessing, a historical example is the Adolf Eichmann trial of 1961, held in Jerusalem, which was the first example of a complete court proceeding recorded for television broadcast. This case demonstrated many of the complexities in the concept of broadcasting legal events. According to filmmaker and writer Eyal Sivan, historians and scientists have largely ignored the trial footage archive as a reference source, despite it containing testimonies from over one hundred victims, and the words of the perpetrator. Sivan points out that the trial has been systematically reduced to a few minutes of iconic footage, which, he argues, is indicative of how these forms of archiving often fulfil political agendas, reiterating linear narratives, rather than activating more complex processes of enquiry and interpretation.[35] Societies usually focus on a 'duty of memory' (Sivan 2002: 284) towards the victims of historical events, on a concern with reinforcing through visual means, constructing agreed truths. Paradoxically, complexities in representations, e.g. the rhetoric of perpetrators, and the examination of their thoughts and motives generally exist more comprehensively in fictional representations than in documentary forms. Sivan comments:

> There is no question of truth here; the beginning of an answer might be the question of the function of collective memory. The act of filming allows an emphasis on the spectacular function of the event: some images, mainly of victims, help to create icons of memory – what we used to call "monuments". (Arendt 1964: 282)

Therefore, part of the perceived importance of validating history, as it is witnessed taking place, is that the spectacle as monument holds an intrinsic value in itself. An extension of this idea is the contemporary practice of gathering data from global forensic satellites, detailing suspected political atrocities (Weizman 2010). Although the scientific processes of verification and monitoring mean that the forensics gathered could potentially be considered legally conclusive, in practice such evidence is always augmented by human testimony. Consequently, it is in the repetitious multi-layered telling of atrocity, its unpacking through demonstrative telling, that remains the momentous trace.

ALMA SULIJEVIC[36] LECTURE, UNIVERSITY OF ULSTER, 2007

Since 1997 the Bosnian artist Alma Sulijevic has been developing a project entitled, 4 Entity, in which she works as a volunteer involved in removing landmines from the areas across Bosnia and Herzegovina that were carpet bombed during the Bosnian War from April 1992 to December 1995. The title of the work ironically indicates the political subdivision of Bosnia and Herzegovina into three ethnically homogenous territories namely: Repub-

35 Hannah Arendt attended the Eichmann trial and mediated it through philosophical, non-sensationalist writing, see Arendt (1964).

36 Alma Sulijevic is an artist and professor at the Academy of Fine Arts in Sarajevo.

lika Srpska, Federation of Bosnia Herzegovina and a city district called Brcko District. Sulijevic's suggested fourth territorial entity is the zone still covered in several hundred thousand antipersonnel landmines. I experienced the work of Sulijevic while working with her collaboratively on a project entitled Appropriate, in 2007, during which time she gave a lecture at the University of Ulster. In this lecture Sulijevic adopted a testimonial approach; in effect she asked the audience to participate in a form of witnessing to the aftermath of war, by engaging with the evidence that she demonstrated through both spoken testimony and physical residues. What we witnessed was threefold, firstly the artist's rhetorical performance, articulating the scale of the humanitarian crisis through the lecture format. Secondly, there was the screening of a video artwork documenting the act of landmine extraction from the fields; and thirdly there was the sale of hand-sewn bags of decontaminated earth extracted from around defused landmines. Additionally a certificate of authenticity was signed with every bag of earth. In this transaction of selling the earth, Sulijevic makes palpable the idea of lost territory, the zones of unusable land implanted with the long-term residue of warfare. She knowingly uses the context of the art world to disperse this evidence, in that the earth has clear symbolic value, which is converted into financial capital and used to continue the land mine clearance operation. The decision not to sell the actual landmine devices is one which effectively deflects the fetishized aspects of the machinery of destruction.

Additionally, through the action of selling the decontaminated earth, what is evoked conceptually is the loss or the void and the deaths sustained from the bombs, yet, also the idea of growth and what is required to make the ground fertile once again. Sulijevic relates how the land clearing is mainly undertaken by elderly women and describes the intuitive qualities of the physical action, learning how the earth feels when you probe it for mines, the experience of surfaces beneath the ground:

> *There is a very sensitive instrument that is used in the field. Each time you drive this tool into the earth you have a certain feeling of tactility. You are very sure if you find glass, which is very slick. You start to get a sense of the materials in the ground. Actually, you think about the mines, and then you do not think at all. (Peace Women 2012)*

Sulijevic's lecture in some respects replicated the methods of the courtroom by utilising spoken testimony, visual representations and physical forms of evidence, completed by the signed certificate as a quasi-contractual agreement between the buyer and the artist.

In her lecture she compellingly communicated the idea of hidden carnage, and brought the audience into contact with the fear involved in the continuing effects of warfare on everyday life. And although, or perhaps because, she described her actions without drama or self-importance, Sulijevic's presence conveyed the visceral sensations of working with the unknown and the uncontrollable.

EMBODIED ACTS OF WITNESSING

The lineage of most improvisational practices in art goes back to DADA, Surrealism and Fluxus. It has always been an oppositional stance to existing social values, the impetus of searching beyond what can be explained, evidenced, or proven (Bürger 1984). By exploring methods to embody acts of the unconscious, art has often functioned as a rejection of patriarchal, rationalist structures, and ultimately a rejection of war. In describing his conception of various stages of the developments in social mourning, and issues of representation after Auschwitz and Hiroshima, political theorist Gene Ray makes interesting observations about the relationships between repressed trauma and creative activity manifesting as 'play'. Ray describes that within the process of artistic 'acting-out' there are inherent features of control and structuring, but that in order to engage traumatic elements hidden in the unconscious, these elements must be approached elliptically, the process is necessarily indirect:

> Acting out – a symptomatic way of avoiding the repressed by displacing it into repetitive forms of behavior – is I think best grasped as an early phase or opening in the process of working through, rather than rigidly opposed to it. This helps us to see how art can function as a relatively privileged field for the initial processing of these kinds of collective traumas. In strictly psychoanalytic terms, acting-out is an unconscious manifestation of resistance. But art of course is never completely unconscious: it has often enough mobilized the unconscious and its contents, but only by subjecting them to some degree of conscious, formal control. So some kinds of art can be thought of as a practice of acting out

> that is partially conscious and that incorporates elements of a more critical working-through: "playing-through," we could call it. "Play" may at first seem an inappropriate category for grasping responses to qualitative events of genocidal violence, but the fact is that it's not always possible to confront these events directly. Playing with them symbolically – artistically – is a way of first approaching and liberating repressed material. (Ray 2011: 22-48)

Ray's term 'unconscious manifestations of resistance'(Ray 22-48) is particularly constructive in explaining the dynamics of improvisation, i.e. how fear, anger, guilt, shame and any number of emotions can leak from a performer's body, often without the artist's preconception or immediate comprehension of what is triggering these responses. In discussing the layered effects of violence and pain, Venna Das has stated that, 'Denial of the other's pain is not about the failings of the intellect but the failings of the spirit. In the register of the imaginary, the pain of the other not only asks for a home in language but also seeks a home in the body' (Ross 2003: 49). The argument is essentially a question of embodiment: to what extent it is possible to inhabit the sphere of another's pain, and if in fact pain can be transformed through acts of interpersonal sharing. Representations of pain in performance art form the traditional canon of artworks from the 1960s, and the issue of masochism has been a significant theoretical concern in relation to the medium.[37]

The work of artists such as Boris Nieslony, André Stitt, Htein Lin, Alma Sulijevic and Roi Vaara in relation to different issues and questions of violations has an influence on how the nature of the violence expressed in contemporary practices is perceived. According to Ray it is a form of psychological working through, testing behaviour, perhaps even a testing of social forgetting, especially failures of communication. And, returning to the idea of testimony, the actions are perhaps most often intended as offerings to evoke not reactions of shock, but of compassion.[38] However, this change can usually only become credible in the moment of transitioning from another more abject state. The emphasis is in the transitioning and how the

---

[37] For discussions of masochism in performance art see for example O'Dell (1998). Also 'Rupture', Jones (2006: 79-85), and Alfano Miglietti (2003).

[38] See for example Weintraub, Danto and McEvilley, (1996), Phelan (2003: 16-27) and Jones (2006).

audience and performer mutually understand the contract of responsibility running beneath the process of disclosure.

LIMINAL ASPECTS

The core ideas within this discussion are essentially about instability and the transitional, liminal or oblique aspects of artworks when considered in relation to legal methods of evidencing. In the ideas introduced by Ray above, it can be recognised that there are factors of displacement and disorientation between conscious and unconscious understandings of creative actions, as a means of beginning the release of suppressed traumatic content. Therefore, doubt is essentially a process, not a fixed state. The sense of existing inside moments of historical change, whether on a micro level of individual human responses, or a macro level of political processes, these transitional conditions can create states of stasis and regression, but also of potency, aliveness and political agency. In the midst of these polarities, the value of doubt is in that it has a way of addressing the interim moment, void or threshold, where decisiveness is curbed, and positive and negative values allowed to circulate simultaneously without hierarchical judgement. Central to the issues of societies in transition is the frequently expressed desire to create 'certainties'; this usually means an undervaluing of the present state, and the process of 'arriving'. In this space, and within the actions of remaking identities a society emerging from violence must choose what to discard and what to preserve, what to memorise and what to constructively silence or forget.

The writings of American anthropologist Michael Taussig, whose concept of the 'space of death' (Taussig 1987: 4), which he describes with regard to the aftermath of colonial violence in Peru, is an introduction into ideas of liminality through politically created voids. Additionally, the work of Brandon Hamber (2009) in analysing processes of social transformation and the psychological aftermath of violence, provides an important perspective on how change manifests in different political settings, using the word 'ambivalence' to convey the uncertain spaces of transition. There are numerous other examples of how people, incarcerated or held within dehumanising circumstances such as refugee camps, resort to using the final layers of deprivation by making a weapon of nakedness, filthiness and ultimately starvation in order to shame their captors. In certain societies, the naked female human body is still regarded with trepidation, and is sometimes used as a curse. Recent examples such as Nigeria, 2003, where a group of women invoked a curse on Chevron Texaco, and in 2008, hundreds of women from Liberia living as refugees in Ghana staged a prolonged naked protest beside a highway against the Ghana government. These kinds of protest demonstrate the continuing power of bodily display and the forbidden aspects of what different cultures denote as the boundaries of taboo. The photographs taken by US military personnel inside Abu Ghraib prison reiterate the fact that these boundaries are exploited in times of war, since the calculated nature of the sexual humiliations that the soldiers perpetrated on their captives were strategic uses of culturally defined prohibitions. Therefore, when faced with extreme situations individuals enter into liminal spaces, unfamiliar to so-called normal society.

Additionally, just as the bodies of those murdered for political reasons disappear and resurface in many extraordinary forms, both physical and spectral, there are aspects of the practice of performance art that function within liminal space, and exhibit interim behaviours beyond the parameters of social orthodoxy. In this regard, the durational works of Teching Hsieh, Alastair MacLennan, Stuart Bristley, Mike Parr and Marina Abramovic are exemplary of acts of will pursued through a self-imposed contract that goes beyond ordinary levels of deprivation into realms of what would ordinarily be considered torturous. Yet, this physical actuality is continuously undercut by the implicit understanding that the deprivations are self-constructed, therefore drawing the works back into a lineage of understandings that, whilst in ways echoing human rights violations, can also be related to hermetic, spiritual practices.

In the chapters, it is not my intention to directly compare actual situations of human rights violations with art actions, although many performance artworks are made as direct, visceral responses to the suffering of others. What these artworks indicate is more to do with the transmission of trauma and the ways in which physical improvisation often utilises ritual properties of gesture and utterance beyond ideas and purposes of representation. This marking and unmarking of the human subject is important in questioning how artists can reflect difficult political content in their actions, without resorting to literal representations, or indeed becoming implicated in acts of propaganda.

WITNESSING AND MEMORY

NEWCASTLE UPON TYNE, 11TH NOVEMBER 2009

Two minutes silence is announced on a Newcastle metro train, the driver speaks to the passengers in a pensive tone of voice, 'ladies and gentlemen would you please join me in observing two minutes silence'. A tall young man has just got on with a pincher dog who responds to the sudden stillness by whimpering, cowering beside its owner, the man touches it lightly on the muzzle with the fingertips of one hand. Someone in front of me coughs, the sound male and throaty, I catch myself sneeze suddenly in reaction, otherwise the train remains silent. The carriage seats are positioned so that passengers correspondingly face each other; the silence makes all of us lower our heads, inadvertently we replicate from our moulded plastic chairs the stature and expression of grieving. A small yellow leaf on the floor of the carriage moves lightly in the breeze from the open doors. No mobile phones ring, nor does any sound enter from outside of the train, everything is subdued in this circumstantial moment of public commemoration, so ordinary, and yet so fragile this silence. The engine starts to turn over, the carriages vibrate beneath the seats, as an automated voice announces 'doors closing'. A few seconds later the driver speaks through the intercom 'thank you for your cooperation'. A brief termination of progress within the margins of a train stop, the doors seal shut.

To 'observe' two minutes of silence in remembrance is to participate in a form of secondary witnessing, the carrying forward of traumatic memory across generations embodied in a gesture of stillness that oscillates between passive and active. In some respects the witnessing only becomes active through its enactment as collective presence, the proximity of bodies marking a precise timeframe of inward reflection.

Andreas Huyssen in *Present Pasts: Urban Palimpsests and the Politics of Memory* (2003) describes the predominant shifts in international debates around memory congregated on the Holocaust as the inscriptive narrative. He states:

> It has been all too tempting to some to think of trauma as the hidden core of all memory. After all, both memory and trauma are predicated on the absence of that which is negotiated in memory or in the traumatic symptom. Both are marked by instability, transitoriness, and structures of repetition. But to collapse memory into trauma, I think, would unduly confine our understanding of memory, marking it too exclusively in terms of pain, suffering, and loss. It would deny human agency and lock us into compulsive repetition. Memory, whether individual or generational, political or public, is always more than only the prison house of the past. (Huyssen 2003: 8)

This statement has acted as an important reminder that discussions of memory should not be dominated by the past to the degree where there is no longer dynamic space for catalytic thinking. Huyssen and others argue that the legacy of accumulating global archives of traumatic material appears to have negative implications for human agency in constructing futures.

Legal proceedings are inherently bound to issues of witnessing and memory since trials must generate forms of reactivated evidence, usually evoked through the perspectives of witnesses. Therefore, legal processes can exacerbate the suffering of survivors and families of victims, some of the negative implications of societies' dependence on legal structures are discussed later. These negative effects are a consequence of the fact that the witnessing that occurs in courtrooms, often involves the re-enactment and in many respects re-embodiment of traumatic events. Yet, despite this, for many people it remains a vital step towards discovering the truth of events and in so doing beginning to deal with their loss. In an essay entitled, *The Terrorist Bombing in Oklahoma City*, Karen Sitterle and Robin Gurwitch examine the impact on survivors of the trial of the bomber Timothy McVeigh.[39] They describe how:

> In Oklahoma city, most citizens welcomed the trial of Timothy McVeigh as an important step towards closure for the survivors and the Oklahoma City community. However, few survivors were prepared for the emotional toll the trial took, as intense, gruesome stories about the bombing unfolded and were broadcast in the media daily. By the end of the trial, the community reexperienced the tragedy with the same intensity as when it

[39] The Oklahoma City Bombing took place on 19th April 1995, when a terrorist bomb destroyed the Alfred P. Murrah Federal Building. 168 people were killed in the explosion.

> occurred and reexperienced all the symptoms associated with the original trauma and its complicated bereavement. Involvement in the legal system can produce a secondary traumatization for victims for years after the actual incident. (Sitterle, Gurwitch 1999: 187)

The jury, relatives and media gather to establish the truth of an event, the trial is a recognised form of witnessing, but it is in effect, obscured, or indeed blind witnessing, since what is reconstructed is always based on the examination of residues and remembered perceptions of events. Thomas Macho describes how since the sixteenth century the figure of Justitia has been represented as a blindfolded virgin holding a sword and scales. According to Macho, the blindness of justice changed meaning from initially being a mockery of the blindness of court rulings, to becoming '[A] guiding maxim: the law is no respector of persons. The wealth, reputation or facial features of an accused person are not to distract the court; there must be no eye contact to cast doubt on the impartiality of the judgement' (Macho 2012: 177). This impartiality before the law is one conception of blindness, in effect placing the jury in the opposite position from that of the witnesses, since they are placed in the role of having to reconstruct vision from what is demonstrated rather than directly observed. But another understanding of blindness is that it can be the basis for developing a heightened sensitivity to other forms of perception. It is this position that Phelan adopts when she describes how it is the failure of vision that, paradoxically, can make us more attuned and aware of the empathetic forces beneath the gaze:

> [I]t is exactly because the gaze is "not all" that empathy and Symbolic identification are possible. Opening up of the "not all" of vision requires patience with blanks, with blindness, and with the non-productive. To take the humility and blindness inscribed within the gaze seriously, one must accept the radical impotency of the gaze. This impotency understands the broken and incomplete symmetry between the self and the image of the other. (Phelan 1993: 18)

In accepting these failures or blindness, there are rules for how a renewal of vision might take place. It is my proposition that it is only in valuing the ephemeral and sensorial aspects of events that we learn or remember how to have empathy for the people around us and the environments we inhabit. This has implications for the relationship between memory and audiences, since an integral part of performance art is that the performer is always accessible and responsible to the audience. As such there is an innate reciprocity and vulnerability to the relationship. For the audience to engage with what they see is an act of conscious witnessing, and to retain memories of an action is an act of will.

The Performance Of Human Rights Violations

> [S]pecific lives cannot be apprehended as injured or lost if they are not first apprehended as living. If certain lives do not qualify as lives or are, from the start, not conceivable as lives within certain epistemological frames, then these lives are never lived nor lost in the full sense. (Butler 2010: 1)

This chapter first deals with issues of the spectacle of terrorism, how the mediatization of violence has created a culture of atrocity based on the power of images. This exploration of mediatized representations is then developed in comparison to the texts, actions and images of artists, as acts of interpretation of what is perceived as precarious content or values. The second part looks at political funerals, censorship and blind spots, in particular the concept of 'the space of death' in relation to politically controversial deaths, and artists' interpretative representations of the threshold of life. Inherent in Judith Butler's statement quoted above is the idea of the value of human life being dependent on epistemological frames in order to uphold, reduce or evade the impact of loss. Both sections seek to reclaim territory from the distancing techniques of the mediatization of everyday life, which forms the crux of societal insecurity in admitting or adjusting to the ongoing unaccountable loss of human life.

Part 1: The Spectacle of Terrorism

The Spectacle of Terrorism explores what can be considered the limits of art's potential to make interpretations of real world events, in a situation of perverse reversal, where some of the most acute and memorable images of our times are those constructed and staged by terrorists. The visual aesthetic consciousness being employed by terrorists as an unequivocal form of weaponry has an impact on visual artists relegating the potency of representations made in opposition. And, since the performance of atrocity as media spectacle generates fear within populations, this has meant the impact of witnessing the visual act can actually supersede in significance the numerical effects of the actual loss of human lives. Therefore, whilst many artists are drawn to grappling with the visual content of atrocity (either appropriated from sources or constructed as fictions), this is viewed within the art world as an inadequate, but still a necessary effort to continue to challenge the veracity of the imagery that otherwise becomes entrenched into collective memory.

In his 2007 novel *The Falling Man* American novelist Don DeLillo created a character called David Janiak, a performance artist known as the Falling Man. This fictional character is described in the text appearing at random in public spaces, free falling from conspicuous buildings in a climbing harness. Janiak's performance is to hang in a static position, mimicking the infamous image of a man photographed falling from one of the World Trade Centre towers during the September 11th attacks. DeLillo describes one character's reaction to the artist's actions:

> He'd appeared several times in the last week, unannounced, in various parts of the city, suspended from one or another structure, always upside down, wearing a suit, a tie and dress shoes. He brought it back, of course, those stark moments in the burning towers when people fell or were forced to jump. He'd been seen dangling from a balcony in a hotel atrium and police had escorted him out of a concert hall and two or three apartment buildings with terraces or accessible rooftops.
> Traffic was barely moving now. There were people shouting up at him, outraged at the spectacle, the puppetry of human desperation, a body's last fleet breath and what it held. It held the gaze of the world, she thought. There was the awful openness of it, something we'd not seen, the single falling figure that trails a collective dread, body come down among us all. (DeLillo 2008: 33)

The character Janiak is unscripted throughout the novel and the motivations for his performances are only articulated through the responses of other characters, until eventually the physical extremity of the performed action leads to the character's death. The reoccurring sightings of the suspended 'Falling Man' caught in a freeze-frame of his own volition reactivates for other characters the horror of 9/11. Janiak's action of dropping head first in free fall into the memory shadow of the twin towers photograph becomes a motif, which is progressively replicated as the reader comes to understand that in fact all of the novel's characters are caught in various forms of descent. Each person is falling within states of inner grief and at different rates of velocity.

On 17th January 2009, an Internet search under the keywords 'Falling Man' brings up *Esquire Magazine* website (Junod 2012) and an article written by Tom Junod.

The article begins with analysing the situation of photographer Richard Drew, who took the iconic image, and the subsequent history of that photograph, including the search to identify the 'jumper' as the press dubbed those who fell. The identity of the man is still unresolved, and the article reflects possible reactions of would-be relatives, repudiating that the photographed man is their loved one.

The falling man has a goatee beard, light brown skin and beneath a white catering tunic an orange vest; this distinctive article of clothing has still not conclusively identified him. The article suggests the man remains unidentified because someone wants to protect his memory from the infamy of this image. Initially the image was reproduced and broadcasted all over the world, creating a storm of protest. This and other images of the 'jumpers' quickly came to be understood as taboo. One website interestingly acts as a hoax, luring people to read about the number of people who died by jumping, but instead the website attacks the searcher for voyeurism and perversity.

Copying the article across from the website into a word document, it takes a few moments to load before the image drops, fits into place, 'select all' flickers and perishes from the surface of one document in a split second transaction, before illuminating inside the next. Again the figure reappears, cast against the straight lines of the buildings behind. An almost impeccable symmetry, the body mysteriously static, elegant as if poised beyond time, then the horror implicit in this beauty, the reality of a body falling at 150 mph. My impression of the image is that it is too beautiful. Exactly this beauty is the crux of its disturbing power. I find myself, while looking at the image on the screen simultaneously viewing and averting my eyes. Or perhaps more accurately

scanning, sifting the components of the visual information, which depending on personal interpretation either gives the figure the perceived at-

titude of acceptance of fate, or heroic dignity. It is this ambiguity, which made the image instantly iconic, as the (alleged) pastry chef falls headlong; only in two frames of the nine shots photographed of him does his head face towards the camera. Others people photographed while falling displayed physical torment and desperation, as did other frames of the falling man, only this one image projects outward the quiet lie whispered into the consciousness of a terrorised state, the 'poetic justice' of heroism within the turmoil of destruction: you see what you want to see, or scan through the shock of looking at the images so widely prohibited as to become considered terror pornography.

The captured moment of the victim falling from the tower exudes a privacy, which makes the act of the photographer feel like an acute transgression. Yet, the persistent protection of the falling man's anonymity maintains an enigma around the photograph, facilitating its symbolic value as representative of all who died. Returning to DeLillo's novel, in using a character that obsessively repeats until death this one action of 'impossible' stillness, the writer attempts to state something about reactions to trauma and grief. Janiak is compelled to mirror the reality of the photographed falling man, to move beneath the illusory quality of the surface of the image into the actuality of experiencing the fall. Just as grief can be a form of psychological and physical suspension or numbness, trauma can also be a catalyst for replication and mimicry. The trajectory is of a visual moment forming a language of known gestures, which can then be manifested and replayed through cultural forms such as performance art and theatre, but also significantly the power of mimicry in spectacle within politics and terrorism. Seamus Kealy (2008: 49-91) in relation to the writings of Slavoj Zizek, reiterates the idea that Hollywood films in their repeated depictions of devastating mass destruction, in effect, created an appetite among the American population to experience in actuality the images they had consumed, initiating over time a corrosive process of transference from image simulation into 'a wish for destruction to appear in the Real' (Kealy 49-91). And, that this is a consequence of intensive mediatization, which creates psychological distancing from shocking truths of the Real. Kealy describes these phenomena as the complex infiltration of state politics into patterns of behaviour in daily life, fusing aspects of the machine of war with the machines of fantasy and illusion.

THE ACTS OF A MADMAN OR A SELF-STYLED MARTYR: THE PERFORMANCES OF MICHAEL STONE

Taking aspects of the fictional example of DeLillo's character, some of the same characteristics of mirroring occurred in the real actions of Michael Stone, a twice convicted terrorist killer, infamous in Northern Ireland especially for two acts of terrorism (he has also claimed other murders). Stone's actions are examined in this chapter through the broadcast media events they provoked, and the subsequent court proceedings, which formed a secondary discussion of retrieval and interpretation of aftermath. The events focused on are the Milltown Cemetery Massacre 1988, and secondly an attack at Stormont parliament buildings in 2006, which Stone has described and defended in court as a work of performance art.

On the 16th March 1988, Michael Stone, a member of the Ulster Defence Association, mounted an attack on the funerals of IRA volunteers Dan McCann, Sean Savage and Mairead Farrell[40] at The Milltown cemetery in Belfast, resulting in the deaths of three people and leaving sixty injured. This attack warrants the term 'massacre', and was discussed at the time for its audacity, seemingly a suicidal mission ending in Stone's capture by republican mourners who almost succeeded in killing him prior to the intervention of an RUC[41] patrol. In his autobiography *None Shall Divide Us* (2003), Stone describes his perceptions of the scene of his terrorist attacks at Milltown cemetery:

> [T]he streets and roads were clogged with men, women and children making their slow pilgrimage to the funeral mass. I stood on the steps of the leisure centre and had a good look around. I could see two of the coffins had arrived. I could see Danny Morrison organising media crews and pointing out the best locations for cameras and reporters. I felt I was watching a really bad movie about Northern Ireland. I heard the click-click of a nearby camera. (Stone 2003: 131)

The spectacle of Stone's attack on the IRA funerals was pre-staged to a significant degree, it was his stated aim to execute a high profile assassination in revenge for the Remembrance Day bombing/ Poppy day Mas-

[40] All three were killed by the SAS in Gibralter during Operation Flavius.

[41] Royal Ulster Constabulary.

sacre 8th November 1984.[42] The prior knowledge that his actions would be broadcasted as media spectacle was an important incentive behind the attack, and from the outset of the global release of the pictures, the media dubbed Michael Stone with the persona 'Rambo'. This attachment of a fictional character onto a living murderer instantaneously merged a layer of mythology and celluloid onto horrific circumstances. Although this fictional naming was not instigated by Stone himself but by the media, his notoriety as a terrorist thrived on the persona established in reaction to a perceived mimicry of a macho and violent Hollywood film character. Also significant in the idea of the Rambo character is the aspect of 'righteous' anger, that the violence perpetrated in the film is for a 'just' cause and in this regard is part of the American way.

The element of self-constructed identity is noticeable when Stone recounts the first time he had the opportunity to watch the broadcast pictures of Milltown, in the courtroom during his trial,

> [T]hen the television was switched on and I looked up. It was Milltown. I could see the gravestones and see the crowds. I could hear the voices as clear as a bell, the thuds and cracks as grenades went off and shots were fired. I looked at the press out of the corner of my eye. I didn't turn my head to look at them because I knew they were watching me. They were much more interested in my reaction to those pictures than watching the images themselves. They would have seen the footage a thousand times.[...] The press never took their eyes off me and I knew as the images of Milltown were played, rewound and fast-forwarded, they were conjuring half-truths and exaggerations for tomorrow's papers. (Stone 2003: 208)

This passage is characteristic of the tone of Stone's autobiography in which he frequently describes events through his self-performance, as if seeking to manoeuvre the reader towards his viewpoint.[43] An inner analysis of mental preparations and self-consciousness, the text relays like a film script the moment of the murders at Milltown reopened from a unique angle. Throughout the book, by giving the reader the inside 'intelligence' of how the killer surveyed the situation, he deploys a tactic of first person

---

42 11 civilians were killed by an IRA bomb.

43 See also Dillon (1992).

identification, making the reader become part of the moving head, eyes and body replaying the violence. The reader has to separate from this tightly narrated viewpoint, in order to analyse the situation of Stone as a narrator who is mechanically retracing his actions, with an air of self-detachment ordinarily identified with the movements of a fictionalised character.

Stone received a sentence of 684 years for the Milltown Cemetery attack, however, this was curtailed because of the early prison releases made under the terms of the 1998 Good Friday Agreement. In subsequent years, he developed a career as an amateur artist with the support of a London gallery and taught painting to local children in East Belfast. But, on 24th November 2006, he dramatically re-entered the public domain when he orchestrated a spectacle at Stormont parliament buildings in an attempt to disrupt the talks between political parties over power sharing and the election of the First Minister. Stone attempted to enter the main entrance of the building through revolving doors, but was trapped there by two civilian security guards. Yet he managed to throw a bag of implements into the main foyer area. A group of security officers dragged him out of the building and pinned him down within view of media cameras. The action plays back in video as an inept and futile gesture, however, the credentials of Stone as a mass murder obviously infuse the spectacle with the heightened aspects of memory. Stone was widely ridiculed in the press for his attack on Stormont as a prank, and this has been further exacerbated by his continued explanation of the 'event' as a piece of performance art. A claim he backed up in court, with various interpretations of the dysfunctional or 'amateurish' weapons which he used. His Defence Lawyer Arthur Harvey QC claimed it was 'a piece of performance art replicating a terrorist attack'. Stone stated in court:

> [I]f I was going to kill them why swap the magazine of the starting pistol for a piece of sponge. The sponge was to represent Harold Wilson's speech when he referred to people here as spongers over 30 years ago.[...] he claimed the arsenal of items were merely "props" with symbolic significance, the nail bombs for "nailing the truth". (Higgins 2012)

However the explosive devices Stone was carrying were deemed as 'viable' and Stone was found guilty (among other charges) of the attempted murder of Martin McGuinness and Gerry Adams.

The Stormont attack is considered by the general public in Northern Ireland as an embarrassing incident, perhaps because it reminded people of the kind of sectarian thinking that had currency during the Troubles, but in re-enactment was understood as an unacceptable display of sectarianism. However, the act of mirroring and reusing gestures with traumatic resonances in the public memory is an interesting tactic of terrorist organisations. Therefore, when Michael Stone produced an action that in several respects mirrored the past, he used the symbolism of terrorism, and whether or not its implementation was in effect a parody of violence, it is the image of the past that reverberated among viewers. In echoing so literally the tactics of paramilitary violence (and his own infamy within that visual language), Stone was unable to construct a 'symbolic' language around his actions as he claimed, but only a gesture of narcissistic reiteration. Whether or not it was his intention to kill, Stone's abortive and disenfranchised action at Stormont should not be considered as a performance artwork, primarily because its intention communicates emphatically as an act of violence, rather than one of either satirical or transformative value. There is insufficient content in Stones's enacted gesture to generate new meanings, from either the objects he used, or the manner of his physical presence, which in no way departed from previous perceptions of his behaviour. However, if the gesture is viewed as one of protest, then in some regards it could be considered within a different lineage of public performance, one that emphasises the legitimacy of direct effect rather than of a symbolic act.

Traumatic events can leave a void of incomprehension in the general public. The representations of circumstances that we accept as authentic are those captured directly as events transpire, either through verbal testimony, written report or mechanically recorded. The next layer of distribution occurs through transcribed works, those that in some way replicate the essence of the original. The Falling Man of De Lillo's book is an obvious shadow of the reality of the victims falling from the Twin Towers. Similarly the Stormont attack could also be perceived as a secondary gesture, mirroring the terror of Milltown, as if the actions are refracted back through the lens reformulated but dissipated. The body of Michael Stone trapped between the rotating doors at parliament building, becomes an emblem of intransigence literally stuck in the process of change. The importance Stone placed on the necessity of creating media spectacle in both the Milltown and Stormont attacks in some respect contravened the traditionally rather anonymous and invisible displays of Northern Irish paramilitaries. For, although both loyalist and Republican terrorists created acts that had the hallmarks of spectacle, most paramilitaries, especially the Republicans, did not develop a cult of the individual. Loyalists such as Stone and notably Billy Wright and Johnny Adair did seek public notoriety, and it was Stone who initiated this shift into creating a media presence. The flouting of the rules of visibility and invisibility is developed later in this chapter in regard to political funerals.

ARTIST STRATEGIES OF RE-ENACTMENT

In the courtroom there is a complex relationship between memory and refreshed memory, where evidence is used as a prompt for the witness in order to stimulate remembering. There are parallels between this and artworks that test memory and perception. Some artists use strategies to build knowledge through re-enactment of a fact-based situation or event that has happened, but in which the replicated reconstruction deviates from the original archived outcome. Re-enactment strategies have been criticised by writers such as Dora Apel (2002) because it cannot satisfy the 'real' that it seeks to reactivate, yet, it stimulates a simulation inside which the artist/producer/audience can mentally perform the machinations of what has been in an objective way known, however the traumatic content remains elusive. Apel identifies the gap between real and interpreted experience as a '[C]ompulsion towards forms of re-enactment by those who did not experience the original events' (Apel 168). She argues that re-enactments, '[E]nd in a kind of crisis, a greater sense of traumatic history's elusiveness but also its persuasiveness and its imminence' (Apel 168).

This contestation between the 'real' of historical trauma and its representations is especially problematic in documentary forms where the focus is on presenting valid ways of understanding past events. In a lecture given to the Western New England Institute for Psychoanalysis in 1990, Filmmaker Claude Lanzmann made an angry response to the audience, berating them for what he termed as 'the obscenity of understanding' (Lanzman 1995: 202). Lanzmann's argument was developed in opposition to intellectual attempts to understand the acts of Nazi perpetrators, their endeavours at searching for the truth of why 'evil' can be perpetrated. Lanzmann's response was that by trying too hard to 'understand' you deflect the effects of the atrocity; you posit the attention endlessly on the perpetrator at the expense of the victims. He stated:

> Well, is it because of all these conditions that the children have been gassed? This is what I called the obscenity of the project of understanding – and more than this, it is not only obscenity, it is real cowardice, because this idea of our being able to engender harmoniously, if I may say so again, this violence, is just an absurd dream of non-violence. It is a way of escaping; it is a way not to face the horror. (1995: 200-220)

What could be construed as the perversity of creating representations of violations and the methods of arriving at contentious ideas of truth-making, are explored in complex ways by artists such as the Vienna Actionists, Artur Zmijewski, Thomas Hirchhorn and Santiago Sierra. The artworks function sometimes through the restaging of acts of human violation, or even create situations that transgress again a secondary re-embodiment of a specifically charged ethical boundary. An example of this occurs in Zmijewski's video work 80064, 2004 (Arns & Horn 2007: 154-158), in which Zmijewski interviewed a former Auschwitz prisoner, Josef Tarnawa in a tattoo studio. Tarnawa is questioned about his experiences in Auschwitz, including Zmijewski asking him if he tried to resist. Eventually the artist persuades the 92-year-old man to have the tattooed identity number from Auschwitz re-inscribed. Tarnawa objects that this action will destroy the authenticity of the faded marks, but finally agrees. This repetition of the historical act ascribes the role of victim back onto the body of the Holocaust survivor in a way that disturbs the viewer.

Artist and writer Dave Beech discusses some of the ethical implication of Zmijewski's artworks such as 80064. He states:

> Zmijewski uses the politically obscene encounter as the very basis of the relationship between the artist and his 'public'. He does not compensate for these troubling and traumatic encounters with the social niceties of tolerance, kindness and conviviality. In fact, to do so would be utterly objectionable, as if genocide could be made less intolerable with diplomacy and delicate handling. (Beech 2010: 62)

There is an echo here of Lanzmann's perspective, that if Zmijewski were to instigate his troubling artistic propositions and undertake them in a politically correct manner, this could in fact be a hypocritical position. In effect, the method of 'participation' in many of Zmijewski's works is not facilitated in a benevolent open manner, but authored and authoritive to the artist's position. What is interesting about Zmijewski's strategies is that they can induce a degree of trauma on those involved in the filming process, sometimes deliberately incorporating people in the role of victims, and that this is accomplished usually with the complicity of those who decide to be involved. Participants in the films (occasionally) show awareness of their own victimhood, but they remain passively engaged within its machinations. Zmijewski's artworks often platform extreme or objectionable opinions provoked by the artist, that undermine the notion of a blank unprejudiced state of viewership among art audiences, and posit doubt and conflict into viewing positions. In effect, what this produces is not an empathetic witness stance as is generally pre-conditioned into artworks, but a tension introduced into watching, which can occasionally make the viewer become a witness to their own prejudices.

In watching news broadcasts the repetitions of media footage take hold, on a daily basis 'real time' becomes 'arrested' time becomes 'default' time, while the world plays catch up with the enormity of events. Historically, if the footage of Milltown cemetery did not exist, the events of that day would be remembered differently. Boris Groys has commented in relation to the phenomena:

> Video art in particular has become the medium of choice for contemporary warriors. Bin Laden is communicating with the outer world primarily by the means of this medium: we all know him as a video artist. The same can be said about videos representing beheadings, confessions, etc. All these cases represent consciously and artistically staged events that have their own easily recognizable aesthetics. Here we have the people who do not wait for an artist to represent their acts of war and terror: instead, the act of war itself coincides with its documentation and representation. (Groys 2008: 10)

In the aftermath of Bin Laden's death, Groys's point remains important, that terrorism has reversed the terms of the ongoing cultural debate about photographic and cinematic truth, since the images of beheadings disseminated by terrorists are accepted unequivocally as true. Although, there remains a degree of leverage and divergence between what a country's media chooses to transmit, nonetheless, art can in no regard compete with the power of the images produced from staged atrocity, and the mandate on truth that such images possess in the global imagination. This belief in the authenticity of terrorist-constructed images held by global audiences, is based on how these representations feed on underlying fears and suspicions. Terrorist images are compelling because of their facticity, yet Groys claims they are not beyond critique and indeed must be interrogated, because they exist primarily within the realms of media, and within this framing the images have limited diversity and are constantly renewed and overlaid in sequences of present tense. Groys argues that art's only validity in the sphere of representations of war is in the potentiality it still tentatively holds to facilitate reflection on terror, and critique of the images produced by terrorists within the context of history. Therefore, art should not reproduce the spectacles of terrorists but challenge the authority continually reactivated by the global media around these events and images that become seemingly unassailable.

MIRRORING GESTURES IN PERFORMANCE ARTWORKS

In many respects, Stone's protest, attack, or performance at Stormont was not radically different from the subversive mixtures of shock tactics, hoaxes and guerrilla strategies utilised by both political activists and some contemporary artists. But, what is more common in contemporary performance art is the making of images and gestures that function as acts of commemoration or connection to the history of place. Gene Ray, writing in relation to the actions of artists post World War II, describes the diverse approaches that emerged as artists searched for forms to address the immense shift in global consciousness after the events of the Holocaust and Hiroshima. Ray deftly positions the worth of the artist's body as a malleable but essential form of evidence within the process of an expanded idea of mourning. He states:

> [B]ecause the human body is the object of political violence and terror, because, in the end, it is in and on their bodies that the victims of history must bear all the traces of their pain, terror, torture and destruction, the body will always be the basic reference for all artistic mourning, all artistic modes of remembering historical trauma and disaster. And this is of course central to the way in which performative practices, conditioned on the physical presence of the performer's body, produce their effects. (Ray 2011: 34-35)

This idea of 'artistic mourning' is an ongoing issue within performance practices, the cultural diversity of work being produced means that the work of artists who have, or are living through conflict has a powerful visibility within the artworks exposed internationally. There is a trajectory of impact on audiences from this possibility to experience directly the work of artists who have witnessed war, and inclusive of artists living in countries with ongoing states of political repression. The value of this work is that it contains, solely, within the artist's precise presence, qualities of emotion from rage to gravitas that communicate outwards a testimony of mourning. However, this embodied form of evidence has limitations, and there are inherent difficulties in using performance to respond especially to mediatized events. The singularity of a human body moving in the 'neutrality' of a gallery space is capable of evoking a range of challenging and resonant emotions in an audience, but the method of communication is innately oblique. Performance artists in general resist the 'telling' of information, what they can do compellingly is give testimony through their physical demeanour, usually without verbal language and using limited if any technological staging. These kinds of body-based practices, function especially through the developed use of silence, stillness, vulnerability and intimacy. One variation of this however is the protest gesture, which in contemporary performance work is frequently understated and diametrically opposed to the graphic and immersive nature of media based spectacle. Through a sparseness of means the artist's aim is to construct a physically charged empathetic connection to the audience, and it is this energetic encounter with those who witness the work that holds the proposal of resistance.

The most potent of these kinds of acts tend to be specifically crafted singular actions made by artists in response to the history of place. One example is the action of Finnish artist Roi Vaara (Vaara & Ferre 2005: 38-

41) performed in 2000, in Tiananmen Square, Beijing. In this work Vaara stood completely still for one hour and twenty minutes positioned within the vast scale of the infamous square, facing the monument to the People's Heroes, arms by his side, straight backed in a sentry like position, wearing a formal dinner suit and black sunglasses. For the duration of the action photographic documentation captures the reactions of Chinese citizens becoming aware of the abnormality of the gesture of this Western presence. The work quickly aroused the attention of the Chinese police who approached and questioned Vaara but allowed him to continue, until the number of Chinese people seeking to interact with Vaara and have their photograph taken provoked the police to react by dispersing the crowd and asking Vaara to leave. This performance clearly emphasised the mirroring of a previous gesture fixed in collective memory – that of the unarmed protestor known as 'Tank Man' (Front Line 2012). The protestor's name and his fate after the infamous exchange with the military has not been verified. 'Tank Man' stood in front of a column of tanks during the Tiananmen Square protests of 1989, at one point standing on the turret speaking to the soldiers inside, until pulled away by the crowd. From a Western perspective Vaara's action reads as one of solidarity with the protestor, yet the documentation suggests that those present perceived the action in a variety of ways from humorous subversiveness to intrusive, and perhaps mocking behaviour. Vaara's body and intention has to be unravelled from both Western and Asian perspectives, it is neither neutral nor universal. Similarly, the action of total stillness displaced within crowds is also adopted by the South Korean artist Kim Sooja whose performance series (8-part video installation) titled *A Needle Woman*, 1999-2001 (Sooja 2012), uses the 'passivity' of her gendered and ethnic presence as a catalyst within various international street contexts. Sooja stands silent and motionless framed with her back to the camera, which records the reactions of passers-by in response to her body as a marker in public space, revealing that her body and its 'lack' of gesture cannot be perceived as neutral, but always a zone of contestation.

These kinds of physically reduced gestures introduce through their directness one strand of the language of protest. By being in place, in effect obstructing, such actions can hold a sense of bearing witness; they can occasionally be actions of despair, or of complicity in resistance across time. And although these artists are making themselves visible, this is different from the intention to re-enact or make a spectacle. In effect, they utilise their presence in space and enable the context to become activated, which is markedly different from Stone's actions of conspicuous spectacle.

PART 2: POLITICAL FUNERALS, CENSORSHIP, BLIND SPOTS

> The space of death is important in the creation of meaning and consciousness, nowhere more so than in societies where torture is endemic and where the culture of terror flourishes. We may think of the space of death as a threshold that allows for illumination as well as extinction. Sometimes a person goes through it and returns to us, to tell the tale. (Taussig 1987:4)

The concept of 'the space of death' (Taussig 4) that Taussig proposes is relevant to Groys' call for artworks that reactivate the freeze-frames terrorists have imposed on mass memory. One of the most emotive and controversial issues in the representations of violations is the conduct and handling of the dead, whether it is the bodies of perpetrators or victims, corpses (or the absences) exude a power to create psychic disturbance in familial and societal patterns. An example of this is the continuing use of images of the IRA Hunger Strikers in multifaceted re-framings as propaganda symbols, and as fictional interpretations.

MICHAEL 'MICKEY' DEVINE'S WAKE WITH INLA HONOUR GUARD[44]

Eight people are visible in a room spaced around a coffin. The face of one, Mickey Devine is distorted beneath a coffin veil, visibly the skin is seen in contrast to the complexion of the living, yet, paradoxically it is this face that is the most accessible in the room. Two figures, dressed in black with paramilitary hooded faces stand guard: ceremonial presences among the domestic situation of grief. Three young children and a woman seem the proper recipients of the situation. One child stands beside a partially opened doorway leaning against a wall, perhaps, inadvertently holding the

[44] Information available at CAIN (2012). The image is at: http://www.hungerstrikes.org/funerals/devine_funeral01.html. Accessed February 2012.

same posture as the guards, arms tucked behind back, an ambiguous gesture that might express respect, but could also denote discontent. Behind the two guards a poster on the wall portrays a male face, its appearance links it to the dead man in the coffin, in this reproduction the face's expression is seen to be smiling. This poster on further viewing gradually becomes the focus of the photograph. Placed on the wall higher than the head height of the two guards, it hovers above them with a dominance derived from its incongruous emotiveness located between the two masked faces. The mother and children have softly blurred features, the three have their hands raised in prayer partially covering mouth and chin.

The room is domestic in scale, presumably a bedroom. One other figure is partially visible standing beyond the range of the camera lens on the extreme right of image, this figure at first gaze would appear to be another guard, but on closer inspection the fragment of face is not masked. Still, this figure was probably deliberately excluded from the image frame to protect identity. The image wavers in a peculiar way between a propagandistic souvenir, and the excruciatingly private; the intimacy of, presumably, the wife and children standing and kneeling at the edge of the coffin, and the marked distance to the guards against the back wall, whose proximity, however, suggests their acceptance within the family circle. Even the child's (accidental) mimicry of the guard's pose demonstrates in some ways the degree of absorption within these exceptional circumstances of mourning. The smell of the room, the colour of the carpet can be surmised. The family a congregation of facts, they pull into the future away from the liminal presence of the corpse. Death in parting brings together the secrecy of the paramilitary organization within the sacred circle of family. The room incubates both grief and resentment a constellation of emotions. Defiance can be as quiet as this, as quiet as hands paused still at waist level, the family becomes the aftermath, the funeral a gesture of anger perpetuated into the future.

This image of Irish republican prisoner Michael 'Mickey' Devine's wake can be read as quietly shocking because of its complex domesticity. Even aspects such as the aesthetic properties of the cheap camera used to take the photograph, adds to the pathos of the muddied image, giving it an illicit, unofficial quality. The image begs the question: was it constructed for the camera as propaganda, or is it a commemorative fragment of family portraiture? Initially it would appear to be a family document, however, there is a cultural reticence about photographing the dead. The poster on the back wall speaks of an ongoing state of protest, the home as a battleground of activism throughout the Hunger Strike campaign. It disturbs, perhaps, because of the tangible manner the family are visualised implicitly within the mechanisms of paramilitary war. Since even in grief the status of the body is shared between family and the republican cause, the prayers and grief on the relative's faces marks a perfect polarity to the faceless guard figures. The impression this image creates is of the worth of the dead man's body that becomes a valuable political property, a weapon of warfare actually rendered more potent in death.

Conflicts over the rights of burials were repeatedly demonstrated during The Troubles, when RUC officers frequently converged on wakes and funerals, attempting to disrupt proceedings, and in particular attempting the seizure of the tricolour and republican insignias, forbidden under the state's Flags and Emblems Act. These emblems ensured that there was communal recognition of the deceased's role as a soldier within an officially organised unit. Also, the ritualised procedures around the burial demonstrated acceptance and belonging within nationalist communities. For these reasons funerals became pivotal viewing experiences for the Northern Irish population. In some respects, the nightly mediated images of funeral processions became the accepted substitute for broadcasting footage of violence, and funerals were often used as a way of demonstrating by those who organised them. To some extent this centrality of funerals as broadcast events during the political conflict meant that the spectacle of funerals came to be read as a form of quasi-court proceeding. With the bodies concealed, the traces of violence were integrated into formal spectacle, so this became what was available for the public to 'judge', framed through the tone of voice and interpretation of the broadcaster.

REPRESENTATIONS OF MARTYRDOM

British filmmaker Steve McQueen's film Hunger (McQueen 2008) is based on the 1981 Hunger Strikes in the Maze Prison, Northern Ireland, and focuses in particular on the republican prisoner Bobby Sands. In the film McQueen for the most part portrays Sands as a provocative, and to some extent, flawed and volatile character. Most of the character representations in the film are constructed in long sequences of physical actions, with minimal verbal narrative. This use of relative silence in Hunger, in conjunction with protracted scenes of single shots, functions as devices that heighten the visceral impact of the physical violence represented, and exacerbates a sense of tedium and inhumanity of the prison situation. This conceptual use of ambient sound is only altered in one central sequence of dialogue, filmed in an unbroken 17-minute shot, where Sands' motives for instigating the second wave of Hunger Strikes within the prison is scrutinised in a dialogue with a priest. This dialogue is used to articulate the moral conflict of religious doctrine concerning suicide, and Sands' understanding of his proposed death as political sacrifice to the republican cause. Sands' body essentially becomes an item of political investment, and indeed weaponry. This idea is developed in later sequences in the film, when McQueen presents an infiltration of the body of the dying Sands, attempting to convey the inner mental journey as the disintegrating physical body becomes motionless. McQueen uses cinema's capacity to revise plot or character through devices of reframing, inclusive of dreams, and in the case of Hunger projections into the hallucinating mind of the dying figure of Sands back into childhood. However, this interjection of the past-tense creates a sense of romanticism, indeed sentimentality into the narrative that is incongruous to the intensely visceral handling of the preceding events and script. In a way these devices encrypt the representation of Sands firmly back within a popular mythologizing as poet and martyr. Essentially, in death Sands is placed beyond the violence that governed his life, distancing him from the identity as an IRA operative previously constructed in the film. It is important to note that the covert, privately taken images of the Hunger Strikers in death, such as the image of Mickey Devine's wake described above, are not the typical representations used for public displays of commemoration in Northern Ireland. In the communities where the Hunger Strikers lived, the most common forms of memorials are traditional murals that usually depict the men through smiling portraits. These public memorials emphasise the men's remembered community face as opposed to what happened to them under internment and imprisonment. And in so doing, they extract them backwards in time from their violent deaths to reinstate them in a more humanised and familiar form, also one in which they become freeze-framed in time as young and virile. These memorials can also be interpreted as propaganda, since the smiling portrait can be used for the purposes of vindication;[45] an example of this is the quote from Sands often used beside his portrait: 'Our revenge will be the laughter of our children'. The ongoing preservation of commemorative sites is essentially a project of producing lasting models of heroism, yet, these images can also reinforce identities of victimhood in that the hero, martyr and victim are unified. From this second perspective of victimhood, the political aftermath of the Hunger Strikes has created an ongoing memorializing through religion-based iconography, for example mural depictions on the Falls Road, Belfast, which place Sands in the position of Christ. The other men who died on Hunger Strike, including Mickey Devine, are remembered in less symbolically evocative ways.

However, the surviving 'private' images of the Troubles, such as the funerals of the Hunger Strikers, provide a secondary form of propaganda. These images stimulate a sense of looking into a prohibited space where it feels like a transgression to view the faces marked in death by their final suffering. These images are not glorious, but corporal and utterly disturbing because of the mortal recognition they evoke, which prompts the nature of the suffering to become opened once again for consideration and reflection. These images have gradually become widely accessible through the Internet, but their initial release into public circulation would have been prohibited within the republican community, since there is a long tradition in warfare of never showing 'your soldiers' in death. Therefore, this seepage out into the public realm is a contravention of the tradition of protecting your ranks. But, the retrospective release of these images within the changing social climate of the peace process shows a changing emphasis in the republican propaganda message, which becomes one of seeking justification through empathetic methods of communication. In this regard, these images can be compared to McQueen's film, since *Hunger* also utilises both shocking and emotive representations, which produce in some moments an elusive sentimentality that can be interpreted as politically simplistic if not propagandistic.

45 Interestingly, it is also a device now used by the British media to represent the deaths of military personnel through family photographs, which Steve McQueen has used as a factor in another artwork, entitled *Queen and Country*, 2007.

STATE MOURNING

A comparative perspective of mourning is circulated in mainstream media representations of soldier's funerals, which galvanise an idea of ceremonial dignity and by extension honour, without the savagery of witnessing the cause of death. The practice of 'embedding'[46] journalists, so that they continuously travel and live with military personnel, has created a sterilised and much criticised form of reporting, concealing scenes of the actuality of the violence of the war being conducted. In effect, the weight of emotional reportage, for example, relating to Afghanistan exists not in the foreign reports but in the bodies and reactions of soldiers' families in Britain receiving the (concealed) bodies back for burial.

BBC NEWS BROADCAST, 22ND DECEMBER 2009

The bodies of three British servicemen are brought back to England from Afghanistan. The broadcast moves through the naming of each soldier, to the rites of military repatriation, the coffins are shown arriving at an airfield and awarded full military honours. The broadcast shifts geographically to the village of Wooten Bassett, where the streets are shown lined with mourners. A low angled shot of the road indicates a civilian undertaker, who is viewed walking into centre screen, an entourage of hearses moving slowly behind him. Military flags are evident on the side of the screen held at the roadside by mourners, some of the crowd step forward and hastily place bouquets of red roses wrapped in clear cellophane on the rooftops of the hearses. Shots of individual mourners are filmed in gestures of grief, shots of men weeping, heads lowered, and embraces of comfort. A shot of a single man's face is emphasised as he crosses his arm around a woman who is turned away from the camera. The last shot captures the bowed head of a mourning female, her face covered by fallen hair as she leans over bent in grief holding the roof of a static hearse: a moment of stillness in the momentum of the cavalcade as it travels through the narrow streets. The actual church services relating to each of the individual soldier's burials are generally kept private, away from public viewing. Therefore, the two defining stages of broadcast reaction are: the first deploying

[46] Introduced by US military in 2003 Iraq War.

the visual formality and spatial alienation of the military airfield footage in keeping with government decorum; and the second, the direct emotive reactions of the crowds at Wooten Bassett.

These street scenes increasingly present an improvised public event, where the protocol of military cortège has altered to facilitate the depth of public feeling visualised as patriotic grief. The scenes of mourning are presented on the screen in silence, without commentary, with only low-level ambient audio from the location. Social commentators have dubbed this evolution of public grief around state deaths as 'Dianification', referencing Princess Diana in regard to sentimental demonstrations of public compassion. The rituals continuously evolving at Wooten Bassett have perhaps developed at least in part due to the media attention, which reacted to what had previously been private actions.

DIFFUSED REPRESENTATIONS OF WAR

Returning to Groys' arguments stated earlier on his perception of the role of art being to challenge the 'truth' and authority of terrorist spectacles, Andrew Hoskins and Ben O'Loughlin (2010) convincingly argue that the long view of aftermath regarding war images is one of convergence of both the official mainstream approved broadcast content, and increasingly the friction and subversive mirroring that occurs in the internet transmission of material rejected by the mainstream guardians. Increasingly the mainstream media has been forced to make available (after short time lapses), material that it had previously curtailed on grounds of 'unacceptable' viewing. Watching, for example, the YouTube footage available on Michael Stone or the Hunger Strikers gives access not only to the original media footage, but also an excess of amateur material made in response to it, that either is derisive in tone, or enshrines those depicted in it as cult heroes. These confrontational interpretations create their own currency and circulation. This has implications for what Hoskins and O'Loughlin describe as the phenomena of 'emergence', that is the latent capacity within mediated material to expose or transform meanings of events sometime in the future. This diffusion of war representations, they argue, functions increasingly in tandem within the realm of the casual acts of dispersing familial home footage, tourist images etc., so that images from Abu Ghraib startlingly begin to share a dialogue with the mundane content of social networking sites. The implications of this for artists is that interpretations of terrorist spectacle are increasingly mutating entities, regenerated both from within terrorist organisations themselves, but also from the acts of artists and activists engaged in subverting diverse forms of information and representations.

STRATEGIES OF DISEMBODIED VIEWING IN ARTWORKS

American artist Bill Viola's series of video works, titled *The Passions*, 1995, directly references historical religious paintings. An example of this is the 2002 work *Observance*, based on Albrecht Dürer's altar wings, *Four Apostles*, 1526. In this video work eighteen performers form a line of 'mourners', moving in procession slowly towards the camera/viewer position. As they step into the frame they move from neutral expressions into displays of individual evocations of grief, an inner turmoil that is sometimes solitary; but at other times connective gestures occur through supportive glances and touch. The enacting of these powerful emotions sits within a context that clarifies the situation as a staging. On arriving at the centre of the shot each actor then proceeds away from the camera, relapsing from intense expression into a calm normality. The source content provoking these feelings is not revealed, and the viewer is placed in the blind spot where this image/object situation is sited, becoming effectively the other that is reacted to. Technically Viola utilises a radically decelerated speed of the film frames, which significantly alters the movements of the actors and interrupts audience expectation of real time narrative expression. What is left is a suspended uncertainty around the heightened, clearly simulated acts. The 'pain' of revelation each actor displays raises a plethora of imbedded historical memory, which carries the intricacies of representational gesture from western classical art, yet is also inclusive of conventions of cinema and television.

The most immediate interpretation is that these are studies for figures at the base of a crucifixion, but what is most perplexing is how these movements of individual response are choreographed both into and out of emotions. As each actor exits the shot, they look downwards, out of frame, or sometimes peering towards the viewer. This creates a rupture in the screen, a lapse into the viewer's space. By concealing the visual cause that the performers are reacting to, the piece becomes contemplation on the culture of mourning, as if staring into the space of death reflected backwards through the eyes of the living. However, the simulated construction of the work raises uneasiness in viewing, the transparent drama of the actor's technique makes perceptions of the work feel insincere. As with McQueen's dream sequences in *Hunger*, the erosion of palpable corporal presences undermines the articulation of the threshold of death. The viewer is returned to fantasy constructs that pull away from the mortality of flesh, which, in its visceral enactment (especially in *Hunger*), is the most compelling component.

Film theoretician Laura Mulvey has analysed the struggle to excavate truth from film, a hidden truth, something we sense to be imbedded despite the insistence of the surface. Mulvey describes the features of a freeze frame and our relationship to viewing film, the ability through digital technology to cease and revive content and shift linear narratives,

> [A]s stillness intrudes into movement, the image freezes into the 'stop of death',[47] taking the aesthetics of cinema that leads back to pre-cinema, and to photographic and psychoanalytic theorics. The blurred boundaries between the living and the not-living touch on unconscious anxieties that then circulate as fascination as well as fear in the cultures of the uncanny. This shudder, however consciously experienced, is a symptom of the unconscious difficulty that the human mind has in grasping death and its compensatory capacity to imagine an afterlife. (Mulvey 2006: 32)

Mulvey's analysis of film articulates the mechanisms of rehearsed or perceptible 'deaths'. What it is the viewer excavates from seeing, in ways that stall narrative gratification, yet activate memory into configurations that sometimes jolt the touch of death, or perhaps the sensation of touching the dividing points. If this is true when do we experience mortality? Is it as Mulvey suggests, when we are taken back to the 'thenness' of when the image was made, the inexplicable aspects of how an image was composed and within that the staged and accidental qualities coalescing? We touch death when we separate stills because then we insert memories and emotions around the framed moment.

---

[47] Raymond Bellour termed it as the 'stop of death'.

In relation to Mulvey's ideas on the transferences between the past of the image and the navigations of memory, the Northern Irish artist Willie Doherty in his single channel video installation *Ghost Story* (Doherty et al. 2007) creates an audience experience of internalisation, where the focus alternates between corporal and disembodied presences. In *Ghost Story*, a male voice relates a monologue of personal reminiscences, some of which contains fragments of traumatic memories that are strongly tied to a sense of place. As the monologue is spoken, the viewer watches scenes taken from a steady-cam operated camera moving initially along a country pathway among hedgerows. The landscape presented is diffuse because of the camera speed and movement, but gradually it becomes haunted by the images poetically evoked by the narrator. 'I wondered about what had happened to the pain and terror that had taken place there. Had it been absorbed or filtered into the ground or was it possible for others to sense it as I did?' (Doherty et al. 162) The shifting pattern of the voice is in itself a form of travelling, a form that interchanges between estrangement and intimacy. Occasionally events are seemingly prompted back sharply into the present tense in the narrator's mind, but the event is concealed and eludes the viewer. In terms of liminal space, the mesmerising airy movement of the camera seems to separate from any fixed or corporal form. Additionally, as the camera moves through a landscape of situations deliberately non-specific and unoccupied, such as hedgerows, an alleyway behind houses and car parks, the voice draws a sense of presence towards its locations, engendering a series of associations. Do the dead follow us, or do we pass over them unsolicited? Are they where we left them, or where they are most disassociated?

The ghost story text is a narrative of memory, some of which is apparently first-hand experience, other parts respond to mediatized events; a commemoration without the residue of orthodox documentary form in that it is left ambiguous who is talking and why and where they are travelling. This created liminality is a slender suspension of the mind, making palpable a slither of memory both personal and historical. The viewer seeks to connect the voice to an identifiable position in order to reactivate known historical events; the context builds during the monologue by positioning the traumatic fragments offered within an existing template of possible narratives hinted at in occasional shots, such as a close-up of a woman's eyes and a moving car in a car park. Therefore, what is unfocused or unspoken is as potent in relaying something of the speaker's identity. In ways this replicates some of the methods of broadcasting censorship used by the British government during the 1980s[48] such as subtitles, dubbing or lip-sync of actors' voices, or insertions of silence and blank screen. In a propaganda war, these censoring devices created voids and absences that in effect became a palpable intervening form of presence, the loss more potent through being denied. Doherty's work resuscitates aspects of the afterimage of political violence in Northern Ireland, without resorting to the mirroring of original broadcast reportage, which is only obliquely alluded to through the use of language.

DURATION: THE SPACE OF DEATH IN PERFORMANCE ART

In her book *Mourning Sex* (1997) Peggy Phelan discusses the persistence of live art forms and theatre within contemporary culture. Despite the surrounding economy based on reproducibility, Phelan posits the idea that these forms survive, because they, '[R]espond to a psychic need to rehearse for loss, and especially for death. Billed as rehearsal, performance and theatre have a special relation to art as memorial' (Phelan 1997: 3). The most prominent realisation of this concept in performance art practices is within the form of durational actions. In durational works the timeframe of an action can extend across days, months or even years, during which period the artist is understood to be continually interfused within the process of the action. Therefore, durational work traditionally involves intense commitment and discipline. It is valued because of the physical and psychological difficulty involved in sustaining a circumstance that pressurises the artist beyond normal social perceptions of acceptable limits. Occasionally it reflects some aspects of historical religious practices, such as hermetic solitude, pilgrimage, fasting, and in this respect is identifiable with spiritual practices and a questioning of mortality. However, because of the extended timeframes, these works are necessarily difficult or impossible for audiences to view in their entirety. So, the viewing experience is often limited or exclud-

48 See for example Rolston and Miller (1996).

ing, and therefore most durational works function extensively through the evidence of documentation.

Seminal examples of durational performance are the artworks of the Korean artist Tehching Hsieh who entered America as an illegal immigrant in 1974 and between 1978-1986 produced a series of five one-year long performances. In each of these actions Hsieh radically restricted his freedom of movement through various constructions of voluntary confinement. During the *One Year Performance,* 1978-1979, Hsieh sealed himself into an artist's studio constructed as an 11'6" x 9' x 8' cell. During that year Hsieh set rules that he would not converse, read, write, watch television or listen to radio. A friend facilitated the piece by bringing meals and clothing and discarding waste. Every third week the room was opened to the public, so there were nineteen viewing days. Hsieh has commented on reflection of these public events,

> Eye contact would have caused interaction with an audience. It was to be avoided. If you look at the pictures of this piece when I was inside the cage, look at my eyes, and you can see that I was inside myself. In order to make the space inside the cage bigger, I treated the corner with my bed as "home" and the other three corners were "outside." I would take a walk "outside" and then come "home". (Heathfield & Hsieh 2009: 327)

Hsieh's statement contains an important truth about the nature of durational work, since such work is generally constructed from an almost entirely interiorised perspective, an audience's gaze or contact can be corrosive to the immersive quality of the physical experience. Being watched negatively affected Hsieh's imposed captivity, given that contact, even if only through a distanced gaze, intrinsically changes perceptions of time. The camera is the true witness for the *Lifeworks* performances, each image is designed as evidence and as such holds the quality of police records, the artist's body viewed like an object of surveillance, especially in the first two works in the series, which were concentrated in a single room with a fixed camera viewpoint. To enter the work is to enter the intransigent aspects of the documentation produced from the actions, which effectively deflect emotive readings. Hsieh archives himself almost completely devoid of expression in a uniformly neutral self-portrait, a façade that fascinates, because it reflects back on the viewer questions of their own relation to time rather than the fate of the artist, who after all created these restrictions. Additionally, the camera provides a momentum through the ritualised act of recording, structuring the monotony, and in that function becoming the defining law of the work.

In *One Year Performance,* 1978-1979, Hsieh not merely stalls time, but staggers or palsies it into emptiness. The abandonment of stimulation from time-filling activities reveals a vacancy structured directly into the core of the work, rendering time as increments to be 'worked' through without traces of quantifiable worth. Conceptually Hsieh's objective within this process was to fulfil quotas of unrepresented labour that nonetheless required mental and physical endurance. The performance examines aspects of human obedience, our ability to be consumed by discipline. In this way the action is simultaneously dehumanising and yet, intensely human.

In some regards the actions can be read as a critique of capitalist society, especially the third action in the *Lifeworks Series*, when he decided to live outdoors for one year in the urban environs of New York. Notably, Hsieh does not discuss political interpretations of his actions, although the work could be read as a statement of immigrant activation and deactivation of the working body to desist from attainment and integration. In many respects, each *lifework* deepened the separation from society, even the fourth work *Art/Life One Year Performance* 1983-1984, in which he was attached by a rope eight feet in length to the artist Linda Montano, yet even in this circumstance they agreed upon a rule not to touch. Therefore, by voluntarily suppressing his own freedom through five distinct and rigorous methods, Hsieh does something important with the idea of immigration: he takes his illicit freedom in America and converts it into containment, but containment validated and executed on his own terms. Therefore, the physical constriction is replaced with a philosophical victory of entitlement, a freedom residing in the mind if a human has the will to access its potential. Returning to the Hunger Strikers, the point of their struggle was to attain the status of political prisoners, meaning an avouchment of their validity as soldiers conducting a war, not as criminals. That this distinction was considered to be worth the degrees of suffering endured by the men and women, who undertook both the 'blanket protest' and/or Hunger Strike, is an avouchment of the questions of motivation and will when humans decide autonomously the worth of their own beliefs and convictions.

Significantly, the final *Lifework* in 1985 was conceived to be undocumented and undocumentable. In this one-year work Hsieh made a declaration of intent to 'not do ART, not talk ART, not see ART, not read ART' (Heathfield & Hsieh 2009: 55). In this and subsequent works Hsieh instigated his own deeper withdrawal firstly from the art world, and then in 1991 an attempt to disappear entirely from human contact which lasted six months. All these later works exist in a pending state of belief between the audience/witness and the artist's statements, the only 'proof' offered is the rigor and utter commitment demonstrated by Hsieh in the foundational artworks.

In counterbalance to Hsieh's work, a less well known but significant durational performance was created by the Chinese artist Yang Zhichao, who in an artwork entitled *Jiayu Fort* (Berghuis 2006: 182-183) had himself incarcerated in a mental hospital for the duration of a month (30th December 1999 to 30th January 2000). Zhichao admitted himself to the hospital with the assistance of his sister who made a statement about his mental instability and gave payment to the institution. During the month long stay he was subjected to electric shock therapy and acute doses of sedation. The performance was documented through the artist's written diary, which was published in an underground arts magazine, and a series of sporadically taken photographs and video recordings made surreptitiously by his brother-in-law who visited the artist for that purpose. What is significantly different about this durational work and those of other artists, which are generally made within supportive arts structures, is that the artist voluntarily capitulated his personal autonomy to an institution, where his body and mind were subjected to the will of others outside of his control. This loss of independence over the parameters of what might occur makes the work frightening and quite separate from the underlying principle of most performance work, where the artist assumes control and responsibility for the situation they have put in motion. Zhichao created the performance in order to connect with those who are outcast from Chinese society because they fail to, or are unable to conform to socially correct behaviour. This work directly explored the actuality of those incarcerated, and as such is a powerful statement on state control over the individual.

Both this performance by Zhichao and some of Hsieh's actions emphasise the act of recording as an intrinsic component of the work, and the legitimisation of these images as evidence of the duration, which actually circumvent the necessity for public witnesses. However, most durational actions are validated by their audiences' presence even if the contact is sporadic, and the momentum of the work usually draws energetically from the indirect presence of witnesses. In general the communicative quality of performance art is empathetic; it exists in the viewer's own private capacity to enter into the physical state of the artist, whose body therefore becomes in some respects a receptacle for a shared experiment in self-will, pain, shock, exuberance, trance. Meanings shift as the work progresses, the audiences leave and enter, transferences of energy and attitudes come with each person who arrives. Every artist working with duration in performance is establishing different contracts with time, essentially manipulating time as matter in different forms, and under individuated rules. Their actions represent the framing of a precise moment in existence amplified, or set apart from life. The extraordinary moment is compartmentalised in order to examine something of the human condition, and done so with the presence of witnesses.[49]

SPACES OF MEDIATION, TRANSFERENCE, ABSORPTION

Peggy Phelan in describing the origins of our understanding of performance has remarked that:

> Tragic theatre embodies the agonizing force of existence-as-rehearsal. In such a world, nothing ever happens once, not even death. The characters in Sophocles' play discover that what is truly tragic about death is that they survive it, at least once, only to realize that having survived it once they will have to face it again. (Phelan 1997: 13)

Within war tribunals, amnesty trials and reconciliation processes, it is the resurfacing of corpses that can create corrosive memory: those who brutally disappeared become the fragmented body parts that defy containment

[49] See also Phelan (2003: 16-27). This durational artwork was created in 2002 at the Sean Kelly Gallery, New York, in relation to the events of 9/11. Over the course of twelve days Abramovic did not eat, speak, read or write, however the public had access to the performance to engage in what was termed 'energy dialogue' with the artist.

within legal processes. Although, in some contexts this re-emergence of bodies can also be a positive breakthrough depending on how the situation is handled. Therefore, funerals are potent political emblems particularly if the correct procedures and traditional rituals are denied. Ultimately, the absence of the bodies of victims, martyrs or enemies marks the limits of suppression – and the funeral is the moment of taking back symbolic power. For a grieving community this can be a process of reabsorbing their human sacrifice as fuel for resistance, so in effect, instead of creating fear, the gesture of suppression creates bitterness capable of surpassing fear.

The psychologist and theorist Brandon Hamber describes the legacy of Bloody Sunday as a process of protracted protest, aggravated by the deeply sensed need to clear people's names of false accusations. There is an acutely felt necessity of restoring innocence to an individual, or family name, in order to survive the circumstances of a disgraced death. He states that:

> The disappearance of bodies through political repression creates an ontological uncertainty among survivors and a psychological experience of what Freud termed the "uncanny"[...] Both the survivor and the dead inhabit a symbolically liminal space; that is both a part of society but removed from society. Put another way, the Latin root of the word liminal means "threshold". The disappeared person inhabits the threshold between being dead but also potentially still alive, and the families of the disappeared can find themselves psychologically preoccupied with the same existential space. (Hamber 2009: 81)

How we conduct ourselves in grief is a socially and culturally measured etiquette. Political change can create different rules of normality, such as establishing new measures of acceptable expressions of mourning. For some people the wave of prison releases and political co-operation between former enemies underpinning the Good Friday Agreement has cut short their ability to grieve without their mourning being regarded as protracted and excessive by the broader public, perhaps less personally affected by the violence. Reparation must take some form of symbolic exchange, but death does not have a financial equivalent, and is understood by many as distasteful, 'blood money'.

FEBRUARY 2012

Viewing articles on the Internet to map the continuing fluctuation of meanings around The Falling Man photograph. The image appears to have undergone a transformation: from initially having been widely denounced as obscene in the wake of 9/11, it is now being reclaimed by many in America as sacred. The paradox is pivoted on the shifting political climate, where the original offensiveness was located in the body's abject solitariness, its radical un-fixity, at a time when America needed icons of unity, communality and stability. Now this human presence as singularity has come to epitomise public consensus on the continuing consequences of the attacks. The body is rendered as iconic if you reconsider it as being 'everyman', and in this regard its continuing anonymity registers it beyond monumentality, like tombs to the 'Unknown soldier', its pertinence is its unknownability, measured also by its seizure in a precisely fixed moment of time. Comparatively, because the identity of 'Tank Man' is also still unresolved, this figure too is a reminder that fixing identity is a habitual method of taking consolation from history. By consigning the identity and therefore fate of either man back into the containment of a family or community context partially closes over the void that is otherwise projected around these bodies as troubling markers of the potentiality of chaos that encompasses us all. In some regards, this is a reinforcement of the formulas of empathetic viewing developed through the reporting of famines, earthquakes, etc., primarily sited on constructing stories around one individual, whose suffering becomes emblematic of those around them. The naming of one identity becomes the in-point of emotive reaction, but that these filmed subjects speak, and are given the 'rights' of having a voice, changes their status, they are humanised and their suffering is located as mortal. As discussed earlier, the legacy of ambiguous perceptions around the Hunger Strikers' deaths has left a residue of complex notoriety extending to ideas of martyrdom. This legacy contends that the ten men survived death, or perhaps they could also be considered to be perpetually dying. Whereas The Falling Man and Tank Man leak into the liminal spaces I described around the Hunger Strikers, these bodies have not been claimed back into communities, and therefore they remain isolated iconic spectres.

SUMMARY

Returning to Butler's quote at the beginning of this chapter concerning the human lives and absences that are never acknowledged as having been lived, Jacques Rancière concurs with an interesting statement on the media saturation of images of suffering by claiming we see too few of these images, meaning the 'nameless bodies'. He states:

> [W]hat we see above all in the news on our TV screens are the faces of the rulers, experts and journalists who comment on the images, who tell us what they show and what we should make of them. If horror is banalized, it is not because we see too many images of it. We do not see too many suffering bodies on the screen. But we do see too many nameless bodies, too many bodies incapable of returning the gaze that we direct at them, too many bodies that are an object of speech without themselves having a chance to speak. The system of information does not operate through an excess of images, but by selecting the speaking and reasoning beings who are capable of 'deciphering' the flow of information about anonymous multitudes. The politics specific to its images consists in teaching us that not just anyone is capable of seeing and speaking. (Rancière 2009: 96)

Rancière's statement emphasises the importance of the identities of those who have voices and who therefore have the potentiality of a returning gaze. Since artists are part of this production and disruption of visual informing, this chapter explores some of the inherent rules and responsibilities for how the issue of human rights violations can be addressed.

Strategies described, such as various forms of stillness, stasis and re-enactment, are some of the different ways that artists have attempted to produce diverse interpretations against the background of mediatized representations of violence. Occasionally this is possible through the manipulation of video imagery to draw out different kinds of gaze, or develop interjections of narrative from alternative perspectives. Also, shifts in perception can be evoked through the temporality of performance actions, which reactivate the persistence of gesture as memory fixed precisely to location. What artworks seem most adept at exploring – compared to the spectacle of human rights violations in the 'real' – are the conditions of rewind and reframe, by the insertion of stillness and emptiness into the frame. Perhaps these strategic lapses can be interpreted as surrogates for the un-representable, the ineffable.

The space of death exists as a space apparent to the living; known but concealed from daily consideration. Artist's various attempts to represent this threshold of mortality such as the given examples of McQueen, Viola and Doherty, seem to necessitate the formation of a blind spot somewhere within the artwork, a space reserved for the viewer's own attention and reflection. Therefore, the space of death is often manifested in art paradoxically through a regression from the position of visibility and indeed tactility. Video and film have the technological sophistication to create voids, and mark absence by de-centring the viewer, or making the audience collude as a mirror in the position of the camera. On the other hand, durational performance practices aim to inscribe corporal presences into conceptions of time (despite the limitations of direct viewing and subsequent documentation). The rejection of simulation in the practice of performance artists such as Hsieh, MacLennan and Abramovic renders the process within palpable terms of control and sacrifice. Conversely, and usually in more extreme depictions, a terrorist's use of images insists upon ideas of second death, exhorting a sense of fear and culpability in compelling viewers to re-enter the past and view the savage depictions of the violence that they wish the viewer to understand as 'sacrificial deaths', which is one form of terrorist violence. Moving through the various embodiments encapsulated in the debris of information and misinformation, these ghosts of the murdered and the disappeared persist. The deaths of the named and the unnamed become a seepage of seemingly insurmountable presences.

Spectrum Of Testimony

> We must distinguish between two things: what is established by the Law, and what I have discovered through personal experience; you must not confuse the two. In the code of the Law, which I may say I have not read, it is of course laid down on the one hand that the innocent shall be acquitted, but it is not stated on the other hand that the judges are open to influence. Now, my experience is diametrically opposed to that. I have not met one case of definite acquittal, and I have met many cases of influential intervention. It is possible, of course, that in all the cases known to me there was none in which the accused was really innocent. (Kafka 1977: 170)

The word testimony resonates with connotations across political, legalistic and religious contexts. To testify is to create (or attempt to create) verbal evidence from lived experiences: it oscillates between belief and disbelief, essentially weighted on the credibility of the person who testifies, which in itself is a mediated construct. In this chapter, I will be exploring diversity in the performance of testimony from legal, theatrical, community and art perspectives. The purpose of establishing a spectrum of testimonial constructs is a method to question the potential of arts-based approaches, as a comparative framework to the orthodoxy of judicial process, and give consideration to what is missing from legal channels that can conceivably be developed through alternative approaches.

In exploring different examples of testimonial situations, I will begin with the quasi-legal staging of the People's Permanent Tribunal (PPT) on War Crimes in Sri Lanka, which occurred in Dublin, January 2010. This Tribunal was an independent enquiry into the Sri Lankan government's alleged treatment of the Tamil people, especially during the final phases of a thirty-year war against the Liberation Tigers of Tamil Eelam, when the Sri Lankan military resoundingly defeated the LTTE in May 2009. The PPT exists as an independent organisation based in Milan and is not aligned to any nationality or government. Therefore the PPT functions similarly to a legal structure but without the authority of statehood. This political staging is then used to evaluate the purpose and potential of theatre-based formats, which often facilitate variations of testimony inclusive of factual and fictional content. *We Carried Your Secrets* was a theatre production developed by the Theatre of Witness Company in Londonderry/Derry, Northern Ireland in 2009. This production was made in collaboration with untrained actors who performed a script developed directly from their own lived experiences of political violence.

From this basis of collective activity, I will then consider more singular acts of private testimony, such as those that frequently exist within performance art practices. Among the examples discussed are two performance artworks created for arbitrary urban audiences, one made by the American artist Joanne Rice, the other by André Stitt, originally from Northern Ireland. Both works involve actions of personal testimony formed in protest against historical acts of violence. These and other works explore the possibilities of repositioning where art practices intersect within this sphere of legal, political, and social representation of conflicting and often marginalised voices.

Paul Virilio stated in his 2002 essay *Unknown Quantity* that:

> By progressive habituation to insensitivity and indifference in the face of the craziest scenes, endlessly repeated by the various "markets of the spectacle" in the name of an alleged *freedom of expression* that has transformed itself into a *liberation of expressionism* – if not indeed an academicism of horror – we are succumbing to the ravages of a *programming of extravagance at any cost* which ends not any longer in meaninglessness, but in the heroicization of terror and terrorism. (Virilio 2003: 9)

Following on from the discussions raised in Chapter 2: Violations, Virilio's vitriolic statement criticises the excessive proliferation of globally transmitted images of horror, which ultimately, in his interpretation, create a climate of apathy, meaninglessness and glamourisation of the very things they purport to condemn. But, beyond the technologies of mediatization, what this chapter aims to map are the occurrences of diverse forums of address, and indeed redress, that function outside of the traditional spheres of power. One such construct is the development of people's courts such as the People's Permanent Tribunal, which functions as a forum for moral redress, facilitating international tribunals that allow civilians the opportunity and right to examine the acts of Governments. The tribunal met on the $14^{th}/15^{th}/16^{th}$ January 2010 in Foster's Place, Dublin, a building that was originally part of the complex of the first Irish parliament that closed in 1800. The purpose of this Tribunal was to construct a new body of witness-based evidence and adjudicate over accusations of war crimes in Sri Lanka committed against the Tamil people in 2008-2009. The views stated in this chapter are not an examination of the specific issues of the Sri Lankan political situation, which is beyond the scope of this enquiry. In describing this specific Tribunal, what I am exploring are some aspects of the staging within this kind of spectacle of political justice, and in what ways it can be understood as effective or ineffective as a method of creating political awareness of contentious situations.

On the 16th January, watching the piece-by-piece staging of the tribunal scene was a slow visually inert spectacle. The proceedings involve five circles of influence, the panel of jurors positioned around an L-shaped table exert the central influence, their words and actions structured and watched through a second circle of media technical crew, the observers sit behind the cameras in ranks of seating facing the jurors. There is also an outer circle of observers standing in doorways and corridor spaces, among this group appear to be people intimately involved with the proceedings, representatives of the Tamil community in Ireland, volunteers and organisers stand intermingled in anxious groupings. As the verdict documents were read out by five jurors, many aspects of the evidence that had been collated was so shocking as to be almost unimaginable for the majority of observers sitting respectfully in the room. Yet, in many ways the situation was emotionally static; the divide between intellectual consideration of the facts and the physical embodiment of the war described creates numbness, as if we had all unintentionally consigned the acts of violence into a historicised and distanced archive.

Virilio's statement outlines some of the essential difficulties in such forms of moral undertaking. Although, there appears to be a considered need among populations to address the helplessness experienced in the face of global atrocities, in general the mechanics of processing this distanced horror are in themselves forms devoid of expression. They are in many respects the antithesis of the drama of terrorism, and as such the translation of legal findings are difficult to reconnect back into living contexts. Is it therefore about archiving moral dissent, or marking events into historical classifications, even as these events are superseded by the next atrocity?

The discourse of condemnation is patterned from a formal vocabulary of argumentation and expression. Emotion belongs to the witnesses, it is their purpose to institute it within the proceedings, but they are not present in the tribunal; for reasons of personal safety the core testimonies had to be gathered 'in camera'. The role of the jurors is to deliver condensed findings based on these testimonies and other evidence, in a manner that indicates a minimised residue of emotional influence or persuasion. However, while watching and listening to the verdict the atmosphere of the situation grows, and gradually the jurors' voices carry indications of anger, indignation, and sadness as a resonance buried into the delivery of the factual information. Each speaker holds tightly the pages of the verdict document, or one hand usually holds the microphone while the other hand turns the pages. There is constriction evident in the throat of Mary Lawlor, her face is the most vivid as she speaks. Her eyes often flicker in reaction to speaking certain passages; her body language indicates the pressure of holding to the rigidity of the document. The situation is not one of actual testimony, but of the mediation of testimony. This transference from the hidden first hand embodied accounts into international political channels via the voices of respected intellectuals in the field of human rights is an interesting evocation of the interconnected flow of ethical communication. The speakers assume the authority to speak for the rights of those disempowered.[50]

Entering the tribunal I was required to give personal details to the organisers and was then given an observer's badge to be worn whilst in the building. The term 'observer' implies a passive context of watching, imbued with attentiveness, to notice and watch carefully, even analytically. Yet, also there is a formal separation from doing, since the observer is neither directly involved in, nor by extension implicated in, what is seen to happen. However, this function of watching carries some onus of preserving the memory of the content delivered. Perhaps the role has a value exactly because it exerts a sense of objective distance, a parameter of non-relatedness, hypothetically to stand outside of directly emotional considerations with

---

[50] Mary Lawlor is Director of Front Line – the International Foundation for the Protection of Human Rights Defenders, see http://www.frontlinedefenders.org. Accessed March 2012.

only the power to listen, watch and consider the evidence autonomously. But, this sensation of objectivity is also a construct, for within observing there is also awareness that there are forces of persuasion inherent within the situation that must be balanced.

The absent grouping is that of the accused Sri Lanka government. This absence is potent, in that each delivered verdict from the jurors is met with concentrated silence from the observers, there are no expressions of dispute. The delivery of the judges is formal and authoritative. The importance of the words, articulated after a three-day process of deliberation, carries gravitas. Condensed into factual categories, point for point directed towards international law, on each element on the agenda there is condemnation not only for the Sri Lankan government, but also a much broader condemnation of other governments such as the UK, US, and EU community for its lack of ethical responsiveness to the crisis situation in Sri Lanka as it unfolded. There are some accusations that these governments profited from the war situation, although these accusations are not expanded in depth. The jurors make recommendations for the future, involving further investigation and negotiation. In this way it has the ambience of a suspended sentence, in effect a depositary for future investments of directing and utilising shares in the international technology of blame.

Sections of the verdict reiterate the points of evidence reoccurring under different categories: systemic rape, deliberate blocking of food and medical supplies into the IDP camps termed as 'welfare villages', descriptions of conditions, sickness, bombings and starvation. But, on the central accusation of genocide by the Sri Lankan Government, the tribunal is unable to categorically name the events as genocide without further investigation. This limitation in the verdict comes after stark unremitting condemnation and description of crimes, which appeared to be leading to that pronouncement. In summary the Chairperson François Houtart ends by praising the courage of the witnesses in coming forward, what was at stake for them and what they had already lost: the conclusion points back to the human cost beneath the judicial enquiry again, stating that:

> The PPT cannot conclude its work without specifically recognizing the fundamental contribution of those eyewitnesses who had the courage to come forward to testify on facts that have touched their lives profoundly and forever. They are the most qualified representatives of the victims,

> whose numbers will never be known and whose suffering could never be described in full. The recognition and protection of their rights are the reasons for the existence and activities of the PPT.[51]

The public discussion following the reading of the verdict was brief: only four people responded. The first man, a journalist, spoke about his belief that the verdict had no standing internationally or impact on the Sri Lankan government. He spoke about the Tamil Tigers regrouping and emerging again in different regions. His responses to the verdict were negative, emphasising the ongoing issues of decommissioning and dismantling of paramilitary groups. Another speaker from the Congress of Trade Unions spoke about processes of activating interest through trade union organisations, creating a force of lobby to bring Sri Lanka further into the foreground of international political discussions. The last two speakers spoke of the necessity of broad dissemination, opening conduits to develop international pressure on the Sri Lankan government. Perhaps if the panel of tribunal Jurors had remained in the room for this discussion, there could have been a more complex, thorough debate. However, this would have compromised the structure and formality of the preceding three days of legal contestation. Most of the audience members, like myself, perhaps felt confused by the implications of the practical implementation of this verdict. The event received very poor coverage in the Irish media, although the related website received close to one million hits in the following hours, a result of the intense interest of Tamil Diaspora groups.

On reflection, I found the tribunal's lack of 'spectacle', its reduced theatricality, to be an interesting phenomenon. In effect, the weight of communication lay in the resonance of the chosen words and the impact of individual delivery, all of which placed the emphasis of interpretation onto the observers. The value of the verdict was understood as compromised, since its worth is largely dependent on those present being prepared to act upon its findings. In this regard the event of the tribunal facilitated a shift away from spectacle, the emphasis placed on the impact of the newly created information, and perhaps the civic responsibilities this knowledge potentially

[51] The PPT verdict document is available at: People's Permanent Tribunal 2010. http://transcurrents.com/tc/2010/01/full_text_verdict_of_the_perma.html. Accessed February 2012.

contains. From a sceptical viewpoint (as was expressed in the public discussion) it rendered transparent the concept of a judicial body without the actual mechanics of sentencing; therefore there was only the letter of the law without the armature of connective power. Viewed in this way a people's tribunal existing outside of the control of any single government or legislative system is revealed as a fragile entity. The small number of Tamil and Sri Lankan people present in the room, i.e. those for whom the verdict had direct implications, stood on the sidelines apart from the Irish public. In short the weight of the verdict falling on foreign soil left a vacuum of power and begs the question of who owns this judgement.

In order to consider the potential value of the tribunal, it is necessary to reframe the event through its supporting bodies. The initiative to bring the PPT to Dublin was due to the Irish Forum for Peace in Sri Lanka (2012), a group involving arts practitioners such as Brian Maguire and Jenny Haughton among other academics, peace campaigners and development workers, who lobbied and fund-raised extensively to make the tribunal possible. Maguire in particular part-financed the process with institutional support from the National College of Art & Design, given to support his personal research. Therefore, in many respects, the tribunal had an underlying artistic framework, developed out of art practices intervening in social issues. This support structure changes to some extent the meaning and purpose of the tribunal: to see its underlying intention as based on the symbolic economy of gestures and the ethical weight that such gestures can transmit, which was the organiser's intention. This role of symbolic economy is one of the ways that art can persist in a role of agency, even if somewhat hidden within the mechanisms of an outer structure that pertains mimicry of the authority of government or international law. This is not to say that the mimicry is deliberately deceptive, but that the validation of ideas and actions often requires the appearance of that which it opposes, in order to become visible.[52]

[52] The PPT directly inspired a collaborative performance with artist Dominic Thorpe in which we took on the challenge raised during the public discussion after the verdict statement to become involved in attempting to further disseminate its findings. The performance we developed entitled *Due Process Pt1* directly utilised the PPT verdict statement as both an audio recording and textual document. These items were released to us by the Irish Forum for Peace in Sri Lankan, with permission to use them appropriately. *Due Process Pt1* took place one month after the tribunal and involved a performance

THEATRE CONSTRUCTS OF TESTIMONY

The social anthropologist Fiona Ross has written in relation to the experiences of women who participated in the South African Truth and Reconciliation Commission. In *Bearing Witness,* 2003, Ross describes the inherently unstable aspects of testimony:

> [G]aps emerge between experience and words and between words and what they purport to represent. They instantiate a puzzling relationship between interlocutors and others. Acceptance of testimonies rests on the presumption of congruity between event and description, yet this raises problems of representation. Narration performs the bridge between event and knowledge, yet in so doing undermines the ontological certainty of the former and the epistemological confidence of the latter. Time is implicated. (Ross 2003: 77)

Ross emphasises how testimonies do not exist in a coherently structured manner, they are co-created by the context of speaking, by those who mediate, and also by those who engage as listeners. Yet, subsequently most testimonies are presented on record as unmediated narrative, with the contextual forces undocumented. These issues of developing testimony are also significant in the production of theatre works that introduce their intentions as being socially orientated and witness-based.

One recent example in Northern Ireland of community-based theatre, designed around reconciliation objectives, was The Theatre of Witness Production entitled *We Carried Your Secrets*. It was performed on 16th January 2010, at the Waterfront Hall in Belfast. This production was developed from the gathering of first hand stories about political violence, a process comparable to the gathering of legal testimony. The stories were then embellished and scripted into narrative structures configured around issues of witnessing. In the case of *We Carried Your Secrets*, the script was devised through a process of interviews facilitated by the director Teya Sepinuck with more

---

which evolved into the public reading of parts of the verdict text selected by the audience and an open discussion, which significantly differed from the original event. This performance was not a re-enactment but a considered attempt to reactivate the verdict's findings into a more empathetic and responsive form of engagement and discussion.

than forty people, then refined by meetings between a core group of seven invited to work together on the production. *We Carried Your Secrets* describes itself in the programme as 'A new vision for performance where art and social justice meet'.[53] The stated concept of the production is to promote greater public openness and discussion of how people suffered during the Troubles. The production attempts to represent all sides of the conflict in such a way that the stories intersect, and are understood as interdependent. This is achieved by the involvement of all the cast, assisting in the acting out of each story, regardless of the political identity they openly state whilst giving their own story.

The form of the production consists of ensemble acting sections, in conjunction with video inserts, and live music sections. But the primary method of storytelling is through monologues delivered with a direct testimonial quality. The psychotherapist Ingrid Agger (1994) has written:

> 'Testimony' as a concept has a special double connotation: it contains objective, judicial, public and political aspects as well as subjective, spiritual, cathartic and private aspects. Testimony thus contains the quality of uniting within its structure the private and the political levels. (Ross 2003: 78)

This psycho-social perspective on testimony, directly linking the act of making public statement about traumatic events with aspirations of psychological and social healing, appears to coincide with the intentions of this production. The emphasis is on a process beginning with the traumatic experiences of individuals, who then through the evolution of collaborative relationships, are enabled to speak publicly within a protective structure.

The director Teya Sepinuck explains:

> To me this is a form that sits somewhere between art, social change, politics, education, spirituality, it addresses all of them, but it is basically, I would say, the idea of bearing witness and that I use theatre as the vehicle to bring audiences together to bear witness. A by-product of this work is that I hope it is healing both for the performers and for audience mem-

---

[53] *We Carried Your Secrets*, publicity programme given to the audience at the Waterfront Hall.

> bers, who either see themselves in the stories, or see the other as self if it wasn't your own particular story.[54]

However, Sepinuck rejects the idea that the work has a therapeutic basis, stating that the cast is carefully selected during the interview phases to try and ensure that no one is too vulnerable to undertake the process. She clearly signals the spiritual intentions in the work, and that the emphasis is not on relaying the suffering, but on utilising past trauma to find a transformative element coming through into the present. This spiritual dimension is an important aspect of the understanding of the act of testifying, but it is difficult to define, particularly because it is culturally divergent between religious practices and in specific contexts. This issue of spiritual implications within the idea of testimony will be returned to later in connection to art processes.

The proliferation of recent theatre initiatives, such as Theatre of Witness, and other community-based initiatives that utilise theatre methodologies, would seem to be providing a situation for capturing the seepage of conflicting dialogues around reconciliation and judicial issues: a signal perhaps that parts of the population regard story-telling as liberating alternatives to either political amnesia, or the protracted channels of legal inquiries. This is especially pertinent since for many people legal enquiry has implications involving further trauma, because of their deep distrust and alienation from policing or judicial bodies. Given that *We Carried Your Secrets* makes the agenda of peace building explicit, this and other such productions could be seen as attempts to intervene in a perceived space of public silence concerning the legacy of violence. An important aspect of this is that each person participating in the production is doing so on a voluntary basis. The benefits for this participation are neither financial nor career-motivated. Also, significantly, the content of the script and acted scenes are not fixed by constraints that are legally binding, therefore the structure is flexible to inconsistencies and lapses in memory. In ways the production could be construed as an interim space, where the dominance of delivering incontrovertible fact and evidence is suspended in preference for a cathartic working through of suppressed emotions of anger and fear.

---

54 Interview by the author with Teya Sepinuck, The Playhouse, Londonderry 16th February 2010.

At the end of the theatre piece, there was an intermission after which the audience was invited to stay and discuss the production: most remained. When the audience was asked to suggest one word they felt in immediate response to what they have seen, people swiftly offer the words 'powerful', 'redemptive', 'timely' and 'courageous'. The panel of performers and director sit in a straight line on the stage facing out, no longer performing but still under public gaze, and they exhibit an array of intense facial expressions. There is no certainty that the audience will not ask difficult questions, but in fact each person who does raise a question begins with thanks and appreciative comments to the cast. Generally, the questions are formed more as observations or reactions personal to the speaker. Some in the audience choose to reveal aspects about their own background, in effect positioning themselves in relation to one of the performers. Indeed, one of the ideas that emerges from the panel during the discussion is the one of the Northern Irish population being a jigsaw of people who feel themselves to be inside or outside of the frame, in terms of considering themselves as traumatised. An aspect of this production is the attempt made to speculate on existing perceptions around victimhood. The fact that three of the cast are aged 21, 23 and 26 respectively brings a clearly defined dimension of generational transference, for just as the older cast members speak of the degree of their involvement in the Troubles, the younger cast articulate the destructive lineage either of spaces of silence amid a repressed family history, or destructive behaviour emanating from what they describe as lawless, apathetic and uncaring environments. Their second generational responses to past violence is represented in their stories as being as angry and acute as those of the older generation, who, in their perceptions at least, had a sense of purpose or ideals upon which to base their actions.

Sepinuck shaped the script from stories gathered in interviews, then adapted them depending on the cast's reactions. She describes how for some participants the moment of receiving their own words back in a scripted form is highly emotional: the impact of the written word formalises the content of their interview contact and is in some regards a validation of stories that until that point might have seemed vague and disconnected, rendered now as a distinct cohesive narrative. But, with this formality also comes a sense of estrangement as the cast have to re-learn their own words. The scripting, therefore, is a deliberate distancing device, helping the performers partially to separate from their emotions during the rehearsal phases. The words become disembodied, in a sense elastic during the rehearsal procedure, until they can again be activated or owned during the public performances. So the function of the script is as the primary means of creating an armature onto which the participants can continually pin ideas and find support.

Noticeably, in watching the piece, the controlled nature of the scripted narrative makes it evident that there had been careful consideration given to how to pitch the emotional content, and how to preserve some privacy around what the tellers were each prepared to give. A consequence of this was that the most explicit voicing of trauma occurs in inserted video sections, used as devices to shield the impact of these statements, splitting the presence of the teller simultaneously between stage and the screen backdrop. This is sometimes visually problematic, because the person depicted, perhaps, crying on the screen, is also functioning in a more neutral, controlled manner within an ongoing crafted narration. Often a moment of intense feeling is passed over, when what was given once to the camera as testimony becomes conflicted in the retelling without spatial separation. One cast member showed clear signs of anxiety and grief that increased across the duration of the performance: there was no place for him to release this spontaneous emotion, which creates a dissonance for the audience, aware that the grief occurring instantaneously was outside of the production's created structure. So, there are clear risks within the production that there is no ultimate safeguard to stop aspects of personal traumatic content reoccurring.

The most extreme example of the use of video as a staging device is the inserts of a former police officer, who in the interests of his personal safety and that of the rest of the cast could only be represented on video. This marked absence was interesting in terms of putting parameters on what is still considered physically impossible and, in effect, what still can and cannot be said. This situation was further complicated when one of the cast makes direct accusations of RUC collusion with the gunmen who murdered his Father. This man's story is a clear appeal for justice. It could be said that this kind of reiteration of the past is a form of stagnation, a perpetuation of the trauma. The question arises: what do the cast gain from repeatedly performing their stories, which then become enmeshed in a narrative logic; is there ever a point when the narrative releases the teller from the hypnotism of the testimony pattern?[55] During the interview Sepinuck touches on this issue when she refers to part of the process of gathering stories, as the 'medicine',

> We all have stories, and we all have stories about our stories, and we have a certain way of looking at our story, and often times we're stuck in our story, and the idea in a sense is to transcend it, to see the story to be able to go fully into it, but also to be able to go through it and see that you are not caught by that story. And, often, I find that people's strength, what I would call their medicine, the thing that can actually help them go through their story is usually embedded in it, it's usually right there but they don't always see it, I mean sometimes they do but not always, and so that's my job.

So, in this way the rehearsal process is about identifying some way to unlock a transformative component hidden within the traumatic recollections, perhaps a different route to understanding past actions. In the writings of Shoshana Felman and Dori Laub regarding the impact and necessity of gathering the testimonies of Holocaust survivors, they state that 'Testimonies are not monologues; they cannot take place in solitude'. (Ross 2003: 3) They emphasise the necessity of public reception or acknowledgement, 'The absence of an emphatic listener, or more radically, the absence of an *addressable other*, an other who can hear the anguish of one's memories and thus affirm and recognise their realness, annihilates the story' (Agamben 1999: 3).[56] Therefore, the transference from private rehearsal process to public performances is crucial to the concept of the production, because without the audience's receptivity, the act of witnessing is absent. Knowing that the work will reach a public takes it beyond the personal aspects of reconciliation: there comes a sense of purpose that the telling might help others to reflect on their own traumatic memory.

Being in the theatre there was a sense of protection coming from the audience towards the stage. Many people, including myself, approached the cast before leaving the theatre to exchange some personal comment or

---

55 The lineage of this argument goes back to Theodor Adorno see Adorno and Ashton (1973). Subsequently developed by theoreticians such as Giorgio Agamben, see for example Agamben (1999).

56 See also Caruth (1995).

gesture. Therefore, as the 'addressable other' the audience was responsive, respectful and genuinely touched by the performances. These spontaneous gestures at the end were an attempt to cross and humanise the distance between cast and audience, and to credit the rawness of the performances, which was due largely to the emphasis of the stories remaining embodied within the teller. Judith Butler states in *Excitable Speech* (1997) that, 'In speaking, the act that the body is performing is never fully understood; the body is the blind spot of speech, that which acts in excess of what is said, but which also acts in and through what is said' (Butler 1997: 11). Since this production did not create anonymity through the creation of fictional characters, it made a virtue of its physical directness. Essentially therefore, what the audience responded to was the authenticity of the performers' presence. The words and the voices rang true, and at certain moments the cast were able to re-enter and re-experience their own words, not merely as acted script, but as something they are continuing to work through in their lives.

Within the act of telling there is frequently the visual substantiation of catharsis; details and emotion, blockages and blanks become apparent in the moment of speaking: it is at times difficult to watch. But, from other psychological perspectives[57] arises the idea that this kind of public truth-telling, inclusive of all of its appropriate and inappropriate emotional anger, gives survivors a feeling of greater connection to their community and a sense of serving that same community. That rage, if it is dealt with constructively, can be a positive force for change in a society where there is often a vacuum of power between those left feeling justifiably angry from injustices, but disenfranchised from the channels of political discourse.[58] Arguably, this facilitation of traumatic retelling in the arts opens certain avenues for people to explore past experiences and turn them into something visible, or palpable. Bringing bad memory into visual and verbal forms requires a submitting of the individual's story into a collective situation, where it is then 'abstracted' by group processes which construct it into something that can be worked with collectively, thus changing the emphasis from individual pain into a matrix of shared pain and empathetic reflection.

In essence, the objective of Theatre of Witness in using actual testi-

---

[57] See for example Agger and Soren (1990: 115-30). See also Herman (1992).

[58] See Zinner and Williams (eds) (1999).

monial voices instead of professional actors would appear to be about a stripping away of the artifice of second hand testimony. But, in watching the cast's stories, what is going on for the audience? Arguably the method creates sufficient objective distance to enable the audience to participate through the act of witnessing. Yet, the method also attempts to bridge that objective distance through empathetic connection, since it is pivotal to the impact of the production that the audience accepts the entire cast, not just those actors who reflect the viewpoint of the viewer. There are elements of this which coincide with the quasi-legal authority of truth commissions, where the construction of evidence is layered with an added emotionality, in a sense the performative qualities of eruptive emotion is a double authenticity directly validating other forms of gathered evidence. The value of victim's testimony in this system is as an informing voice confirming traumatic events, but also purposefully as an embodiment of its consequences. The commission environment facilitates a rendering of the truth where the victim's presence evokes a re-enactment of the original circumstances. The body continues to perpetuate traumatic readings recycled into the present tense. In this way, political constructs can utilise persuasion through emotions: the victim is inadvertently re-enacting a narrative that assumes there is always a traumatic reaction to a traumatic incident. Therefore, what evolves is a narrative linearity that simplifies or erases most other contextual considerations and the variety of reactions people have to traumatic incidents over time. This can be seen as part of a global shift away from ideas of the 'stoic victim',[59] to the actual creation of public expectations of expressions of victim-hood. Fiona Ross indicates that in some incidents of testimony during the Truth and Reconciliation Commission in South Africa the situation of testifying actually created 'victims' under cross examination, which sometimes misrepresented the person's own sense of priorities regarding what had happened to them. One such example of this is the testimony of Yvonne Khutwane at the TRC. Subsequent to testifying at the Commission, aspects of Mrs Khutwane's statement, which involved sexual violation (and which she had not intended to speak publicly about), became

[59] The term is from Peter Novick's book – *The Holocaust in American Life* (1999), where Novick argued that society's attitudes towards victimhood and values of stoicism have gradually been replaced by sensitivity.

the focus for interventions by psychologist Ms Gobodo-Madikizela[60] in the court-room, and were later reinforced through the media. Ross describes how 'the event of sexual molestation was interpreted in ways that gradually repositioned Mrs Khutwane as a victim of sexual abuse, and was depicted in both the print media and the Commission's Report as the defining feature of her testimony' (Ross 2003: 92).

However, unlike political and legal processes of staging testimony, what is relinquished here in a theatre format, is the absence of factual evidence and a facilitated contestation of perspectives and consequences, which would also evolve and change over time. Such a contestation would involve a Brechtian stylised intermediary voice. Or as in the methods developed by Augusto Boal's Theatre of the Oppressed, where a central part of each production is the empowerment of audiences to enter the framework of a scene and work through contentious issues by intervening repeatedly in the space of the action in order to generate different outcomes (Boal 1998). Boal's 'spectactors' embody different roles, and in so doing experience the dissonance of being victim, perpetrator or witness in numerous mutable ways, yet always with the possibility to step back and assess what can change in the situation. Within *We Carried Your Secrets* there are oppositional voices giving testimony: each person has reconciled their anger to merge within one centralising narrative. What we are watching, in effect, is a hybrid of truth, re-enactment and self-justification. As an audience we are positioned hypothetically as witnesses with a degree of objective distance, but in another respect the particularity of the cast's physical address is for empathetic understanding. As already stated, at times this creates uneasiness in the audience, and in this regard the public discussion became an integral part of the production because it offered a way for the audience to reconnect to the cast, normalise the space of shame and grief that had been opened, and taking acceptance of what had been spoken. Essentially the process in itself cannot empower those who choose to participate, unless they begin to activate their own opinions, hopes and connections within the armature provided, and as part of a multiplicity of supportive approaches.

60 Pumla Gobodo-Madikizela, a psychologist and Human Rights Violations Committee member, who was assigned to assist Mrs Khutwane during the testimony process.

OTHER FORMS OF STAGING JUSTICE ISSUES IN COMMUNITY SETTINGS

The rituals of justice and our expectations of them remain extraordinarily high. Western societies appear to be unable to relinquish their concept of the 'theatre' of legislation as the primary place of moral hierarchy and debate. The spectacle of oppositional voices protecting or contesting constructions of 'fact' is a battleground of linguistics, behaviour, persuasion, power, worldviews and epistemological belief that is understood still as a cornerstone of liberal democracy.

In response to this desire for legitimization, other forms such as internal community hearings are initiatives that have occurred in Northern Ireland, for example The New Lodge Six Community Inquiry 2002 (New Lodge Six Inquiry 2002). This community-led inquiry took place on the 22nd and 23rd November 2002 in St Kevin's Parish Hall, North Queen Street, Belfast. It was an investigation into the killings of Jim McCann, Tony Campbell, Jim Sloan, Brendan Maguire, John Loughran and Ambrose Hardy which took place on the 3rd and 4th of February 1973 in the New Lodge area of Belfast. The families of the six men killed and the New Lodge Six Time For Truth Committee developed the trial, with a jury predominantly of legal professionals working in Human Rights law. The motivation for the event was to bring broader public attention to the New Lodge community's charges of collusion between the British forces and Loyalist paramilitaries in carrying out these murders. This inquiry took place thirty years after the killings and was a challenge to the British government to undertake a formal investigations process. The committee report states:

> Now that we have moved into an era of unprecedented potential for political transformation, and given the British Government's stated commitment to open and accountable government, there is an opportunity and a particular onus on the state to assist us in our endeavour to arrive at the truth.[61]

This type of hearing could be seen as positioned between Government-led legal enquiry and the authored nature of theatre-based testimony. These

---

[61] Paul O'Neill, Chairperson, New Lodge Six Time For Truth Committee, December 2002. (New Lodge Six Inquiry 2002).

community hearings are localised responses to a perceived absence of state justice. In taking the constructs of state law, such quasi-legal processes paradoxically emphasise the desire for the legitimacy of legal formality and resolution.

There is a bitter irony in Northern Ireland, that many people do not separate their need for vindication through legal channels from their stated non-acceptance of those legal and governmental bodies that constitute such a mechanism of judgement. Arguably this is because the legal system still has power to make judgement, and even if the system is distrusted there is still an implicit understanding of the underlying potency of this power. Living in a post-conflict society can be a vulnerable situation, even within seemingly benign environments, to volunteer testimony in whatever situation of telling is to risk rejection, or even blame and condemnation. For some individuals speaking out publicly will never be a prerequisite to their own individual private process of healing, but as Ross describes, even those who are silent about the past will undergo a reshaping of thinking and articulation. She states:

> The reworking and re-evaluation of testimonies in different contexts and over time matters in relation to claims that speaking 'truth' gives rise to 'healing'. Once spoken, claims do not rest but are reworked and revised in accord with various conventions. Rather than understanding the reconfiguration of testimony as aberration, a deviation from an original, authentic spoken word, it can be understood as part of the work of forming the everyday in violence's aftermath. (Ross 2003: 101)

Ross describes the importance of weighing the impact of time upon the effects of testimony, as the social political dialogue changes shape across even a decade; what is permissible to say changes constantly, the narration adapts to the updates of both official and inner community commentaries. Testimonies are sporadically transmitted, adjusted and recycled, as part of the social reconstitution that is necessary for people who continue to live in an environment where they have experienced trauma.

As mentioned earlier, testimony carries for many people spiritual meaning: this aspect has been frequently disregarded in Northern Ireland, or perhaps blunted by misuse in political rhetoric. One could argue that there is a legacy of the bitterness of religious testimony, which was cynically incorporated with political dialogue for divisive effect during the Troubles. This perhaps alters in some ways the lineage of testimony as an act, and a manner of language post cease-fire, since the same words are difficult to re-appropriate back into new spiritual or reconciliatory interpretations. Examples of this are the slogans and religious emblems used on paramilitary murals, the depictions of Bobby Sands as the crucified Christ, elsewhere Protestant murals use terms such as 'In God we trust'. Such a lineage means in the present tense that the language surrounding reconciliation can significantly dilute the strongest elements of religious overtones – from overt references to forgiveness, replaced with a more 'common sense' rhetoric of developing the province economically for the good of all. In this regard an interesting feature of the South African Truth commission was the presupposition of using a language based on forgiveness:

> Reconciliation was also interpreted as synonymous with forgiveness, and tremendous pressure was exerted on victims who came before the Commission to 'forgive'. The emphasis on a discourse of reconciliation at the public hearings came at a cost of invalidating displays of 'negative' emotions. Some of these emotions – such as anger, anguish or resentment – are legitimate healing emotions for those who have suffered loss. Their dismissal in favour of forced forgiveness had the potential to do additional damage to victims by denying them the process of natural grieving and healing.[62]

It is significant that the ongoing grassroots battles for recognition of human rights injustices such as those orchestrated around Bloody Sunday insist that forgiveness is not always an acceptable response. And, in some situations internationally direct citizen justice is being enacted on former perpetrators of regimes, in an emphatic shift away from identities of victimhood. An example of this is the Argentinian protest form of *Escrache*, which is a symbolic interaction with place and person developed collectively in defiance of political amnesia.

Escrache developed in Argentina[63] in 1995 as a form of political activism against the unpunished crimes of the dictatorship (1976-1983). They are organised by H.I.J.O.S (Daughters and Sons for Identity and Justice

---

62 South African History Archive, quoted in Ross (2003: 78).

63 *Escrache* is also used for protest demonstrations in Uruguay.

Against Forgetting and Silence). *Escrache* works in practical terms by the public defamation of former perpetrators, directly outside of the properties of the accused, thus doing exact damage upon their social identity. Hundreds of people can be involved in an *escrache,* beginning with the gathering of information and involving interactions with neighbourhood organisations, gradually building support and publicity. The *escrache* events resemble both parades and political demonstrations; they are generally noisy and theatrical using drumming, giant effigies, chanting and spectacles such as painting the pavements and splashing the front of the house with red watercolour. The targeted person's property is generally protected by a line of police safeguarding the occupant, and protests finish with the reading aloud of a declaration with information about the accused and chanting 'We will always come back' (Hemispheric Institute 2012). Because of this there are strict rules and instructions to ensure the protest follows a structure and remains legal, although often courts have ruled the events illegal and used the police to repress the demonstration. These methods of *escrache* are deployed to draw forward the local community into a sense of collective responsibility. Part of the reason for this approach is that H.I.J.O.S. members found it was an unsuccessful strategy to try to achieve government accountability through the methods of giving personal testimony; therefore they switched their emphasis from personal to collective address:

> In order to implicate their audiences, H.I.J.O.S. members needed to move away from embodying the victims. The escrache therefore used a series of negotiations to perform the rhetorical transformation that will authorize its agents as witness; the two main ones are stressing the state's failure to resolve the issue, to which the escrache's very existence testifies, and also H.I.J.O.S.'s refusal to take justice into their own hands. H.I.J.O.S. tells its public: we show you this happens; we will not solve it. (Benegas 2011: 20-30)

Escrache could be understood as a form of active witnessing. It is a method of public shaming, forcing issues of individual blame, and by extension the responsibility is placed on the perpetrators' neighbours to pursue justice: once someone has been publicly denounced, neighbours must respond or become culpable for their passive acceptance. *Escrache* removes the possibility of claiming ignorance and ignoring implications of someone's wrong-doing. That said, the *escrache* only take their protest to the boundaries of the accused properties, they do not exact physical revenge. Diego Benegas, in an essay titled *If There's No Justice* (2011), describes the series of interpellation layers that exist within *escrache*, relaying complex ideas of identity intertwined with justice. For the H.I.J.O.S there is a protracted sense of political injustice, a void left by the state-driven disappearance of a family member. *Escrache* brings a social consciousness to examining access to justice, since not only do the protest activities unequivocally identify perpetrators, but also through the protestors themselves acting out public revenge they are acknowledging their rights to retaliate against the legacies of the state-run human rights violations. So, beyond the personal issues of survivors' identities, the communal qualities of the protest actions draw forward the idea of the whole of society as suffering from the legacy of those social structures that committed or permitted violations to take place.

Escrache relates to performance art through its highly developed use of spectacle and the complexity of its participatory strategies, which emphasise the necessity of involving resident people within the situations in order to promote agency: in effect an active form of commemoration. *Escrache* relates on many levels to the approaches of various international interventionist art collectives such as Yomango and Superflex. And, indeed, for a long time one such collective Grupo Etcetera worked with H.I.J.O.S.[64] Comparatively other international protest groups such as the OCCUPY movement utilise the facts of location as an essential factor in inflicting symbolic damage through strategies of public shaming.

ART CONSTRUCTS OF TESTIMONY

Virilio has put forward the idea that imagination and the power of suggestion is the last valid battleground, where contestations between traditional party politics have been surpassed by that between states and global media. He has argued that:

> The sudden questioning of a *substantial warfare*, which was the product of politics, by hyperterrorism, an *accidental warfare* which no longer speaks its name, is also a questioning of politics, and not just traditional

64 For descriptions of artist-based activist organisations, see for example Sholette (2011).

> party politics. Hence the alternation now, not so much between classic Left and Right as between the political and media spheres, or, in other words, between politics and that power of management (or suggestion) on the part of the news and information media, which are readying themselves to invade the imagination of populations held in thrall by this proliferation of screens, so characteristic of the globalization of "affects"; this sudden synchronization of collective emotions which greatly assists the *administration of fear*. (Virilio 2003: 42)

This idea of imagination as a frontline of state defences, with emotion deployed as the weapon in persuasion warfare, where as citizens we are not guided by what we think but what we feel in response to what we are given to think, is a pervasive argument. But, how does this 'globalization' of 'affects' or 'suggestion' (Virilio 42) function within art contexts?

Testimony is most prevalent in art practices that are categorised as 'relational'[65] or 'participatory',[66] utilising to some extent dialogical processes or mediated encounters to facilitate objectives of social change. Testimony gathered through forms of collective engagement are part of the concept of these projects, raising discussions pertinent to specific issues, locations and communities. A good example of this is *9 Scripts from a Nation at War* by Sharon Hayes, Ashley Hunt, Katya Sander, David Thorne, and Andrea Geyer (Hayes et al. 2012), originally commissioned for Documenta 12, 2007. This artwork exists as both a multi-channel video installation and also occasionally as live performances. The scripts that underlie both formats have been developed from the starting point of the March 2003 invasion of Iraq by U.S. military forces. These scripts provide a diverse range of perspectives on the war and are re-enactments by actors and non-actors comprising of voices as varied as those of a philosopher, blogger, journalist, detainee and veteran. Sometimes, the performers speak their own words and similarly to Theatre of Witness this brings an authenticity to certain parts of the script, which nonetheless are kept in tension through the fluctuation of identities. The artwork has some structural dimension that relates to courtroom testimonial forms, but in this instance the production of evidence is articulated through a proliferation of voices whose identities are

---

65 The term was first developed by Nicolas Bourriaud, see Bourriaud (2002).

66 See for example Bishop (2006).

destabilised, therefore contesting the validation of perspectives around the long term dissemination of war.

Other artworks such as those by Artur Zmijewski, operate often on the limits of controversy and political subversion in terms of what can be said under 'the right to free speech'. This approach of provoking reactions from people on what are usually socially unacceptable opinions can be understood as a method of testimony if it functions to focus those arguments in ways that allow the underlying anger and frustration to be heard from a new perspective. For example Zmijewski's series of documentary films entitled, *Democracies*, 2009 (Burns & Kenny 2010), presents footage gathered from several different countries of events that demonstrated extreme expressions of militancy, such as right wing nationalism, homophobia and racism. The videos collectively create a cacophony of voices and a scale of spectacle that makes manifest issues and attitudes that percolate through democratic societies but are often considered to be marginalised occurrences.

The act of testimony is becoming increasingly complex in a global context where there is a saturation of available information, but also a growing counter-culture of web-based argumentation and activism. Situations such as People's Courts, and long term theatre processes like Theatre of Witness, exhibit a core motivation of facilitating dilemmas of conscience and empathy, without cynicism. But, the processes are always weighted on a line of 'telling' audiences a certain position, or forcing a message through emotional connection. Rancière's theories around the autonomy of the 'emancipated spectator' opens up ideas of interaction between artists and audiences that cannot be easily categorised in polarities of active or passive responses. The movement of information or knowledge in cultural forms is a fascinating dilemma between an artist's motivations and intentions. Rancière describes this movement of ideas and sensations stating:

> It will be said that, for their part, artists do not wish to instruct the spectator. Today they deny using the stage to dictate a lesson or convey a message. They simply wish to produce a form of consciousness, an intensity of feeling, an energy for action. But they always assume that what will be perceived, felt, understood is what they have put into their dramatic art or performance. They always presuppose an identity between cause and effect. [...] There is the distance between artist and spectator, but there is also the distance inherent in the performance itself, in so far

> as it subsists, as a spectacle, an autonomous thing, between the idea of the artist and the sensation or comprehension of the spectator. (Rancière 2009: 14)

Rancière's statement is a challenging proposition for artists, since he deposes the power basis between the artist's experience of doing actions and their desire that the feelings or ideas that arise will transmit through into the spectator's critical awareness. In this formulation the internalised intentions/emotions of the performer actually reduce the possibilities of the spectator's space of interpretation. What is being valued in Rancière's equation is the power of the spectator to derive their own autonomous interpretation, so that neither artist nor spectator have greater rights of ownership over meanings or indeed feelings, but are conjoined in the actuality of constructing entities that cannot be owned.

PERFORMANCE ART METHODS OF CREATING TESTIMONY

An example of this reciprocity and transformative relationships occurred in the ceremonial form of a performance artwork by Skeena Reece, a First Nations Canadian artist who performed in Belfast in October 2010 in the Harbor Commissioners office.

Sadly, just before leaving Canada, Reece was informed of her father's death, and in deciding to continue to travel to Belfast Reece changed her proposed performance, and instead produced a ceremonial prayer circle traditional to her community as an act of mourning. What was significant about this work was the crossing back and forward of colonial messages between the symbolic authority of the Harbour Commissioners' building – expressing the wealth of a former colonial power – and the understated subversiveness of a personal act, which became an action of inclusion in witnessing the past.

The prayer circle broke the formal rectangular structure of the room, its lines fragile, made only of string, the prayers added gradually as small pieces of folded paper. Four coloured cloths divided the circle into sectors denoting the races of the world black/white/red/yellow. A series of testi-

monial audio recordings were played in the first part of the performance, filling the space with the voices of victims of colonialism.

The interviews were with First Nations people who as children had been segregated into state run schools that operated as detention centres, where the children were forced to control each other through a climate of fear. Reece gradually began to involve the audience in small symbolic acts, offering each person a ribbon to be tied to an oak branch, collectively purifying the room with sage. These actions gradually dismantled the hierarchical behaviour established by the environment, until the audience finally moved out from sitting in rows to standing in a circle with hands interlinked. In the final layer people were invited to volunteer their personal prayers into the circle, then assist in the careful dismantling of the circle. Through bearing witness to the funeral rites of the deceased father, the audience experienced an extraordinary intimacy joining in a grief spanning a geographical, racial, generational divide. By entering a sacred ceremony usually restricted to the First Nations community, this act of inclusion drew out an emotion for the loss of others, and intersected the idea of traumas remaining active in a culture as residual dangerous forces. Therefore, in sharing a moment of private grief we became witnesses to the broader grief of the First Nations peoples, our complicity in that history was voiced yet also given credence or possibility for reflection and change. This performance evoked presence as a collective act, filling public and private voids, and it necessitated the appropriation of a privileged environment, in order to assert a different order of knowledge into the history of place.

What is clear from Reece's work is that the nature of exchange in performance art is frequently ceremonial. There is a sense of purpose and complexity to the relationship that evolves with the audience, and the form of this encounter only emerges during the action. Reece's performance was an act of testimony because it created a context for understanding the ongoing effects of historic colonial policies on her peoples in which the audience are separated in stages from their distanced position as observers into active witnesses. The contemplation that occurred in the work was created in the space through the slow individualised and precise nature of how each person was invited into the process, which gave the experience a sense of the irrevocable and that the moment and exchange was unique. In this way the meaning of Reece's testimony is closer to a religious or spiritual encounter than that of a legal process, since the evidence becomes a source of empathetic interaction rather than one of objective judgement.

From 7th October 2007 to September 2009 the Boston based artist Joanne Rice created a performance work titled *The Human Cost of War,* located beside the Trinity church, in the commercial centre of Boston. This performance occurred over a two-year period, starting every day at precisely 12pm, and lasting around one and a half hours. Beside the artist were two signs. One sign was placed daily by the artist and was a simple laminated paper text reading:

> Every day I bring 100 stones,
> In memory of those who have lost their lives in the Afghanistan and Iraq wars.
> I am thinking of those who have died as kin.
> I am thinking of their sacrifice.
> I am praying for peace.[67]

The action was succinct and consciously structured not to create a spectacle, other than an understated but persistent presence. Every day Rice arrived with 100 small stones in a hand-sized box. She then proceeded to stand three paces away from the accumulated mound of stones placed on all the previous days. As each new stone was lifted from the box, Rice conducted a private prayer while holding the stone before moving forwards and adding the stone to the mound. Over the course of the two years Trinity church began to intervene increasingly with the work, which was situated on a small stretch of grass on the margins of the church's grounds. The church received many enquiries about the artwork, and decided to place an 'official' permanent sign beside the mound of stones. The text of this sign reads the same as Rice's own text, except for two details. They frame the work noting, 'Art installation do not disturb', and also put contact information for Mobius Art group (Mobius 2012) of which Rice is a member. In this way the church re-contextualised it as an installation rather than an action, and although ironically the formality of the sign creates a degree of ownership for the artwork with the church, it also moves the responsibility for interpretation back to the artist community. The two signs mark an ethical shift in the audience's interpretation. If it is construed as an 'art

[67] Text by Joanne Rice sent to the author in an unpublished exchange about the artwork.

installation' mediated by the church, then the understanding is of it as a benign act, and the emphasis falls on the mound of stones as the artwork. However, if the artist's own sign is read, then the emphasis is weighted to an interpretation of the performance as one of protest. In the latter the attention falls to the validation of the act of prayer, since the alignment of prayer with the political context of Afghanistan and Iraq creates a conflict over who the prayers are for. The deliberate ambiguity of the word 'kin' makes it apparent that the action is not about one-dimensional patriotism.

As spectacle, the seeming simplicity of the action belies its complicated qualities of devotion, reverence and modesty, qualities that are frequently missing from art. The spectacle of Rice in a succession of 100 daily prayers is so understated that it can seem invisible to passers-by. People were often wary to look at her, deflecting their eyes from her face, and usually only staying long enough to experience one cycle of movement. I observed Joanne Rice on two occasions, once in winter then in summer 2009, as she stood immersed in prayer. The extreme privacy emitted through her physical presence created a range of reactions from the passing public, some reflexes of uneasiness at a static figure, occasionally aversion, but also many reactions of empathy and reciprocation. Often people stood in proximity and said silent prayers in witnessing her action. There was no definite community targeted by this work. A group of homeless people who congregated in an adjacent bus shelter frequently guarded over her. Although, in the first months they had ignored her presence, as time passed they repeatedly became involved in insuring her action was not broken or disturbed by pedestrians. So, it became apparent that a respect had evolved within this group towards Rice's action. Also local artists were involved on a daily basis watching at a distance, initially to guard her safety, but increasingly as other meditative presences echoing the action.

Rice's presence was unusual for an artist positioned in public space, in that she did not seek public engagement, and was probably unaware during the action of any form of audience acknowledgement. It is an unusual circumstance of a performative public artwork to function without any direct impetus for interaction. Essentially, the performance created from the most dispersed of public situations a sustained space for contemplation. The poignancy and meaning of the work developed through the persistence of her human presence. Holding ground in a commercial thoroughfare, the work gradually acted upon the peripheral awareness of passing office workers and shoppers. The impact of such an action is almost impossible to gauge, since the dissemination of the work was both instantaneous, and yet, also reflective because of the disciplined durational repetition. Rice's work echoes Ross's observation quoted earlier (Ross 2003: 101) on how time and the effects of context reshape testimony, since perceptions of artworks are also mutable, and the meanings of Rice's work changed over the two-year period. The work uses the potency of the act of 'prayer', yet is in fact a created gesture, since Rice's hands were not raised palm to palm in traditional gesture, nor was she kneeling or prostrating her body. There is an element in the stacking of the stones of Jewish mourning rituals of laying stones on graves. The stones were gathered from a specific beach near to Rice's home outside of Boston. Trinity Church requested that the mound of stones be left behind on the site after the two-year performance was completed. But Rice decided to return the stones to the beach, so that they would not be misconstrued as a monument separate from their physical activation through prayer.

Another perspective on testimony arises in the work of Northern Irish born artist André Stitt, whose practice has frequently exhibited a highly vitriolic approach to testimony. Several of his works have addressed specific cases of social injustice in relation to the context of selected sites. Taking the instance of his performance in Belfast in 2000, *Conviction*,[68] Stitt used his physical presence directly on the streets of Belfast to activate a spectacle of pain and humiliation, whilst deliberately moving along a route of personal significance crossing the city from his childhood home in Donegall Pass to the Duke of York bar. This work was mediated through the Cathedral Quarter Festival in Belfast and therefore was publicised and attracted some arts audience. But primarily the action was dependant on the artist's direct, confrontational, yet silent address to the passing public, who responded with confusion, upset and also acts of kindness. As with Rice, Stitt used a sign as an intermediary device, in this case a white vest-shape worn on the torso, with three printed images, the image on the front was of Tommie Smith and John Carlos, the two black athletes who on receiving Olympic medals in 1968 had made the black power gesture holding up their

68 See Stitt (2008, 2001).

fists in a salute during the 'Star Spangled Banner'. The image is invested for Stitt with a resonance of the Civil Rights movement in Northern Ireland at that time, and he describes how in his youth this awakened for him a sense of the potency of political gesture. The athlete's image was framed and hung from the front of Stitt's body with two other family images from the 1950s in another frame. These signs acted as a means of presenting his action to the public as premeditated, ceremonial and politically motivated. Stitt crawled[69] and kneeled along the streets, his hands bandaged, upper body tarred and feathered, the face blacked out and the head covered in white feathers. The image spoke of rage and abjection, indeed, a sense of shame that cannot be spoken. In this way of using the body it became openly accusatory, yet simultaneously pitiful.

The image of tar and feathers is one that local people would have understood and remembered from incidents of the past, when women were singled out by the community and tied to lamp posts as public punishments for what were regarded as sexual transgressions. This legacy of community style 'justice' is still enacted through current punishment beatings on drug dealers in some communities. In this regard, Stitt's action bears resemblance to the practice of *Escrache* in that it creates a trail of shame in its trajectory through a precise location, the body rendered simultaneously abject, yet aggressive and insistent. However, the work is fuelled by subjective anger and as such is a solitary gesture, which is the testimonial form that the H.I.J.O.S rejected in their decision to make actions forcibly inclusive, drawing in bystanders and residents into collusion. Stitt's work allowed the localised audience space and autonomy to make opinions inclusive of the possibility of negative physical reactions, and the action leaves only a memory stain of the legacy of inner community punishment behaviours. In *The Trial*, the torturous world that Kafka describes is a place of unexplained accusations, and unceasingly obscure processes of inquiry, where the accused Joseph K is depicted moving aimlessly through a system with no rights of redress, or opportunity to testify to any stated crime. His Trial of farcical 'inquiries' that are never manifested, only rumoured, begin to dominate K's life with paranoia.

69 For related performance work see also the 'Crawls' works by William Pope.L, for example in Pope.L. et al. (2002). See also Jackson (2011: 140-142).

Stitt's dispersive display of anger perhaps relates something of the dynamics of powerlessness that survivors can experience in the aftermath of violence, where their anger circulates aimlessly if there is no clear target for their frustration, and is constantly redirected back and internalised. In regard to the anger of victims, Brandon Hamber has described the situation that emerged in South Africa from the TRC Amnesty trials and that the experience of these trials in retrospect was inadequate to what the victims had lost. Furthermore, Hamber contests that part of the process for creating new foundations for social progress needs to come from a more developed version of transitional justice. He states that:

> [T]his can be done by centralizing victim's rights in transitional justice; labelling compromises such as amnesty as morally problematic and sustaining a discussion on its ethical implications; not expecting survivors to restrain their calls for justice and providing space for them to voice their anger; and by focusing on multiple methods of accountability and reframing justice as an ongoing long-term process. It is only through doing this that an adequate context can be created in which victims can undertake the difficult intra-psychic work of coming to terms with the injustices they suffered. (Hamber 2009: 139)

Hamber emphasises the necessity for creating structures that facilitate the anger of survivors, in order that injustice can be systematically addressed and worked through.

The need to externalise anger is often what compels the act of testimony, and Stitt's performance in some regards encompasses the conflict of emotions that can be simultaneously accusatory and penitent.

All three artworks discussed could be considered as works of testimony, because they carry with them a burden of emotional behaviour, consistent with traumatic or suppressed utterance. Both Reece and Rice created non-denominational evocations of spiritual healing through their methods of testimony. This is not to claim that healing takes place for the audience, but that the performances are a method of addressing conflicts of human rights violations in a manner that aims to bring openness, tolerance and empathy to the experience of considering the violations without the situation being accusatory. In this regard, there are also connections to community-based methods of reconciliation, as discussed through the therapeutic aspects of Theatre of Witness's approach to testimony. Thus, a spectrum of approaches is suggested through these three artists. In the case of Rice the gesture has spiritual and protest implications, an extraordinarily sustained intimate action created in reaction to the telescoped distances of transmitted violent events. Reece created a situation of delicate openness in the face of grief, to address colonial injustice not through anger but through collective reflection and encounter. And in the cathartic approach of Stitt, he returned to Northern Ireland to make this work, which was a personal testimony to past anguish in his own life, reactivated in the location that makes this action a form of indictment and catharsis.

SUMMARY

Francesca Alfano Miglietti, in writing about the most extreme aspects of body-based artworks, notes the comparison to activist protests and states that:

> Both the artists and the leading figures of the protest movements choose to communicate through the testimony of their own experience, their own existence, their own nightmares. They put on display the fragments of their own private lives, and they exhibit their personal effects and begin to think of the traces and remnants of their own lives as material to display, to open discussion, to use as document of testimonial. (Alfano Miglietti 2003: 20)

Testimony remains an enigmatic component of our ability as citizens to stake a claim in either defence or defiance of the laws that govern our societies. In situations of atrocity, sediments of truth often emerge through a multifaceted layering of testimony. It is a complex, volatile form of articulation, often used to speak the unspeakable. In this regard the context and environment of telling can be crucial to aspects of the act of validating what has been said. Quasi-legal forms of enquiry appear to emerge in situations where there is a backwash of social displacement, and outstanding issues of injustice that fail to be sufficiently integrated into the broader political agendas. Art intersects with this spectrum in two forms, either through processes of socially engaged practices where arts practitioners merge with other social bodies developing works based on human relations and social context, or it does so through the singular, insular voice working autonomously against the grain of absorption by other structures, in effect using presence as a method of embodying separations, such as Rice's dividing of the church grounds from the sidewalk.

The perceived insularity of the artistic gesture can also be its strength, because in its separateness it can create a zone of intimacy or room for anger that otherwise appears to be disappearing from other types of situations and spaces. The role of the ceremonial (religion) and the ethical (law) are still critically being played out in society, but increasingly within disenfranchised spaces, and through diverse situations of created publicness. In the case of a perceived absence of appropriate government intervention or inquiry into human rights violations, there is generally a momentum for public responses that often utilises channels that are mimetic of justice. Art has a stake within these response mechanisms, and also within the growing diversity of alternative practices of healing and spirituality.

EVIDENCE: THE INVISIBLE CONVERSATION

> Now, we were immediately confronted with the problem of our maladjustment to the event. Because the first sensation there, in the disaster zone, is that our biological machinery is not adapted to this. We, God's creatures, are not ready for it: our eyes can't touch it. Our biology isn't adapted to it. Our feelings, our ideas aren't adapted to it, because up to that point time was measured with our human dimensions.[70]

> Here's a room. There's a table in it, a few chairs, a fireplace filled with ashes. There's the peelings of an orange. There's a pair of shoes on the floor...There's no laces in the shoes.'[...] see that room in your head. Now I've told you two things. I've put two things in that room...you put two more in...put them in that room. Think of why those things are there? [...] Create a room that you can go into so that you understand why everything is as it is in that room. Search out in your mind all the reasons why that room is the way it is. But first just pick two things completely disassociated from one another and put them in this room.[71]

The presumption made around legal-based evidence is that materials imbed irrefutable proof of their histories, that they are in effect mute messengers of circumstances. In legal situations physical evidence is brought systematically into correlation with sequences of testimony, textual statements, mappings of locations, and timings. The diverse artefacts of incidents become part of a matrix of interlocking deductions, where the objects function somewhat as tangible markers within the conjecture of contested narratives and actions. In trial situations the evidence is often presented as exhibits in sealed bags, it is not to be handled directly, only to be observed. This gives it a transitional status as a visual artefact, and in this condition it can be either discretely insubstantial, or in fact develop an 'aura' through

70 Extract from an interview between Paul Virilio and Svetlana Aleksievich in relation to the accident at the Chernobyl nuclear power plant, which occurred on 26th April 1986. Virilio, Fondation Cartier pour l'art contemporain (2003: 200).

71 Keenan (1992:129). (From a conversation between former Beirut hostages Brian Keenan and John McCarthy, during their joint incarceration.)

separation from tactility where the 'idea' of the object takes on new dimensions such as reverence or even fearful reactions depending on the potency of the human associations. Since in legal process the act of spoken testimony is paramount to how objects function in conjunction with the bodies of victims and perpetrators, evidential objects act as conductors of forensic content, but also as persuasive indicators of the velocity and scale of events.

In comparison to this idea of the legal validity of objects, the erratic aspects of the human performance of giving evidence which underlies the handling of objects also needs to be considered. Within creative improvisation processes the invisible conversation begins closer to what Brian Keenan conceived of during imprisonment: the activation of the space between a shoe and discarded orange skin, unspoken relationships that interplay within the imagination. Keenan describes the mental game of invoking objects as surrogates, in order to suppress anger, fear, and grief for absent persons. Within textual forms the residue of unease is apparent in the hesitancy behind words, or beneath words, a blemish in coherence and grammatical correctness. Or, conversely, in writings categorised as 'magical realism', words reanimate the world with an altered sense of perception framed by the circumstances of the characters within which the reader travels. Similarly perhaps, the beauty of body-based improvisation is in the unplanned moments of transformation, when objects or matter begin to shed familiarity and behave outside of their habitual use, gathering a range of potential meanings. These new possibilities can seem alien or contradictory to the object itself, but are convincing as interactions if what the audience observes is the particularity transmitted in the manner of the artist's handling, which indicates the new status of that object. Therefore, it is not the object that transforms, but the human gesture and cognitions that surrounds it, or even passes through it.

In general a surprisingly limited range of objects are used repeatedly in performance art. The most unusual of object choices are usually directed by an artist's memory connections. The emphasis is upon exploiting a range of possible meanings, some literal, some symbolic, others discrete and secretive – different from objects that often are selected for their familiarity or apparent neutrality. The object as it is commonly understood and used in utilitarian functions is frequently irrelevant to how it is incorporated into an action. The artist's intention and directing of inner narrative coerces objects to emit variations of readings through an acute bypassing of what the object denotes in the everyday. This bypassing is an act of will, which becomes an act of imagination. The objects are used ambiguously, they can simultaneously be literal, symbolic and abstract, yet they substitute (often) indescribable events, function as markers for emotional playback, and activate memories insulated in physical task. The object(s) and sequence are only significant through the specificity of behaviour, and in this way they become individuated to each performer who chooses to use them, regardless (and somewhat optimistically) of the layers of cliché involved in frequent usage. Much of the creativity comes in a raw state from the continuum of everyday life. What is occurring is a nuanced heightening or amplification of attention to what is otherwise known about an object or gesture on a subconscious level, i.e. the over-familiar can be ostensibly invisible, but this invisibility can be penetrated through unexpected physical choices, interwoven with memory.

Other performers use literal objects with obvious emblematic connotations, such as buckets, toys and flags, utilising the pathos of banal materials. Their actions extricate the worthlessness of these possessions, yet they also articulate the depth of attachment that can exist within the kitsch or trivial. An example of this is found in the minimalist actions ofMonika Günther and Ruedi Schill.[72] Often using small, unimportant objects such as an egg timer and tortoise ornament, both artists manipulate their chosen object simultaneously to varying degrees of adaptation, emotion and focus. The variations that are crafted by both artists exist for the audience both independently and in unison: the negative space between their bodies functioning as a buffer through which their differences can be comprehended and appreciated. The delicacy, playfulness and expressiveness of what evolves in each performance is a revelation of the quiet secrecy of objects, the potential and pleasure in de-familiarisation produces an enriching innocence from the object's banality, which they imbue with transient emotions.[73]

Elaine Scarry in *The Body In Pain* (1985) makes interesting assertions about the underlying dynamics of object relationships, about what it is that

---

[72] Monika Günther and Ruedi Schill are artists and renowned teachers based in Switzerland.

[73] See for example Stiles, Museum of Contemporary Art (1998).

we undergo and indeed project into the act of making, whether for practical or creative purposes:

> In the attempt to understand making, attention cannot stop at the object (the coat, the poem), for *the object is only a fulcrum or lever across which the force of creation moves back onto the human site* and remakes the makers. The woman making the coat, for example, has no interest in making a coat per se but in making someone warm: her skilled attention to threads, materials, seams, linings are all objectifications of the fact that she is at work to remake human tissue to be free of the problem of being cold. She could do this by putting her arms around the shivering person (or by hugging her own body if it is her own warmth on behalf of which she works), but she instead more successfully accomplishes her goal by indirection – by making the freestanding object, which then remakes the human site that is her actual object. (Scarry 1987: 307)

Scarry's proposition of objects as fulcra is an effective means to describe human agency within the production and application of objects. Whether its use is as tool or weapon, the ways in which objects are constructed become carriers of symbolic meaning and force. Her statement opens the idea of how human behaviour manifests its innermost projections through the trajectory of perceived and actual needs and the attendant metamorphosis of materials. Scarry's assertion that the act of making 'remakes the makers' (Scarry 307) is a useful concept in relation to our ceaseless seeking of self-worth, self-definition and positioning of ourselves in the world, activated emphatically through the handling of objects. In relation to these ideas, what occurs in performance situations could be interpreted as an unfixing of those self-propositions of being. For an artist there is gratification in transforming or subverting not only the appearance of object or matter, but also to alter perceptions of its relationship to human encounter. To take an example of Joseph Beuys's sculpture of 1979 entitled, *When you cut your finger, bandage the knife* where the blade of a knife is wrapped in gauze, in order to reconfigure the idea of the wound and making the blade and finger interchangeable.

Primo Levi, in his writings on the Holocaust, describes his own self as reflected back to him by those suffering around him, those he termed the 'nonman' (Morel 2002: 92) the barely human beings left soulless on the side of living, still human, but conditioned by having 'been an object in the eyes of man' (Morel 92). This idea of objectification as a factor of dehumanisation was brought vividly to light in an artwork by Htein Lin from Burma, during a performance in Belfast on the 12th September 2009, in which Lin evoked a complex range of transformations from a single length of cloth.

At the beginning of the performance a video projection screened images of state violence perpetrated against Burmese monks, an image of personal significance to Lin's own history. Standing behind a stretched piece of cloth (the same colour as those of the monks) Lin used the cloth to form part of the screen. Subsequently, during the hour-long duration of the action, through a series of precise transitions, Lin (a former political prisoner) manipulates the cloth around his body, moving from the idea of that object as a blanket, shield and shroud, producing in effect a fluid sequence of gestured states associated with passivity, defence and defiance. At one point in the performance the cloth was used to interact with individual audience members. Lin walked cautiously towards the audience with the cloth hooded over his head into a long hollow funnel shape, through which he peered intently at individuals in close proximity, the hood becoming a secret meeting point for two faces to converge. The performance action became a construction of transferred resistance, manifested through humble but innately human gestures. The prisoner, corpse, monk, exile, all became apparent, as the body memory tapped the nervous tissue of gesture without the use of verbal language. Significantly, this work was not about shame or disgust, but about resurrecting dignity through witnessed display, creating inclusion within a ritual connected to the artist's own personal survival expressed in the precision of these movements. At various points in the action Lin's young child inadvertently entered the performance, contravening the space of the performer and audience. Through the child's innocent reactions to his father's movements, their unplanned interactions aroused in the audience a sense of acuteness to the present moment, as Lin simultaneously retained the composure of his action, whilst also responding intuitively to his child.

FORENSIC APPROACHES

In atrocity exhibits and sites of commemoration evidential objects are often used directly as part of public displays, such as piles of human skulls, e.g.

Ntarama Church, Rwanda and stacks of human artefacts remaining from the Holocaust, e.g. glasses, shoes and human hair. Questions arise concerning what these artefacts denote. To what degree are they readable as brute evidence in and of themselves, or what methods or interpretive steps are required in considering them? Part of any interpretive strategy adopted by such public exhibits necessitates performative relationships, whether the viewer is choreographed in their collective movements through the environment by means of interpretive displays, tour guides, or even actors re-enacting scenarios. In general it is understood that these kinds of evidential objects become forms of tactile witnessing: they undergo a transformation that stakes the sacred or sacrificial into the core of the mundane. Handling is also a crucial part of developing tactile knowledge, and the frequently inert manner of museum displays reduces the potential of establishing the compassionate connection envisaged in making these displays public, since audiences easily become immune to the shock of massed human residue.[74]

An artist who approaches trauma through authentic artefacts is the Colombian artist Doris Salcedo.[75] She uses constructed installations to provoke aspects of experiential contact, essentially the transmission from static object into positions of directed embodiment. Salcedo achieves this through the complete or partial burial of personal artefacts of victims of violence into the actual matter of her sculptural works. In a reversal of court procedures, Salcedo's sculptures create a discrete withdrawal of access to the visualised human artefact, instead provoking 'presences' of evidential matter relocated into the mind of the viewer.

Other approaches to real artefacts are evident in the work of Jeremy Deller, Christine Borland (2000) and Nathan Coley (2004) who have all worked with the forensic residue of events, and engaged with the scientific and legal processes attached to the afterlife of evidential objects. Deller and Borland have both appropriated archived legal evidence as source matter into artworks without any sculptural adjustment or intervention. They have redeploying the potency of the objects through shifts in context. In 2010, Deller created a work titled *Baghdad 5 March 2007* (Clode 2010), which involved exhibiting the remains of a car destroyed in a bombing which killed

[74] See for example Clark (2011:1: 68-79).Also discussed by Gene Ray in relation to the work of artists such as Arman and Beuys: Ray (2011: 22-48).

[75] See for example Wong (2007).

38 people in the historic Mutanabbi Street Book Market in Baghdad. Deller initially exhibited the destroyed vehicle as an artefact, driven from place to place in the USA on an open-backed trailer and displayed in informal public spaces, such as car parks with the purpose of provoking discussion with passers-by. This approach differs from the viewing of artefacts in museums, since the performance of travelling with and presenting the object as a fact of war makes the artist the mediator of a distanced form of witnessing. Subsequently, the artefact has also been exhibited in The Imperial War Museums in both London and Manchester, where the context of the museum collections created a different set of relationships. In some respects museums can function in a similar way to religious contexts, since the collecting of a work accentuates its status as object, creating a heightened distinction around certain artworks that registers them in a new system of evidential value. Most often performance artefacts are not entered into this value system, although artists such as Joseph Beuys, Marina Abramovic and Orlan consciously produced objects to intervene in that context.

The factors that imbue evidence with value are difficult to pin down, objects linked to crime can develop an ambiguity where they are simultaneously sullied or debased by their associations to violence, yet, they can also be perceived as sacred (such as the blood stained shirt President Kennedy was wearing when he was assassinated). There is an ascendant and descendant tension in the potency of objects, which are observed even within the rational confines of law to have imbedded properties. Some of this 'value' is constructed through what can be excavated from the object forensically, the imbedded 'DNA knowledge'. But beyond this exists a much more ambiguous 'aura' of worth connecting the object to a sense of person, status, judgement and historical moment. Often the qualities of a connected person evoke presence through the inanimate object. There is also a sacredness created through objects or bodies being sealed off separately from the contamination of touch. These objects can manifest for the families of victims magical properties concerning the soul of the departed, whether the object is then seen as benign and protective of the person, or something that needs to be destroyed to release its traumatic associations. Families often remark on the specifics of what a loved one was wearing when they died,[76] and indeed the relationship the person had to that piece of clothing. The storing of it becomes an issue of its sacredness, and represents a porous relationship to the victim's physical being and mortal remains.

When the bodies of those lost through violence or disaster cannot correctly be buried, or if the manner of certain deaths remains contentious, communities sometimes create 'reparation objects' that become tangible surrogate forms around which mourning can be structured. Brandon Hamber has described the importance of reparation practices manifested through symbolic connections, such as memorials or reparation objects created within communities. He states:

> In line with the theory of 'transitional objects', reparations contain a deep internal resonance for survivors of political violence. Symbolic reparations, like the transitional object, need to exist in both the internal and the external world for the survivor, and they must have something sacred or even magical about them to have an (individual) and social (collective) meaning simultaneously. If they exist only in the external world (for example, a government memorial project that is more about nation building than individual victims), the survivor will feel estranged from the significance of the object, and this will not serve as bridge between troubled internal feelings and feelings of social belonging. (Hamber 2009: 111)

To consider this parallel between D.W. Winnicott's ideas of 'transitional objects'[77] and Hamber's observations on reparation objects, there are difficulties of quantifying or even naming the 'magical' entity that people know instinctively has to exist in an object for it to register as sacred. Partly the 'aura' is conveyed through the context and presentation of how and where something is seen comparable to the drama of a religious relic, only viewed on a specific day of the year under controlled circumstances. But in the case of contemporary community-made commemorative objects, what brings sacred or magical properties to such objects is a sense that something of the victim is secreted within its matter. This transference of a 'presence' of the victim is not only symbolically conveyed, but physically enacted in the action of making restorative objects, the labour involved becomes in-

[76] For further discussion of sacred objects see for example Hamber (2009). See also Vamik Volkan in relation to trauma and objects (Volkan 1997).

[77] See for example Davis and Wallbridge (1981).

trinsic to its commemorative value. Perhaps, this relates in a similar way to how a child secretes its own scent and secretions into a transitional object (e.g. most often a blanket or teddy), and this integration of bodily matter is of primary concern to the child who will reject powerfully the effort to 'clean' the object. Significantly, the most potent commemorative objects are a product of the makers being physically merged to the objects by labour: a replication of touch, which on some level grafts into the sense of spiritual worth.

The work of Palestinian artist Emily Jacir has dealt with issues of reparation as actions, and the making of objects as a means to gather together a Diaspora community. In 2001 Jacir developed an artwork titled *Memorial to 418 Palestinian Villages Which Were Destroyed, Depopulated, and Occupied by Israel in 1948*,[78] in which an authentic refugee tent was embroidered in black thread with the names of former Palestinian villages that had been destroyed. The embroidery work was created over a two month period in New York by a mixed group of volunteers, largely Palestinian, some who had family connections to the places named, but also some Israelis who had grown up on the remnants of these villages, and other interested individuals. Jacir's artwork is a good example of the potential of an object to activate and facilitate exceptional conversations, in this case one based on displacement. The communal space that evolves around the object is as potent as the object itself, since those who gather around it can enter into dialogues of experiences, including anger and grief, supported by the collective activity. The object partly becomes a reconciliatory space for the contemplation of emotions that are often buried in daily life. Additionally, since the tent is an inherently portable and utilitarian structure it continues to speak to the present circumstances of refugee camps in Gaza.

Hamber's observations that reparation objects must be handled correctly in order to develop symbolic meaning emphasises the difficulties of government roles in brokering acts of commemoration. The processes of transference and acknowledgement between victims and society is pivotal to its success, on a psychological level demonstrating to victims that they are valued and their pain is being addressed with respect. Consequently, a reparation object made by a community harbours within it a spectrum of at-

[78] See for example Modern Art Oxford (2004).

tendant emotions, some of which can be negative, a grievance. In addition, if this object is formally accepted within a different sector of society, such as government, the accepting of it may not constitute a generative transition into acceptance or apology. Conflicts of interpretation can occur when such objects leave the environment in which they were made, since an object displaced from its original community cannot always be properly understood and valued.

THE HUMAN PERFORMANCE OF EVIDENCE

Another way to think through ideas of evidence is to analyse it as it is manifested through human behaviour. In this respect, four categories could be considered, namely: fear, irrevocability, silence and actuality. All four terms are used in parallel between describing creative improvisation practices and social processes. Fear is developed in relation to both activation and suppression of social responses. Irrevocability marks the moment of encounter, instances of either conflict or epiphany regarding circumstances. Silence relates to absorption, inner reflection of what has happened. And actuality is considered as a process of coming to terms with events, finding meaningful methods of coping, including compassion.

FEAR 1, TERRORIST CELLS, NOTTINGHAM[79]

A room cut off from breath, the air sealed in and sterile, in order to preserve the relics of violence, enable the gathering of forensic debris, ballistics from skin, fingernails, nasal passages, the threads of clothes. From here terrorism takes us into a second skin of microscopic munitions. Here the suspicious are sifted from the treacherous, the lethal from the malleable, the extremist from the radicalised, curtailing the spreading forms of the enemy, countered, examined, reformed, the probing reaches under the legal skin of the host nation. A room without surfaces, untouched and untouchable, the human entity becomes magnified within its emptiness. Walls pre-cast to create a room without seams or edges, cracks, fissures or texture, slippery in its intensely refined visibility. Imagining a room for the containment of a

[79] Bridewell Police Station, Nottingham, viewed by the author during a private tour of holding facilities given by police officers in 2003 for research purposes.

person stigmatised from contact, its unfurnished perfection, the air replenished with oxygen preserved unchanging behind a vacuum door. The space of a human subject transferred into the space of a human object, the viewing time occupied in analysing the smallest stifled movements. Two such holding cells wait side by side holding in exact proportions the scale of state insecurity.

The ultimate form of evidence is the human body; this is explicitly highlighted after the death of historic figures, the most recent examples being Bin Laden and Muammar Gaddafi in 2011. In these instances the decimation and humiliations enacted onto the corpses demonstrate the implication that retribution is in essence immeasurable, it goes beyond death. In addition, creating invisibility is the covert reaction of governments to those they perceive as dangerous, whether through the 'disappearances' of citizens in Argentina under Pinochet's dictatorship, or the 'torture flights' method of the USA in removing its suspected enemies to places where they can be detained and tortured outside of the American legal regulations and the International Convention of Human Rights.

Anthropologist Michael Taussig, in his studies of colonial violence, describes a Chilean story told by Ariel Dorfman about the fate of children abducted by witches:

> In order to break the child's will, the witches break the child's bones and sew the body parts together in an abnormal way. The head is turned around so the child has to walk backwards, and the ears, eyes, and mouth are stitched up. This creature is called the *Imbunche*, and Dorfman feels that the military junta under Pinochet has done and continues to do everything in its power to make every Chilean and Chile itself into an *Imbunche*. (Taussig 1987: 4)

Comparatively, Taussig describes how in Miguel Angel Asturias's description of dictatorship in Guatamala, entitled *El Senor Presidente*, even nature becomes an apparatus of the dictator's control. He states:

> [A]s people become like things, their dreaming power passes into things that become not only like people but their persecutors. Things become agents of terror conspiring with the president's need to sense the innermost thoughts of his subjects, who, once sensed, become not just objects

> but disjointed parts of objects. It is the dictator's sensing of people's inner worlds that terror makes nature its ally. (Taussig 6)

The fabric of fear is in its capacity to assimilate and assert itself into every aspect of life. Scarry reiterates this point in describing how the victims of torture undergo a profound destruction of all the elements of their world, that the process of torture destabilises all former norms and beliefs. A powerful feature of this is achieved by the torturers tactical curtailment of the idea of home by using domestic objects as weapons. One example Scarry uses is the torture techniques used in the Philippines during martial law where victims described:

> [B]eing tied or handcuffed in a constricted position for hours, days, and in some cases months to a chair, to a cot, to a filing cabinet, to a bed; they describe being beaten with "family-sized soft drink bottles" or having a hand crushed with a chair, of having their heads "repeatedly banged on the edge of a refrigerator door" [...] The room, both in its structure and its content, is converted into a weapon, deconverted, undone. Made to participate in the annihilation of the prisoners, made to demonstrate that everything is a weapon, the objects themselves, and with them the fact of civilisation, are annihilated: there is no wall, no window, no door, no bathtub, no refrigerator, no chair, no bed. (Scarry 1987: 41)

This also relates to issues of the spectacle of terrorism, since terrorists induce fear through their ability to infuse their presence into everyday life, so that travelling on trains, buses, aeroplanes, commonplace situations become sites of fear and create omnipresence as potential threat.

Another aspect of this invasiveness of domesticity and contamination of privacy is evidenced through one of the most striking features of art made under socially oppressive conditions, which is the intense qualities of introversion, almost confessional isolated aspects of the works. Examples of this are found in the archived works of Romanian artists under Ceausescu's dictatorship[80] in the 1970s and 1980s, when artists such as Gusztav Uto, Ion Grigorescu and Dan and Amalia Perjovschi made a number of actions that were produced in domestic settings, usually negotiated around a single static camera as witness. An example of this is Ion Grigorescu's work

[80] Pintilie (2002). For comparable examples of art made under cultural repressive circumstances see also Berghuis (2006).

entitled, *The Kitchen or Art in a Single Room*, 1976 (Pintilie 2002: 68). In this work Grigorescu photographed himself within the confines of a narrow kitchen alternating between a range of actions, some mundane; such as ironing or eating, merged with painting, playing the violin and writing, all of which occurs among the clutter of dishes and furniture.

These works speak eloquently of oppressiveness through evidencing the limitation of 'working' space, in effect the invasiveness of censorship into all forms of living space. What the documentation offers is usually only a limited impression of the artwork on an aesthetic or conceptual basis, but more acutely gives an insight into the psychological conditions that provoked the creative gesture, and the compulsive quality of self-ritual being explored. Other tactics developed involved making temporal acts in landscape in small private groups, such as The Sigma Group and House Party. These actions generally occurred outside of places where they might attract public attention, and often indicate a symbolic relationship to landscape not centred in the political climate of the time. The loneliness of these works breeds another understanding of fear, and the paralysis of the self-censorship that permeates outwards from state oppressiveness.[81]

IRREVOCABLE 1: AUDIENCE TRANSFERENCES

In his extensive anthropological analysis of sorcery in different cultures, Taussig reveals that the invisibility of some objects can contravene its dimensions as located in the imagination. Objects can be untouchable and unpossessable although they can reflect hopes and desires of cures imbedded in the sacred as trajectories of illogical force. Taussig describes how:

> Healing someone of sorcery, for instance, generally involves the extraction of an object, a splinter or a worm or an animal, from the inside of the body, just as sorcery – an intrinsic part of religion and perhaps its most "transgressive" part – involves the placing of these things in that body. (Christian notions of exorcism, confession, catharsis, and purgation, as well as the ready use of Christian concepts to translate key elements of so-called primitive religions, the soul, for instance, are parallel phenomena energized by insidedness/outsidedness.) (Taussig 1987: 168)

81 For further descriptions of performance art produced as political response see also Cohen-Cruz (1998).

The body is the site for these metaphysical and physical transactions, also the source for this malleability of passing through objects, which can be simultaneously concrete and ethereal, the movement of beliefs is necessarily bolstered by the transformation of objects and visceral matter. This undercurrent of the sacrificial and alchemical is still evident within performance practices; an innate sensitivity is involved in touching living matter, which is a crucial and profound element for many artists.

Such factors of overt tactility, such as the smell or sensation of blood on the hands, bring an urgency to what emerges. Physically there always exists a degree of sacrificial purposefulness and persistence in the handling of organic materials, which is particularly noticeable in the actions of the Viennese Actionists, André Stitt, Stuart Bristley and Franko B, among others. In his writings on artistic mourning Gene Ray has identified the particularity of the materials used by artists such as Arman and Joseph Beuys in generating presences of mourning from the Holocaust (Ray 2011). For, as Ray emphasises, the Nazis' application of the Fordist factory model to the production of genocide meant it was not enough to exterminate the Jewish population, reducing the bodies to ashes, but that it was also necessary to eliminate all forms of possessions into component parts, inclusive of hair and body fat, all rendered as base material for further commodities.

This disquieting understanding of sacrificial transformation also extends to an artist's use of their physical flesh as material to be abused, defiled, renewed or transcended. In performance art pain usually represents, from the artist's perspective, a transition point or breech, where the actual pain induced produces internal changes from which the next layer of behaviour is driven.[82] This is an aspect of the 'irrevocable'. The term is taken from Richard Schechner (1988) by which he describes the complexity of human fantasy arrangements, our ability to be absorbed in self-perpetuating fiction as an aspect of our relationship to performative mediums, but also to indicate that some of these transitions are permanent, not abstracted but positioned in the visceral and the actual. Therefore, in performance art it is about abolishing artifice, yet the act of creating actual physical pain is fundamentally a primary spectacle, and the choreography of violence a

---

82 See for example the writings of Stiles (1993), 'Shaved Heads and Marked Bodies: Representations from Cultures of Trauma' http://www.duke.edu/web/art/stiles/shaved_heads.html.

compulsive form of viewing. Thus, often a dissonance exists between the performer's intentional trajectory towards a transformation of content and expression and the possibility that the audience might only inhabit the image of the pain, unable to see beyond it, or in some circumstances embody the pain vicariously through witnessing.

In a correspondence with art historian Slavka Sverakova, I asked her to describe her perceptions of pain as a factor in performance artworks. Sverakova responded:

> Proposition 1: when perceiving a work of art the audiences suspend normal judgement to allow the "make-belief" become a truth.
> Proposition 2: performance art sites itself on the narrowest cusp between the "make-belief" and the real, significantly in relation to the body of the performer. I think it involves rapid oscillation in perception and judgement.
> Watching a performance artwork depends on similar kinds of authority. Illusion, seduction, visual force, scale, timing and the appearance (and sensory data) of the performing body, all contribute to the impact on the viewer. I cannot watch calmly when a living person does anything that may harm them, the difference between who inflicts the harm is secondary. Yet, it is significant to the way I manifest my response: in real life I would try to stop them, in performance I turn away. This is because I assume that the artist is in full control of his/her senses, decisions, judgement and that it is not expected of me to treat a work of art as life.
> In turn, this can be clearly unpleasant to say the least, and it does create a conflict between the respect to let it happen and the desire to stop it.[...]
> Insecure conclusion: perception of real suffering, whether it is written, painted (e.g. Grunewald's *Crucifixion*), acted or performed connects to the aesthetic, moral attitudes of viewers, and their various thresholds of sensitivity to sensory input. I believe that the imagination of the viewer contributes significantly.[83]

In Sverakova's conception of the contract between a performer and audience, the audience has knowingly to allow themselves to be persuaded of the dominant emotion that is aroused by the artist. This is a choice, not an obligation, however it is through this independent decision by the audience to engage that the circumstances for the realisation of the artwork evolves. Otherwise, as Sverakova states, 'If I did not allow it, I would deny at least

[83] Unpublished correspondence with the author from March 2011.

two functions of art: aesthetic transformation and psychological transfer.'[84] So, in this way there is a social 'contract'[85] operating during performances: the audience has come with a prior expectation of this transference, even though the potential of its manifestation is deeply unstable. In another formulation of this contract artists need the concentration and presence of the audience as witnesses to attempt to reach other physical and mental states. The audience is essentially the connection to transformation and transference and in this way energetically the pattern created is reciprocal.

PHYSICAL SILENCE

Aspects of performance works regarding the complexities of gathering testimonies from the survivors of traumatic historical circumstances and the residue of violent experiences that is 'unsayable' can be related to the debates of theoreticians such as Fiona Ross, Elaine Scarry and Veena Das. Chaos and disturbance manifest themselves in multiple forms of human behaviour and the body itself is an object that carries evidence as marks and traces but also the internalised wounds are carried as presence. The incidence of pain is an element in performance practices that is one part of a trajectory of actions and reactions, syncopated and entirely interdependent on the actions that frame it. Often, what the audience remembers is not the moment of impact, but the reverberations of aftermath evidenced in the artist's altered capacity within their body, the change that is palpable in how the body moves deeper into subsequent actions. Physical silence is how I choose to describe the presence that surrounds certain performance artists. It is a state of authority induced by the artist, yet, significantly it is a quality that has to be renewed, it only occurs in a live situation through the endeavours of the artist to activate the present moment of every action that they undertake.

Watching the body of a performer such as Stuart Brisley, Alastair MacLennan or Boris Nieslony, the eye is initially arrested by deciphering movement as signals to locate meaning. Gradually, however, there is a growing perception of the emptiness or silence around that body, where

84 Unpublished correspondence from March 2011.

85 For discussions of masochism and shock tactics in art practices see for example O'Dell (1998). Also Alfano Miglietti (2003) and Weintraub, Danto and McEvilley (1996).

the weight sits, how it forms around the shoulders or the elbows, how it quietens the mind to tread almost imperceptibly into the spaces beyond the body's scope. To reconstruct the ambiguities contained in a single gesture are multi-fold, raising a fist or coiling the spine, every gesture has its home in memory, and every gesture can be registered and reregistered endlessly in the imagination. The inner intention in the moment of making movements conveys what this gesture now means, even as it is visualised unfolding. In this transaction what the audience perceives is the weight of a gesture rendered first in the body, before the eye. This, I propose as the compassionate body, in some respects it appears purposeless, un-sculpted, an undirected body released from the cognitive effort of narrating or telegraphing its intentions. In these fluid moments of improvisation the body appears to forget the compulsion to propel itself from moment to moment, and in this way, a sense of contemplative space opens outwards from the artist's intense absorption in the situation.

IRREVOCABLE 2: 'THE TRUE MOMENT'

Observing the German artist Boris Nieslony[86] give a demonstrative presentation about his practice at PALA 5 performance laboratory created for me an insightful analysis of the most difficult threshold within performance art: the space of cognitive negotiation between the interior and exterior body. Nieslony initially conceptualised the process in verbal language, but then also in stages moved away from the prescriptiveness of these thoughts into a physical embodiment beyond the description.

In the beginning he spoke a few words about identity, 'How moves this body without individuality? Who uses this body? Where? How? Move?' He then adds small fragments of autobiography, describing how as a child he was forced to say 'I', 'me', and constantly to identify himself to adults, an act that caused him confusion and pain, because the purpose of this identification was to be made answerable to control. Therefore, in Nieslony's interpretation individuality as an enforced self-identification is not freeing but a method of containment. There are moments in the action when fingers from both hands are pushed into his gaping mouth, body crouched

86 Boris Nieslony is a leading European performance artist, curator, teacher, and in 1985 he co-founded Black Market International, a collective meeting of performance artists.

over from a standing position, moving back to a wooden pillar, moving forward towards adjacent pillar, the fingers move as if fraying between the teeth, sound is uttered, it moves between adult and child frequencies, the words are partially formed but the voice behaves as a tonal physical presence, conveying a sense of helplessness. Watching Nieslony is like watching someone walk backwards out of language. In ways it feels like a therapeutic encounter, as involuntary gestures erupt from the body seemingly without cognitive relationships. The gestures are often ferocious, then lulling and calm, as language falls into sequences of noise, utilising tongue, throat, mouth and lungs probing in various ways to excavate the sounds from beneath or between verbal language. His breath is filled with continuous, exhausting strands of sound, fluctuating with pauses, whistling, murmuring, mumbling, this fragmenting, sporadic body captured in the desire to eclipse the conscious mind, to lever images out uncut from the substratum of socially customised gestures. All the while knowing that this state can only exist briefly, he glimpses the raw edge of the physical and a place where the body approaches its dis/abilities and mortality.

After the performance Nieslony asks the group what is the 'true moment' for the viewer, meaning by this: at what point did we witness the actuality of the situation beyond the spectacle of a demonstrated idea. Nieslony's performances raise pertinent issues concerning witnessing, because they propose the idea of validating the 'authentic' inner self from the notion of presence. In effect, it is a fracturing of the notion of presence, destabilising who the person is we are watching. The interrogative quality of the act of watching in this instance is centred on locating the points of disappearance. In some respects what is occurring is no longer performance, since this plasticity of the artist's body could perhaps be construed as the antithesis of presence. It can seem to be a disappearance, or metamorphosis: creating uncertainty about the status of subjecthood.

In some respects it is radical in performance to undermine the centrality of the idea of presence, which is focused on the body as authoritive and authentic. When the subject becomes unstable in the work of performers such as Nieslony, what is witnessed is the scratching away of self image, and since theoretically the actual self is always in itself a conception/projection, performance in its most stark and spontaneous forms is a state of denied presence.[87] In such circumstances the performer is utilising an internalised consciousness of self, or is absorbing in external stimulus the liquidity of otherness. Therefore the body is being lived in, or being lived through. This 'invisibility' is a rupture of the reliable, readable subject. The 'true moment' Nieslony articulates that what happens cannot be retracted, it exists in its imperfections.

Is the work a rejection of control and controlling, or a releasing, a form of catharsis? Nieslony states that he feels relief after each action and that the actions are made in response to the signal of a voice. He describes how he feels empty when inside this state: 'somebody took me'. His intention is to make movement that is not based in any one separate performance tradition, eastern or western, also to reside without borders between interior and exterior. His is almost an archaic wish to be outside of culture. Yet, Nieslony acknowledges that within doing these performances, they quickly systematise into a movement method, the moments of potential and invention quickly become patented. Therefore, the significance of the true-moment is literally its brevity and urgency, before the body reforms into habitual images. These are compelling glimpses in Nieslony's actions that cannot be pinned down 'stylistically', and what emerges over time from watching him perform is an increased awareness of what his body has lived, an encyclopaedia of the self, ungoverned by narrative telling. What he presents is an emptiness or an enacted emptying out, a research beyond forms; it is disturbing to watch, he exhausts himself and suddenly the situation is complete. Nieslony's actions would seem to be acts on the edge of the spectrum of evidence. Since neither the identity of the artist nor the cultural form of movement is stabilised, both cannibalise each other in a deliberately subversive suppression of self.

INTANGIBLE CULTURAL HERITAGE

In some respects the kinds of exploration of identity, its construction, preservation, or, as in the example of Nieslony's action, its suppression, is a factor of performance art that relates to other fields of embodied evidence. Internationally there is ongoing consideration of the increasingly fragile existence of tribal peoples and the many forms of heritage that are now

87 For discussions of artistic approaches to self-image see for example Jones (2006).

acknowledged to be intrinsically embodied knowledge. Even in so-called developed societies there is concern over what a culture loses in terms of generational and environmental changes. Intangible cultural heritage was defined by William Logan in 2007 as '[H]eritage that is embodied in people rather than in inanimate objects' (Ruggles & Silverman 2009: 1). Therefore, the development of preservation strategies has accelerated in recognition of the global impact of industrialisation and effects of mass media, and how this negatively influences traditional cultural configurations of beliefs and rituals. Laura R. Graham has studied various reactions by indigenous peoples to processes of adapting contemporary media technologies as a means of preserving tribal cultures. Graham describes how the Yuchi (also known as Euchee) have largely rejected technology in regard to preserving their language, because experience has shown these peoples that they cannot replace the innate learning process of communication between elders to children through any technology, including writing. Any attempts to archive language have in fact been a burden on the energy of the few remaining elders. Graham states that for the Yuchi: 'language is a living process that is profoundly spiritual. It is not a "thing" that can or should be technologically objectified or contained. The Yuchi word for language is "breath" (Ruggles & Silverman 189). Some Yuchi speakers have requested that any archived recordings they participated in making should be buried with their bodies, and the tribe concentrate their efforts on language in their community as a 'spoken, living thing' (Ruggles & Silverman 189). The issues surrounding the gathering and dissemination of intangible heritage resonate with those raised by evidencing performance art, in that both acknowledge the brittle and time loaded quality of extracting something of the 'truth' engrained within performative acts including all aspects of the performance of language.

SILENCE 2: POLITICAL

Fiona Ross makes an interesting proposition of another form of covert 'telling', where those giving testimony sometimes protect themselves consciously or unconsciously by slippages and omissions in narration. Ross describes the significance of the trickster mode of narration:

> There are many different ways to express harm and violence. The repeated use of the trickster trope by older women and young men con-

> trasts with the Commission's insistence on 'victims' and 'perpetrators', that, [...] may reify pain and violence and have the effect of objectifying people and experience. Such objectification implies passivity on the part of those that suffered violence and harm and imputes an enduring damage. Trickster narratives open a discursive space that enables a consideration of the past different from that offered by the models of heroism and victimhood. Yet, the ironic or humorous stories told about 'the struggle' in Zwelethemba may obscure important facets of human experience in contexts of violence. If the Commission testimonies are limited in that they elide the collective then the stories couched in trickster mode neglect pain by emphasising autonomy. Perhaps these stories draw from a cultural repository to ward pain away. (Ross 2003: 157)

Ross describes the reluctance of activists to give statements to the Truth and Reconciliation Commission, because they felt that it disjointed the ideals of collective action, which they believed were central to their struggle. The silence of victims as in the 'unsayable', or in the trickster example, elucidate the value of selective silences as a means of protecting what only the immediate community can understand, and in turn they must come to terms with. This leads to a broader sense of how silence is a crucial entity functioning in different ways over time, ultimately towards formats of collective memory or forgetting. In an essay by Yadh Ben Achour, entitled 'The Order of Truth and the Order of Society', Achour states that:

> [I]n politics the truth may do damage. Sometimes the obligation to remember must cede to the imperatives of peace, order, and security. [...] time needs silence in order to bring about forgetting. Truth may keep alive or even reanimate the thirst for vengeance, thus preventing the return of confidence and calm, both of which require a dose of silence in order to affirm themselves.[88]

There are also elements of invisibility in the political speaking body that is deliberately denuded of excessive gesture. Politicians and broadcasters are trained to minimise their actions and reactions, the flatness of the political body destabilises the possibilities of interpretative readings of body language, and in doing so focuses a maximum of attention onto the spoken word. Therefore, what the viewer tends to scrutinise are both the

88 Achour (2002: 123-134). It is significant that this book was a platform of Documenta 11 and brought issues of global justice into the art context.

verbal pauses and the gestures that elude the speaker's ability to contain them. This restrained expressiveness is especially pertinent in survivor testimonies.

PENNY HOLLOWAY[89] LECTURE AT QUEEN'S UNIVERSITY 31ST MARCH 2011

Watching Penny Holloway, light appears on the corner of an arm, one moment to position the eyes in relation to the general stillness, beneath the weight of looking, another struggle then darkness where the mouth fails to move, only opens a gap, closes, remains tight lipped. Not that you would be conscious of that, or of the same expression found in a movie, or in the middle of a song: the ambiguity of a withheld emotion. She is holding down her son fugitively in her inner most thoughts, she holds him tight in a downcast position, covering his eyes and heart with the breadth of her tangled arms, beneath her words move the signals of aggression that this space of him shall not be violated with loose words, she straightens, adjusts, moves the loose printed sheets of text methodically to the right, apparently methodically, then she turns the edges of the relocated pages back on their spines, levers then between her fingers, her eyes move as if scanning for words, but when she begins to speak again her words show no hesitation, there is no pause, the speech well-rehearsed, structured in a worn groove, driving along the story of the struggle, her nails blunt, sleeves buttoned down, she looks at the notes needlessly, then directs her eyes back straight down the room without stalling on any one single face. She looks inwards, checks that the emotion remains controlled. Sentences begin and end, some parts of the story need reiteration, a second attempt at the explanation (sliding forward) the disturbing narrative, careful, so careful as not to be accusatory, or defensive, careful to alternate tone into and out of textures of concession, she acknowledges the help of those who investigated. When the question comes about sectarianism, she is able to hold it at arm's length, to let the listeners understand the accusation in the slight silence proffered before an answer,

[89] Penny Holloway's teenage son Thomas Devlin was murdered in 2005. Subsequently she has campaigned extensively for justice, including challenging the Public Prosecution service, Irish government and loyalist community, which she claims has protected her son's murderers.

the political response is quietly given, a concession, a concession to the ongoing state of deliberation, only one provocation at a time, softly the fingers fall back on the split pages, equidistant, two stacks: a before and an after or a them and an us. Her hands spread to hold down the two piles, warm them with the palms placed tightly over the facts, guarding what she decides to say or to leave for another day: further revelations, he didn't come home, and for this, there can be no grief until there is penance, no mercy until there is closure, the last part of the case pending, the appeal by the prosecuted. She waits with both arms open, both hands holding down the pages that previously swayed from finger to finger, the questions litter the room only for the briefest moments, then there is quiet around the mother. The murder unrehearsed in each person's mind, she said it would be so in the beginning, knowing that the facts are available, her refusal to satisfy the need for shock is a steady victory she has perfected over time, a pieta is complete, inside herself she carries her child too ungainly and public for her body to contain. Yet, still she nourishes a darkness around his adolescent body, only cautiously does she use his name, she refuses to call herself the victim, asserting twice he was the victim. What is her role, she questions, what is the pain of those who wait ashamed of this pain that cannot be named. She delays his death, carries the weight of the one who never came home.

What matters in performance is not only an expression of the unspeakable, but perhaps also the untouchable, the gaze, or the 'violence' of the gaze: that eyes can lock into each other, decant thoughts, emotions between one body and another, liquefy intention through mirroring physical responses. In live events there is huge diversity in what the viewer experiences through the gaze of the wounded, the complicit or the judgemental. Relations of power become assembled in different ways towards different meanings, breaches and interpenetrations of memory. An important aspect often overlooked is that the audience's eyes also leave a trace on the performer, a reminder that embodied relations are fraught with different presences. Adrian Heathfield makes a significant point about presences shifting and being uncontainable during the course of an action: volatile in that the audience is also a matrix of charged entities. Heathfield articulates this ambivalence, stating:

> [W]hether it emerges from the clash of 'real' time with 'fictional' time, from an actual physical wounding or from the excessive density of enacted events, the charging of attention used by many contemporary Live artists brings the spectator into the present moment of the making and unmaking of meaning. This condition is often decidedly unstable and ambivalent, for whilst the artist's or the spectator's 'presence' in the moment may be a prerequisite, the transient and elusive nature of this presence becomes the subject of the work.[. . .] often 'being there', in the heart of things, you are reminded of the impossibility of ever being fully present to oneself, to others or to the artwork. (Heathfield 2003: 9)

As humans how do we refresh innocence? How do we recycle conscience, and awareness? Learn how to look again at things, which perplex, seduce, or become mundane with overuse? Performance often uses succinct but simple forms to raise fundamental questions about our humanity. It employs the everyday as a sounding board for continuous acts of readjustment to the fluctuations of our living circumstances.

Unquestionably cultural shifts of interpreting pain have altered the perception of visceral acts in contemporary performance art. Aspects of masochism are still present, but obscured behind layers of symbolism both the sincere and the mocking. In fact mockery could perhaps be considered as the primary form of self-abuse that is being manifested in many performances: the lapsing and failure to actualise the anger or shame felt inside. There is seemingly a crisis in how to represent anguish, a bypassing of the corporal, and embarrassment around visceral qualities. Any number of factors from the excessiveness of violence and humiliating spectacles rendered through reality television and cinema no doubt impact on both audience and performer's understandings of what can be credibly staged. These are the reasons why I contend that the most potent actions are in fact those which escape from a body uncontrolled, uncensored and unstaged, those which have such a deeply rooted sense of interiority and inevitability that they can only be understood as living testimony.

ACTUALITY 1

The artist Alastair MacLennan[90] has described his understanding of the ability of the corporal body to transition meanings in the act of communication as a series of integrated relationships within the multifaceted nature of surroundings. He states that:

> The body is both an object and a living organism. It is one, and one of many. It is capable of unspoken discourse for which it becomes both the mover/agent and an objective embodiment. The body as a physical channel for meaning has neither been fully neglected (we pay attention to non-linguistic modes of communication) nor fully attended to (our culture is directed more to the word). (MacLennan et al. 1988: 10)

In this statement MacLennan introduces the idea of the body as an object in the world, with capabilities of being stable, pliable and in turn manipulative. Our understandings of its (exposed and hidden) discourses are constantly in a state of negotiation, both from the internal directives of subjecthood, and the outer objective perceptions of otherness.

Performers can coerce the receiving body of the viewer into activating its own resources to respond. In this regard, performance is never neutral. The body in states of stillness is at its most magnified, because in these moments it resists the need to explain itself through gesture. In this base or concrete form, the mind of the viewer is increasingly caught up in imagining the interior thoughts and using that body as a quasi-metronomic measure of time passing through the transparencies of another presence.

ALASTAIR MACLENNAN, ST PATRICK'S DAY 2011[91]

MacLennan in an impromptu action on derelict ground in North Belfast emptied the contents of several cardboard boxes of performance artefacts from forty years of actions onto the concrete foundations of a demolished building site that was littered with urban debris, weeds and underdeveloped trees. Over the course of two hours he steadily sifted and structured

90 The Scottish artist Alastair MacLennan has lived in Northern Ireland since 1975, currently Emeritus Professor at the University of Ulster, Belfast. MacLennan's practice is internationally recognised for its incisive relationship to location, extensive durational commitment and contemplative values. See MacLennan (2011).

91 This actuation was a private work by MacLennan, to which I was the only witness.

the fragments, gradually interconnecting the artefacts with objects found abandoned on the site. Like a drifting tide line, his slow movements forward and back along the fragmented pieces gradually evolved into a series of ranks and currents, moving without preconception, prejudice or sentiment to any of the amassed range of objects, the motion of arrangement and rearrangement began to state its own purpose, a hierarchy emerging not based on any clear logic of values, his hands apparently driven by a compulsion to re-conceive of each piece, to revive and resuscitate the stored and the discarded into a communion with the situation, until what became perceptible was not the structure of an artwork, but the dispersal of the formerly valued artefacts into oblivion within the nature of this place. MacLennan's actions ceased only when it was no longer possible to distinguish between the art and the accidental fragments. This actuation was rendered poignant by the gentle economy of MacLennan's body, methodically integrating his own history of matter into a state of release, not through chaos or destruction, but a reflective and creative realignment with all the available random resources. In this way, the action was not a commemoration of the artefacts, but the renewal of a lifetime of working methods.

COMPASSION

Reminiscent of Levi's description of the 'nonman' and the Chilean figure of the *Imbunche*, Walter Benjamin described Franz Kafka's recurring use of 'assistant' characters, as:

> [B]eings in an unfinished state.[. . .] neither members of, nor strangers to, any of the other groups of figures, but, rather, messengers from one to the other. [Kafka himself described them as having no other ambition than,] to use up as little space as possible. To that end they kept making various experiments, folding their arms and legs, huddling close together; in the darkness all one could see in their corner was one big ball. (Benjamin 1973: 113)

These satellite characters nonetheless carry a weight of gesture as exploration or even contamination: they manifest unease in their unformed states. Yet, in Benjamin's interpretation of Kafka's bleak vision, it is through these characters that Kafka creates harbingers of 'hope'. An intriguing notion that those least endowed with linguistic and functional abilities, in fact the 'accused persons', could in some senses be attributed with qualities of beauty. Perhaps the implication is that only those who have accepted their condemnation can enter a state of release or redemption.

In law the levels of evidence are nuanced and hierarchical, the ultimate proof being the human body, or in its absence the potency of witness testimony, down to layers of increasingly fragmentary circumstantial evidence and forensic detail. The arrival at an approximation of truth is envisaged to bring some sense of closure to past events, which will enable those involved to begin to come to terms with what has happened. The 'resolution' offered by performance is also that of a method of coming to terms with the past and creating a sense of actuality in the present – as with therapeutic and reconciliation processes the inner stimulus whether founded on rage and guilt has to be transformed. This change is not instantaneous but incremental and often weighted with painful emotions. Performance in some instances freeze-frames the coming to terms with the past, or explores the silence of forgetting.

Returning to the ideas touched on earlier regarding the tendency of viewing performance art through conceptions of the pained body, in comparison the redemptive compassionate body is in some respects more difficult to ascertain and assemble as image and symbol. For many contemporary performers there is a separation in their work between the display of actual wounds and the evocation of pain through tactics of methodical physical restraint. These kinds of actions can create charged situations through the embodiment of a restorative or coping state. And I propose that the compassionate body is one which seeks to align disparate elements to restore order and to coincide purposefully in relation to other bodies, either that of other performers or of audience. This is a process of bringing a sense of cohesion to the shared situation even if only momentarily, or occasionally by returning the audience from 'suspensions of disbelief' back into the realities beyond the performance context. This restoration to normality is in itself a form of discrete rupture, but it is significant – if the resonance of an action carries across from the performed situation into the dispersal of the event back into social space.

ACTUALITY 2

Returning to Michael Taussig's writings on the 'tricks' of shamans performing cures, he describes:

> [T]he performer is neither asking for a gift nor entering into a contract with the spirits so much as gearing into their world through the perfection of his performance of beingness. In later life, Nietzsche saw this as essential to the Dionysian state, in trance or ecstasy, with music and dance, the Dionysian character becomes totally plastic and protean in a rush of becoming other. This is not so much becoming any specific other so much as becoming becoming itself. (Taussig 2006: 140)

Taussig explores the plasticity of the performing trance reactive body, its metamorphosis between animal, human and spirit states, moving in and out of the human body until what is perceived is not the other, but an interfused reality, an essence of the human expanded outwards into place. The contradiction of heightened performance states is that the body usually must exude authority in order to achieve presence and therefore credibility, but that on reaching this watershed it must then leak out, vomit its own identity and the connections founding it in the familiar. The true moment is therefore also the inexplicable one, where what is perceived has the insistence of factual occurrence, it has a clarity, but one that seems to exist outside of the structure from which it arose.

Regarding the aftermath of political disappearances, performance art is often described by its commentators through terms such as 'oblivion'[92] and 'disappearance' (Phelan 1993: 148), words that articulate a sense of absence – both what is excluded/not present and that which is not 'seen' to be present as the core of performative activity.

I focus on the word invisible, because what fascinates me is the dilemma within improvisation to transgress the visible aspects of the live situation, or, in other words, to use the performance situation as a means to awaken oneself and others to a set of possibilities that communicates between and beyond the body. In this regard silence or visceral, irrational utterance is a core factor particularly in the Western European traditions of performance art. This use of studied silence often coexisting with stillness

[92] See for exampleAdrian Heathfield's essay 'Alive' (2003: 6-13).

or precisely restrained forms of movement, I have already termed physical silence: a discipline among other methods adopted by artists for carrying and conveying evidence through the body, in ways that intersect with boundaries of object relations, human interactions and space. Observing my own body ageing, developing compassion over time for the repetitions that inadvertently invade its movements, reminding me of a current of mortality that makes the head or hand react in certain gestures, the body re-inscribes itself in numerous ways each time it performs. Because of this layering of gesture developed over years, defining the exact meaning of a movement becomes increasingly opaque, each day a gesture can seemingly be remade. A secret language of specificity and insularity within a body, motioning in degrees of communication, part open, part concealed, the body retains something of its own core of ingrained knowledge in every act that it works through.

Often this secrecy becomes more imbedded: the greater the fluency and apparent simplicity of reflex-like gestures – as can frequently be witnessed in the work particularly of performers such as Nielsony, MacLennan, Jan Swidzinski[93] and Suprapto Suryodarmo[94] – leaves behind a trace evidence of the body's habitual behaviour and capacity evidence is impossible to separate from presence. This economy of expression is somewhat like Kafka's 'assistant' figures of bodily obsolescence in that the person who reaches a condition of responsive or absorptive ritual is perhaps touching on the essence of human interrelation to time, space and other beings. Conceivably this is why there is often an impression when watching a performance that it is an exceptional encounter, somehow intricately imbedded in the artist's life. The sense is of a private window into someone's interiority, where the action ceases to be art and becomes a rite of passage, an act of mortality or commemoration, dignifying time with human notation set outside of the ordinary, like opening a sleeve through daylight and revealing the hidden room.

---

93 Jan Swidzinski, pioneering Polish artist and writer, known for his theories of 'Contextual Art'.

94 Suprapto Suryodarmo, Indonesian artist, and renowned teacher, especially known for the development of Amerta Movement, a technique evolved from rituals responsive to natural and spiritual sources.

SUMMARY: THE PRICE OF SILENCE

Contemporary art perspectives of performativity encompass a hybridization of several artistic approaches: relational, dialogical and participatory. Whilst all these forms involve many shared qualities with performance art, they often exclude or reduce the value of the body as an expressive medium outside of verbal language. Performance art continues to regenerate itself predominantly as a body-based, non-verbal art form, dependant on its ability to create memorable embodied images rather than, for example the kinds of understated physical transactions involved in relational artworks. This inherently theatrical practice of placing the emphasis of expression on the performer's body is part of the difficulty of validating performance as a genuine socially adaptable practice, since the situation is a hierarchy of overt tactility on behalf of the performer, which is generally not converted into interactions with audiences.[95] Conversely, dialogical and relational artworks are often critiqued for a lack of visual spectacle or sensual stimulus, but the 'loss' is seen as compensation for a heightened potentiality of verbal communication, the shaping in fact of exceptional conversations[96] and the physical rituals imbedded (usually almost imperceptibly) in such speech. The kinds of silences developed in performance art are perhaps relevant as a counterpoint to these kinds of dialogical explorations, the space in effect, for the rituals of communication to be reconfigured and contemplated separately from the dominance of speech.

95 Of course some performance practitioners do develop interactive approaches, e.g. Skeena Reece's practice described in Chapter 3: Testimony, but the strategies they use still foreground the role of the artist as the director of the 'ritualised' situation. This differs from the kinds of interactions that occur in dialogical and relational artworks which emphasise the dismantlement of authorship.

96 See for example Kester (2004).

JUDGEMENT: DOES IT FAIL IF IT IS ONLY ART?

> [N]owadays cities are dumping grounds for globally produced troubles; but they may also be seen as laboratories in which the ways and means of living with difference, still to be learned by the residents of an increasingly overcrowded planet, are daily invented, put to the test, memorized and assimilated. (Bauman 2007: 92)

The Polish sociologist Zygmunt Bauman proposes in his book *Liquid Times* (2007) that utopia has been overturned conceptually into an ongoing state of individuated and insatiable needs. He claims that humanity does not move towards utopia but perceives itself to be inside the motions of utopia, and that this movement is an addictive state. In effect, to reach the conclusiveness of static conditions would be intolerable after the obsessive acts of pursuit. Therefore, sustainable acts of protecting, nourishing and cultivating, Bauman argues, now happen in society as counter intuitive activities. Furthermore he states that the task for humans is to identify from within the turmoil those things which have consequence, gravity, necessity, profundity, and are therefore oppositional influences to the force of incessant change. Bauman suggests there is no way out of this so-called inferno, only small gestures of resistance to its immersiveness.

Bauman makes a case for the value and ingenuity of the communication and social interactions demonstrated in ghetto areas and refugee camps, as models of progressive social behaviours. He argues that it is these places that in fact incubate the necessary skills of future cities by demonstrating the ingenuity required to navigate fractured societies. In contrast, he also describes the growth of enclaves of wealth, deliberately sealed off from such diversity of interaction, where the rich increasingly live in restricted zones that constitute forms of siege mentality. Bauman's argument explores the idea of what he observes to be the task facing global societies to reverse the negative perceptions of what are in fact crucial techniques of human survival. Improvisation exists in its most essential forms in situations of deprivation; however, it seems vulgar, almost perverse, to term the strategies of survival as creative. And, conversely, in the face of real humanitarian suffering and injustices, how should we view the creative skills of artists? Are they in any way adequate or adaptable to produce forms of response beyond propaganda or empathetic gestures? Or, are they in certain ways making matters worse by, for example, allowing those accountable for the condition of socially deprived areas to exculpate themselves by commissioning artists to intervene in politically sensitive community situations?

ISSUES OF CREATIVE AUTONOMY

The last decade has shown a considerable upturn of interest within the international art world in the representation of difficult political subjects, evidenced in the form of controversial international exhibitions like Documenta 11,[97] Manifesta 6,[98] and the 4th Moscow Biennale.[99] However, this trend arguably creates certain difficulties, in that the attention garnered can conflate complex issues of context with conflicts of exoticism, or, as curator Joanna Mytkowska puts it:

> [T]he big international shows have started to resemble catalogues of war and plagues from the most exotic parts of the world, in what is probably one of the last manifestations of the domination of post-colonial discourses, suggesting that wars and conflict happen on another planet and that, in a global context, they can be presented as phenomena pertaining to others. (Mytkowska 2008: 6)

It is debatable what role the international art world actually plays regarding the topic of compassion fatigue, which is fundamentally an issue fuelled by global media.[100] However, it cannot be ignored that art exhibitions do regularly contain representations of atrocity, albeit generally from an intentionally humane perspective. That said, there can still be a sense

---

97 Documenta 11 took place in 2001 and was structured around themes of justice from global perspectives.

98 Manifesta 6, was scheduled to take place in Nicosia, Cyprus, in 2006 but was withdrawn because of the political divisions in the city, which proved intransigent.

99 4th Moscow Biennale of Contemporary Art took place in 2011. It was themed, *Rewriting Worlds* and featured political activists as well as artists.

100 See for example Moeller (1999).

of 'milking' complex, localised conflicts for artworks. In trying to deviate from literal narrative devices, artworks can oscillate in a realm of knowledge that pertains to the factual, but is only quasi-factual, or attempt to convey the truth about situations despite being highly subjective and conditioned for reception by an international art audience. Occasionally artworks make a simplifying universalism of subject matter, drawing parallels frequently more connected to other artworks than to in-depth enquiry of actual events and situations. A danger exists in replicating international assumptions towards certain conflicts, whether or not the artist's intention was to create an interpretation separate from that stance. However, in outlining these kinds of arguments, my intention is not to dismiss or dispute the benefits of artworks and institutions behind them, and that even if flawed, these institutions facilitate the production and reception of contentious and difficult material. It remains significant that within the parameters of art there is still a degree of flexibility and autonomy to accommodate shocking and stigmatised content. The breadth of artists involved in practices termed as 'institutional critique' demonstrates the ongoing presence of dissonance from within arts institutions and networks. So, it is not the situation that these issues are not debated from within the art world, but that artistic methods of political intervention cannot function with the kind of militant values or force that is achieved through activist strategies.

The responses of various commentators of politically oriented art theory such as Gene Ray, Boris Groys, and Gregory Sholette, among others, all provide bleak diagnoses of the possibilities of culture under neo-liberal economic policies. Yet, they still advocate that artists should continue to use the art world as a forum for critical responses, discussions, protest and interpretation. They argue that artists should not be blinded to the inadequacy of this context regarding the construction of real social change, since art world structures fundamentally need to be augmented by other tactical methods and forms. In this regard, the position that is argued is that the only possibility for purposeful change would need to come through radical, anti-capitalist, revolutionary movements and that therefore artists must immerse their energies and resources into such kinds of collective action and ideology. This demarcation of the critical limitations and culpability of the art world within capitalism is a bitter pill for most artists, and creates a dilemma for many practitioners over where their ethical allegiances lie and how their skills can manifest outside of arts institutions.

Ray proposes three models for critically engaged artistic practices, the first being (as mentioned above) institutional critique, i.e. art produced from within the institutions in acceptance of the inherent relationship to capitalism. The second model is to entirely reject the art world, such as the legacy of avant-garde practices, where artists emphatically place their concerns into the integration of art within spheres of everyday life. The third model referred to as 'nomadic', is indicative of Deleuze and Guattari's theories of nomadic 'war machines', where artists alternate between the art world and social spheres according to changing circumstances, Ray states that:

> [T]hey can invoke artistic autonomy and "spend" the symbolic and cultural capital they accumulate through participation in the art system in order to construct a kind of cover or limited immunity that carries over into the sphere of everyday life. In certain situations, such cover may gain them more freedom of action and expression or provide a plausible defence against prosecution for politicized actions on the borders of legality. (Ray 2012)

This mobility does not entirely erase situations of culpability, but it does nonetheless leave a window of potential between the (contested) freedom of speech and autonomy within art institutions, and the possibility to stretch these armatures of privileged artistic expression into other social alignments. The example of the terrorist Michael Stone, demonstrates that the reversal of this process is not possible, since Stone had not accrued credible cultural capital sufficient to overturn perceptions of his identity.

It is also important to remember that many of these arguments and models are not new. Dissonant practices have been circulating in the art world as groups and networks since the artistic avant-gardes became active in the early twentieth century, a model that Ray reminds us still has credibility. But, aside from the schisms between art and its institutions, these issues are directly paralleled by the pragmatic and ethical questions of how artists might otherwise seek to purposefully realign with different kinds of infrastructures and situations in the social sphere. In this regard, in the 1960s the critic and theorist Lucy Lippard began the process of identifying the diversity of strategies artists were developing, in reaction against the materialistic values of the art market, terming these processes as 'dematerialization' (Lippard 1973). This mapping began to reveal the implications of arts-based funding, and how the interrelationships in the mechanisms of the art world have proved notoriously problematic to separate. In this regard, recent commentators such as Gregory Sholette and Shannon Jackson make an interesting analysis of the matrixes that continue to underpin all contemporary art production whether inside or outside of the art world. Jackson's discussion of support structures in *Social Work* (2011), is a constructive way to reassert the fact that art does not exist in a vacuum, it needs supports, and these are multi-layered, systemic and have strengths as well as restrictions. Jackson observes that:

> By emphasizing – rather than being embarrassed by – the infrastructural operations of performance, we might find a different way to join aesthetic engagement to the social sphere, mapping a shared interest in the confounding of insides and outsides, selves and structures. To emphasize the infrastructural politics of performance, however, is to join performance's routinized discourse of disruption and de-materialization to one that also emphasizes sustenance, coordination, and re-materialization. To redirect along these lines is finally to remind ourselves that the Art/Life discourse has a different traction when we recast it as a meditation on the paradoxes of Art and its Support. (Jackson 2011: 29)

By shifting the emphasis onto the act of bridging, sustenance and the mechanisms of re-materialization, Jackson questions the negativity in art circles towards acknowledging the multiple ways art intersects with the social sphere. Since art is habitually used and criticised as the 'sticking plaster' brought into contested situations, then in order to circumvent this position, it constantly needs to address the manner of not just why, but how it participates with communities and structures. Claire Bishop succinctly states the two primary approaches of 'participatory' (Frieling 2008) practices as being either,

> [A]n authored tradition that seeks to provoke participants, and a de-authored lineage that aims to embrace collective creativity; one is disruptive and interventionist, the other constructive and ameliorative. In both instances, the issue of participation becomes increasingly inextricable from the question of political commitment. (Bishop 2006: 11)

In essence, the question of artistic approach or intention has been encapsulated as one of consensus or antagonism. Whether or not the artist perceives their role to be one of telling uncomfortable 'truths', communicating deficiencies and injustices – the artist's exposures may be intended as gestures of solidarity with communities, but can sometimes ricochet negatively, in effect damaging ongoing political negotiations in which communities are involved for example with local government departments sensitive to any negative publicity. Or in the consensus model, the artist is working to affirm and empower local communities or create congenial public situations, and in doing so choosing to underplay contentious questions that might exist around the context. However, consensus and antagonism are not always easy to separate as strategies, and in this regard I concur with Jackson's analysis that most arts practices in the lineage of relational aesthetics are in effect straddling both polarities. Artists who accept the role of mediator or advocate must also accept the conflicts of responsibility and compromise, if the work is to reflect honestly a collaborative process and be in some manner catalytic rather than prescriptive.

These ideas of consensus and antagonism are significant in regard to the ideas introduced earlier, of how artists should align themselves with activist and human rights organisations to enact social change, and how such connective initiatives might best be developed. In an essay entitled 'How Much Politics Can Art Take?' (BAVO 2008: 108-117), a collaboration between architect/philosophers Gideon Booie and Matthies Pauwels puts forward ideas using the term NGO art as a way to describe certain art practices, which respond directly to social situations of injustice with practical solutions. BAVO's argument is that the outrage at social injustices expressed within art world contexts is easily absorbed by the political opposition it is reacting to, because it is too easily categorised as being merely the 'aesthetics' of outrage. BAVO indicate that these arts organisation differ from traditional NGOs through the innovative quality of their problem solving, stating that the emphasis is, '[N]ot so much on symbolic expressions of sympathy or the visualization of a certain critique of the injustices in question: the point is to present solutions, create toolkits and do-it-yourself guides that allow disadvantaged social groups to better their situation' (2008: 109). Yet, because of their reactive qualities these projects are subject to weaknesses in infrastructure, and it is difficult for such initiatives to become sustainable. Additionally, such art projects are also often critiqued in cultural circles for lacking in aesthetic merit and that the utilitarian objectives override the creative innovation. BAVO's description encapsulates the agenda of conscientious thinking and ethical ambitions of many contemporary art practitioners, however in essence what is required to undertake such projects is often a complete relearning of skills on the part of artists. For within the kind of in-depth socially oriented involvements advocated for artists to engage in, traditional art skills are not adequate, especially to the needs of communities with complex psychological requirements. Therefore, it is relevant to ask what it is that artists can offer, and by extension, if what is developed can still be framed as creativity.

To address this problem, one example of a direct and innovative problem-solving artist intervention is *Trampolinhuset,* a project developed in Copenhagen by artist/curators Tone Olaf Nielsen and Morten Goll in 2010. The project directly interacts with asylum seekers and refugees in Denmark, providing a wide range of practical support resources, including legal advice, health clinic, and education. In addition, *Trampolinhuset* provides an alternative social situation for asylum seekers: it is a basic, but warm and welcoming environment, offering a homely interactive space at odds with the institutional housing situations in which most of the participants live, offering kitchen facilities for collective cooking, talks, screenings and other forms of entertainment. Its organisers describe *Trampolinhuset* as, 'A user-driven culture house for asylum seekers and Danes working for a just and humane refugee and asylum policy in Denmark' (Nielsen, Goll 2011). The project is intended as an interface, where not only asylum seekers can connect with and support each other, but also where Danes can meet purposefully to interact with the asylum community, and develop political awareness based on real experiences and discussions. Therefore, it is a hub of cross-cultural learning, as well as a space providing practical assistance in the form of health clinics, hair dressing programmes, computer and language skills, collective cooking and film screenings. Increasingly these activities are initiated and delivered by the asylum seekers' community. A daily roster in *Trampolinhuset* displays what activities will take place, but there is also a second roster of maintenance tasks, and significantly the project is slowly empowering its participants to advance the process and make it a sustainable resource.

Trampolinhuset is a visible art model in the Copenhagen art world; the project has won arts awards and is considered to be an act of curatorial intervention. However, what it is framing is not quantifiable as artistic objectives, but a set of social issues, circumstances and experiential encounters. It is a process that archives the communication procedures of immigration in which the house participants are involved. And, by framing immigration from the perspectives of the asylum seekers, the project takes the highly institutional and repressive aspects of that process, and replaces it with humanising interactions. In terms of sustainability, it is a 3-year project funded by Government bodies, but deliberately its organisers decided it should not be developed through cultural funding or in conjunction with art institutions.*Trampolinhuset* is in many ways an ambiguous project, it exists within creative processes and idealistic aspirations, but is sited within political structures and pragmatic solutions. It is as much a force for lobbying on immigration as a dialogical model of humanitarian interaction. This careful positioning between the mechanics of politics and the rhetoric and visibility of culture makes it a subtly powerful voice in the public asylum debate.

ACTIVISM AND VISIBILITY: WHY PERFORMANCE ART IS SEPARATE TO ACTIVISM

In 1984, Lippard wrote of a sense of fatigue in the art world about the possibilities of 'political art', she responded:

> [N]ow and then I hear artworld denizens complaining about any and all "political art" that "It's like going back to the '60s; the '60s failed, so why try again?" Such attitudes not only demonstrate ignorance of the entire grass-roots cultural movement of the '70s, and of the vast social differences between the '60s and the '80s, but they also recall the treadmill on which avant-garde artists run in place under the impression they're "advancing." [...] Passivity is the fate of the audience in both "high" and "low" art today. The sense that everything will be different again tomorrow and still different again the next day discourages the hope that any action can be meaningful. As on network television, pluralism and posterior fads-post-this-and-post-that movements are desperate tokens of the need to go *some*where, *any*where, reflecting a fear of history, of being

> caught up and forced to deal with history, a fear of being put stylistically in one's place by history. (Lippard 1984: 315)

Reading Lippard's remarks now in 2012, the issue of fears about datedness and corresponding impotence remain prescient. Indeed there is an intensified quality to the insistent pressures of mediatization. In this regard, many artists and curators have created counter psychology methods to address the effects of instant information, by adopting ironically slower processes of witnessing, annotating, assisting, disseminating the complex social environments in which they imbed themselves. Exemplary examples of this are the long term projects artist Mierle Laderman Ukeles has developed with New York Department of Sanitation, and Allan Sekula's durational processes of recording working conditions in service industries,[101] or Suzanne Lacy's projects between police departments and teenagers in disadvantaged areas. What Lippard is voicing is the entrenched fear in many artists that their work could become affiliated with or fixed as reinforcing dominant political hegemonies, or at its most extreme point propaganda.

To clarify my position regarding activism, it is not my intention to pit activism and performance against one another, but to identify commonalities and differences within both. As in Ray's 'nomadic' model I would consider my own work sometimes to be in the shared space between these categories, but questions remain for me of the difficulties that I and other artists encounter in trying to make working alliances with activist organisations, who generally have their own internal identity, ideology and agenda. The matrix of protestors, agitators and activists within contemporary society is perhaps increasingly becoming visible through Internet based social networking sites, but remains a splintering of identities and unclear ideologies. The connections bringing protest and creativity increasingly together in alliances, are perhaps partly grounded in the failure of the art market to deal with its surplus of artist practitioners, as Gregory Sholette has indicated in his book *Dark Matter* (2011) but also the necessity for activism to find a sufficiently benign common tongue or visibility with which to be framed by the media. Examples of this are the types of frequently patronising representations that the media transmit of protestors, such as coverage

---

[101] See for example the detailed case studies in Jackson (2011).

of the Occupy[102] movement autumn 2011. In one instance of a UK Uncut protest taking place on Westminster Bridge on the 9th October 2011, in reaction against changes to the NHS, the BBC broadcaster noted that among the crowd there were 'pensioners, comedians and health workers'.[103]

However, if a protest action is disseminated and perceived by the general public as a creative act, such as a poetry reading intervention beside high street cash machines, it attracts relatively positive coverage and defuses presumptions of anarchistic or anti-social motives. Of course, protestors also use tactics to incite and create disturbance, and in order to draw emotive attention generally use more explicit visual forms than arts practitioners. The literal, dramatic qualities of protest are usually illustrative, demonstrative, and do not demarcate between random or targeted audiences; they use broad strokes of visibility, obstructing space and time in specific locations such as outside St Paul's Cathedral in London from the 15th October 2011 to 28th February 2012, or Zuccotti Park, New York 17th September 2011 to 15th November 2011. These tactics indicate that in order for performance artworks to communicate clearly to broad audiences outside of art institutions, the art has to swallow a degree of literalism, it has to provide a representational framework by which a diverse audience might become attracted and engaged in its messages. However, performance art loses its critical and imaginative qualities when it becomes literal, and this is one of the reasons why it is generally created for a specific and informed audience, with control mechanisms around the parameters of space. The impetus behind most performative 'telling' is composed of autobiographical elements, ethical beliefs, fused to environmental considerations such as Joanne Rice and André Stitt's actions. It is only in incremental and elusive stages that the work begins to communicate outside of its singular subjective position into broader interpretations for its audience, and in this regard it retains the privileged autonomy of its interconnection to the art world.

---

[102] See Occupy Wall Street, http://occupywallst.org. Accessed April 2012.

[103] See for example Ben Ando's report, BBC news, http://www.bbc.co.uk/news/uk-15234363. Accessed October 2011.

HUMAN SCALE GESTURES

Therefore, although there is no simple distinction between the performances of artists and of activists, what both forms of actions are effective in generating is the inexplicable gesture, i.e. encounters that unsettle preconceptions of person or place. Many examples of this can be stumbled across on the Internet where the identities of artist/activist appear interchangeable.

THE SCARECROW, YOUTUBE, 19TH DECEMBER 2011[104]

Watching the video documentation of a young Palestinian art student Razan Akramawy standing on the rim of a flat roof on the boundary wall of a domestic dwelling. The action is titled, The Scarecrow, 2011. In many ways watching this footage, I feel Akramawy's body marks the ambiguity of distinctions between art-based performance and activism, for her physical action – legs brought together, body straight, arms outstretched gently wavering with effort, standing poised on the edge of the wall – is a poetic interpretive gesture. Whereas her white printed T-shirt with the text 'the scarecrow shall prevail', written in Arabic and then beneath in English, is an overt slogan. And yet, the two elements cannot be easily separated, her body transforming, responding moment by moment to its vulnerable station on the wall, embodying its defiance of the immediate environment and by extension the political context. While the slogan fixes the action into a one-dimensional message, it literally explains the act that has been self-consciously composed for the camera. Another factor is the overt symbolism of a standing figure with outstretched arms, which cannot be separated from the image of the crucifixion. However, in watching the video these problematic aspects of literalism are suddenly transformed by a development outside of the pre-conceived plan of the work, for what the video actually documents is an accidental 'failed' interaction with a Jewish man who comes out from a nearby passageway to observe her. The man encircles the young woman from below, then comes up onto the rooftop, and in one brief moment stands behind her and impersonates her gesture in derision, but in so doing he himself is implicated within the footage, where

[104] See 'The Scarecrow', http://vimeo.com/29029591. Accessed December 2011.

the belligerence of his mirroring gesture becomes a charged moment of encounter.

The dynamics of this filmed incident echoes closely with the kinds of testimonial video 'evidences' that permeate from human rights websites, where despite the intentions or preconceptions of the maker, it is only in the un-choreographed moment of exchange, (or in this instance rejection) that what occurs becomes compelling. In effect, it is the breech that is the 'true moment' of improvisation, or the truth-making within the political act. The stillness of Akramawy echoes the artworks of Roi Vaara and Kim Sooja. Both of whom have used the gesture of an obstructive stillness in public space to create different ways of producing resistance, which is also a feature of the actions of Alastair MacLennan. In all these examples it is the exchanges and reactions that are triggered around the artist's body in relation to the particularity of location, that become the substance of fascination and interpretation.

In Northern Ireland the lineage of protest is marked repeatedly through the territorial holding of ground considered to be in some sense 'sacred' because of the events that have occurred there.[105] The culture of murals and enclosed community memorial sites are the dominant forms. These spaces are maintained not only as commemorative proclamations, but also as ongoing protestations of what each community perceives as injustices. As the peace process has progressed these sites have become the default locations of tourist curiosity. Places like the Bogside in Derry receives visitors daily, and to some degree the act of viewing history through the frame of location and preservation is conflicted with issues of intrusion.

THE BOGSIDE, DERRY, JUNE 2009

Standing in the Bogside area as part of a group of tourists on a guided tour, the feeling is uncomfortably exposing, waiting for the group to assemble on a seemingly banal intersection of land. The group huddle in a circle around the 'Free Derry' gable wall memorial, a tour guide, almost inaudible behind passing traffic, describes the significance of the site and explains how the topography has changed since the 1960s. Even though the spectacle of guided tours is repeated daily and is very familiar to local

[105] See for example Purbrick, Aulich and Dawson (2007).

people, it still holds the potential to arouse animosity. The paid excursion to walk across this site functions as an intrusion of memory over normality, and while the guide explains the political history, a group of young teenage boys appeared suddenly around the tour group. They kick a football repeatedly in among us agitating the group, and intervening into the space directly in front of the memorial, tactically reclaiming the territory back from the guide. Since after all, these children gain nothing from the tourist industry, they demand at least our attention. However, stubbornly each one of us in the group continues to face the gable wall and listen to the tour guide who describes in turn the surrounding murals on the walls of adjacent housing, as if we are in a museum where only the pictures are of interest. In the process of these teenagers enacting this small gesture in reaction against their invisibility, there is an ironic replication of the original scenario of the Battle of the Bogside, when local people blockaded the streets against the intrusions of the British army. In a sense, the area is caught in a cycle of abnormality; it is an area, sacred to some, socially deprived to others, held in a stasis of slow urban renewal despite some local initiatives. The Bogside eludes becoming neutralised, and therefore seems fated to replicate its history of tactical defiance on a daily basis.

Tourism is revealed in this instance as an act of controlled aggression, the inadvertent screening out of local people, by the fascination of the 'idea' of place as opposed to its actuality. As described in Chapter 4: Evidence, performance art often functions in a manner that intervenes with 'ordinariness', the mundane qualities of places, forms of movement that merge almost entirely with the rhythm of the prevailing circumstances.

Performance art has an inherent reliance on context and how an audience is orchestrated around an action. Therefore, most performative and especially 'participatory' practices enforce methods of control over the audience, which can be quite subtle, but nevertheless establish boundaries around the kinds of variations of behaviour that might occur. So in this regard, the nature of most performance events is more akin to ceremony than the dissonance of activist events, it needs support structures in order to achieve quality, and by extension the audience requires knowledge of the rules and ritual. Outside of these support mechanisms it is frequently lost in confusion and negative reactions based on audience expectations of entertainment, which undermines the potential of what might emerge. So, in effect performance art is rarely confrontational; generally it seeks to establish fresh consideration or respect for the environment it is developed within.

PERFORMANCE ART IN THE FRAMEWORK OF THE PEACE PROCESS

Simon O'sullivan, writing in response to the 'minor literature' theories of Deleuze and Guattari (1986) notes that:

> minor art is involved in the invention and imagining of new subjectivities as well as turning away from those already in place. A minor art then does not just orientate itself against, or position itself in, an 'outside'. Rather it operates at a more oblique angle (it looks for other entry points). It is at once inside and outside the major, *in* the 'world' but not quite *of* it. (O'sullivan 2006: 76)

O'sullivan's reading of 'minor' in relation to art practices establishes the precariousness of invasions and cross-fertilisation between major and minor creative languages. Part of this quandary of oblique approaches shows that while performance art is an extensive and multifaceted language of human interconnection, yet, it remains for the most part marginalised. This lack of visibility and outreach of performance art is perhaps a condition of its 'nomadic' relationship to the art world. In general performance fluctuates between random, unpublicised, non-spectacular occurrences in public space, or it is programmed by artist-run initiatives as festivals, which occasionally are programmed into museum or biennale contexts as a perfunctory inclusion of live practices. This marginalization, or shifting between inclusion and exclusion can also be mapped in the post conflict environment of Northern Ireland.

For over forty years Belfast has become recognised internationally as a centre for performance development. Founded in the 1970s on the experimental artworks and teaching of Alastair MacLennan, the brief but valuable involvement of Joseph Beuys which initiated A.R.E group,[106] then through the actions of artists active since the 1980s such as Brian Connolly and

[106] Art Research Exchange, see Chan, Lerm Hayes (2011: 118-146).

André Stitt,[107] and since 2001 through the efforts of Brian Patterson and Bbeyond organisation, it has expanded to include a diverse range of emerging practices. I have been part of this history since 1992 as both a practitioner and organiser, involved in the development of three artist-run organisations,[108] and as an artist bringing forward issues of gender into debates of territorial control and trauma. What I have observed in this timeframe has been a considerable shift from works of singular defiance, motivated by dissent and resistance to the prevailing sectarian politics, into new forms of practice (since the first cease-fire in 1994) that reflect actions of collectivity and interaction. Regeneration has formed the (problematic) backdrop of a significant generational shift in changing perceptions of public space and social behaviours in the expanded 'neutralised' parts of Belfast. Although sectarian divisions remain entrenched in sectors of the city, and the peace lines continue to extend, younger artists are no longer dominated to the same extend by the fear induced by territorial interfaces. And, in effect the peace process has facilitated increased interest among artists in developing performative approaches to transitional locations, often employing methods of playful subversion with the civic environments, and the frisson of direct and indirect interactions with the public.

O'sullivan identifies that the conditions of Deleuze's concept of minor literature is that it 'deterritorialises' the major language, and it must be political, collective and immanent. He states,

> Such a deterritorialisation involves the neutralisation of sense, or the signifying aspects of language, and a foregrounding of the latter's asignifying, intensive aspects. This involves a kind of stammering and stuttering – or 'becoming a stranger' – in one's own tongue. (O'sullivan 2006: 70)

Without generalising the diversity of performance practices evolving locally, perhaps the common ground can be summarised in returning to the idea of actuality, an established sensibility of responding in the moment to the immediate situation as it reveals itself. This quality of responding with

[107] André Stitt is originally from Northern Ireland but has developed his career mainly in London and Wales. However, his prolific body of performance works is recognised internationally as having some basis in the politics of the Northern Irish conflict, and has been influential to Irish practitioners.

[108] Catalyst Arts, Agency and Bbeyond.

spontaneity, whether through absurdity, insidious marking of space, gravity, or collective synchronicity (for example Bbeyond have held collective monthly actions since 2008 in randomly selected public spaces), the changing nature of performance here is a process of responding intuitively to the changing political circumstances. In this regard, I believe performance remains relevant as a method of mapping the social terrain, acting upon the opening up, or excluding practices of the newly commercialised public spaces, and the imbedded layers of social permissions and behaviours contained in these changing boundaries. These artistic approaches are heavily indebted to the strategies of the Situationist International movement, whose tactics of *Detournement* – tactical defacing of structures and images to reveal ideological dissonance – and *Derive* or drift – a tactic of interruption in the fabric of public space – continue to be highly influential in art discourses. Although these interventions cannot be termed as politically challenging or activist, since the intention is not to confront, but it is a form that infiltrates and tracks social awareness and tolerance, in this way it is more effectively framed within the ideas of relational art.[109] Performance art has the possibility to intervene in the common perceptions of place, through these kinds of incursions or juxtapositions of socially orthodox behaviour. Therefore, as a minor art it is nevertheless proving itself to be self-sustaining, flexible and responsive to patterns of social change.

A SPACE FOR FAILURE

Improvisation is not telling, or knowing, it is questioning and testing in motion. Activism is – ironically – a stance of authority, albeit counter authority. To be successful it must assert and inspire confidence in its message. This is diametrically opposite to most improvisation where the 'message' is generally oblique, and subjective. Yet, in reconsidering the proposed 'worthlessness' of art in situations of conflict and deprivation, the words of the Polish theatre director Tadeusz Kantor are perhaps worth considering:

---

109 Nicolas Bourriaud's theory of art that produces '[R]elational space-times, interhuman experiences that try to shake off the constraints of the ideology of mass communications; they are in a sense spaces where we can elaborate alternative forms of sociability, critical models and moments of constructed conviviality', as cited in Bishop (2006: 166).

Reality can only be
"u s e d."
"Used" is the only appropriate term.
Making use of reality
in a r t
signifies
an annexation of reality.
The phrase "in art" demands that
This annexation happen outside the practices of life;
That it be
c o s t – f r e e,
g r a t u i t o u s,
u s e l e s s, and
p u r p o s e l e s s.
(–)
During this process,
reality
t r a n s g r e s s e s
its own b o u n d a r y
and moves in the direction of the
"i m p o s s i b l e."
the annexed reality contains in itself
real objects,
situations,
and an environment described
by time and place.
Their r e a c t i o n s to one another,
the i n t e r c o n n e c t i o n s among them,
the annexing g e s t u r e
of (as if casting a spell on reality)
r i t u a l,
are substituted for
the process of moulding,
which is out of place here. (Kantor & Kobialka 1993: 96)

The Polish artist and theatre director Tadeusz Kantor (1915-1990), was an important figure in the advance of post-World War II theatre, because he created several radical methods and theories concerning attrition, and attitudes of developing vision, poetry and movement from situations of depravity. Something in Kantor's statement touches on Adorno's theory of negative representations and the troubling point of proximity to reality, for Kantor articulates that art needs to be in fact withdrawn from directly interfacing with real issues, in order to create tools to reflect on that conflicting reality. This is the conceptual and interpretive distance that activism does not in general engender or facilitate. Kantor describes the space of art as an annex away from reality, in a sense a breathing space that replicates a living reality that has become recognised as overwhelming. He imagines the possibilities that inside such a valve there is an incubation of repetition, disorientation and experiments in simulation, playing out in order to create new potentialities. But, this is not to say that dissonance and disturbance are evaded; the circumstances in some ways replicate reconciliation practices where the incubation of extraordinary circumstances allows the unspeakable to be addressed through both direct and indirect methods.

SUSTAINABLE ACTS

To return to Bauman's hypothesis on the dichotomy between cities as simultaneous dumping grounds and laboratories, and Kantor's concept of art as an annex space, both these formulations stimulate impressions of extra-societal spaces, perhaps spaces reserved for the plausible acting out of repetitions of failed communication. Within such a space, there are rules of engagement, whether through the dividing of humanity partitioned into enclaves of wealth and race, or conversely the explorative rehearsals of contact. In the example of *Trampolinhuset*, there is the ideal of a haven within states of temporality. A place is created around de-institutionalising the process of asylum seeking, which generally is a process that conspicuously alienates and dehumanises those requesting asylum. Somewhere in intersecting these three models is something inherently different to the political solutions of Western governments to design social regeneration through tightening border controls and expanding urban master-plans.

Artist and theoretician Kristine Stiles, in describing the development of art movements such as DADA and Surrealism, observes that the direct use of the artist's body as the primary matter in the making of work:

> [D]eveloped as a viable independent visual art medium in Japan, Europe, and the United States in the 1950s, and, I think, must be correlated directly to the corporeal threat experienced by populations living in the geographical spaces most terrorized with destruction. The actualization of destruction in performative works of art was a cultural sign, I suggested, a *techne* for making one's life into an aesthetic coefficient of survival. Such art not only bore witness to various survival strategies by converting invisible trauma into a representation, but, more immediately, into a presentation. Simultaneously representational and presentational, this art offered an alternative paradigm for cultural practices, one that appended the traditional metaphorical mode of communication, based on a viewing subject and an inanimate object, to a paradigm of exchange, based in the connectedness implied by metonymy. In this model, the human body held the potential for an exchange between individual subjectivities.[110]

This statement, not only links the use of the body to destruction, but also crucially to survival, and the method of such survival perhaps is about an enhancement, and a trusting in the fragility of presence as the site for exchange; the presentation of a body in space, acting as a sign or a signal, making apparent, indeed a display of invisible wounds. The ongoing global perpetuation of violence designates there is a lasting need to respond and find ways to address the renewed cycles of trauma. The methods of physical, body-based performance may seem exhausted after sixty years of experimental artworks and critique, and perhaps it is appropriate that much of what is understood as contemporary performance art practice has diffused and morphed into participatory processes, or has come to be incorporated into the proliferation of growing strands of activism. This multiplicity of performance forms is possibly a coming of age for the medium, a realisation that it cannot be contained to one specific canon but has hybridised across several. Throughout this investigation I have attempted to describe different facets of performance artworks, where what the viewer experiences is the demonstration of the body as weapon, as victim, as testifier,

[110] Stiles (1993), 'Shaved Heads and Marked Bodies: Representations from Cultures of Trauma', http://www.duke.edu/web/art/stiles/shaved_heads.html. Accessed January 2012.

as martyr, as authority, all of which exists in a nebulous zone of remaking protest that alternately uses procedures of subversion, attack and embrace. The lessons of the peace movement have not been forgotten, yet neither have the tactics of revolution and terrorism dissipated.

The artist and activist Gregory Sholette in his book *Dark Matter* (2011) has effectively traced the diversity and patterns of socially orientated and indeed subversive art practices that have been evolving since the 1960s under a profusion of terms and categories.[111] Sholette describes the seepage effect of many art based activist approaches such as Tactical Media, stating that the effects of these artists exist as:

> Small, spontaneous, nearly tactile actions whose aggregate effect on the dominant system is real enough, even if it will never fall like a blow of a hammer, but fester within the system like a low-grade fever. TM counts on the ability of this viral communicability to thicken in connectivity and to seek out other, similar pathogens, nomadic swarms, and ephemeral counter-networks. It is within the evanescent realm of cyberspace that this image of distributed collectivism is most clearly made manifest. (Sholette 2010: 147)

There is undoubtedly a growth of global networks sharing information and arousing mechanisms of humanitarian concern, participation and interaction. Within these mechanisms of generative dialogue, artists are contributing in stances of agitation, mediation and interpretation. However, Sholette makes a valuable precautionary statement when he suggests that separating the instinct and ethics of protest movements has become a seemingly impossible task. He describes the shift from former types of rebellion to one made possible by the emergence and availability of technology, and claims that the contemporary 'everyday rebel' has become:

> Patiently anti-ideological and decentralized to the point of sheer dispersal, the apparently indefinite politics of this "tactical resistance" leads some theorists to conclude that an entirely new form of activism has emerged directly opposite to that of earlier generations. (Sholette 34-35)

---

[111] See also for example Gene Ray's account of the G8 in Genoa 2001 protests, *On the Conditions of Anti-Capitalist Art Radical Cultural Practices and the Capitalist Art System*, www.eipcp.net. Accessed December 2011.

Although Sholette contends that much of this outpouring of art based activism generated through the Internet is seemingly not motivated by ideology, that is not to say (and not his intention to suggest) that the shift from overtly stated political affinities is a movement away from essentially humanist agendas. The 'lack' of ideology is therefore not construed as a lack of ideas, and the apparently chaotic growth of organisations can be interpreted as a potential strength instead of weakness, because it clarifies the grass roots community orientation of many activist and social justice movements. In some regards this spreading of ideas in an apparently chaotic manner relates to Deleuze and Guattari's theory of 'rhizomatic' networks that engage existing systems of communication and utilise methods of connection that become flexible to merging divisions and inconsistencies. Simon O'sullivan in describing this concept, states that,

> A rhizome is a system, or anti-system, without centre or indeed any central organising motif. It is a flat system in which the individual nodal points can be, and are, connected to one another in a non-hierarchical manner. A rhizome, then, fosters transversal connections and communicates between heterogeneous locations and events. (O'sullivan 2006)

However, if these unclassified forms of resistance are not led (exclusively) by the spectre of war, or class ideologies under capitalism as were earlier manifestations of civil unrest, then what shapes its drives? The apparent lack of ideology somehow makes these new forms of resistance appear more dangerous and uncontrollable. An example of this is the rapidity of social networking sites' demands for reactions to political situations and human rights issues, creating waves of involvement that are targeted by being emotionally predisposed. In an interesting adaptation of compassion fatigue, the Internet makes emotionally charged campaigning suspiciously effortless and one-dimensional. Therefore, somewhere between technological and body-based versions of activism, there remains a critical need to utilise the knowledge patterns that have evolved from necessity and austerity.

PRE IRAQ WAR PEACE MARCH, BELFAST, FEBRUARY 2003

A moment of participating in public dissent makes you realise in yourself how deeply entrenched the pressure is to conform, to not be one of the protestors standing on some civic collection point, placards and signs unfurled. The performance of protest involves costuming, staging, arranging, becoming a visible entity. Among this crowd a faction of young men emerged wearing Palestinian headscarves, and scattered throughout the gathering crowd other interest groups infiltrate the situation: ecology, Christianity, symbols and signs interspersed. A giant costumed figure of the Grim Reaper arrives on stilts, towering over a group of assembling drummers, swaying precariously to the rhythm and whistles that begin to take hold. This assembling of the crowd has rawness as the different elements of activism come together, fragmented but gradually solidifying into one entity, all under the chosen slogan of 'not in my name'. This is true even for those who come with no distinct plan, wearing the hypothetical uniform of neutrality – standing without a banner, without a slogan. Even this stance reads as a quantifiable identity among an orchestrated demonstration. Neutrality is the sacrifice you make the moment you cross into the lines of protestors. The crowd checks its own numbers, headcounts the weight of presence, aware that numbers count. Then the rows of people steadily move out from the gathering point, walking in ranks converging towards the City Hall. Some move with glee, the exuberance and momentum of tight groups bonded in friendship. Others walk separately, quieter, watching the margins of the protest lines for the first instances of police presence. Moving in this predictable carnival the gaze gradually adjusts to glancing exchanges with pedestrian shoppers, who watch with mixed expressions the progress of a protest that they have decided has no immediate bearing on their lives.

It feels somewhat uneasy as the stream of protestors move through the commercial heart of the city and the two strands of citizen pass through each other; those who have decided not to participate become static bystanders. Their inertia can partly be explained by the fact that activism is charged by its own localised history. It is a long tail of interconnections that mean even this pacifist global event, carried within it the debris of the Civil Rights Movement, the Peace People, and numerous civic protests of injustices, the cacophony coalesces briefly into the speeches from a stage erected in front of the City Hall, silencing the crowd into reflection on the potentiality of the mass destruction of human life.

There is a dissolving quality to how one's own public presence is incrementally mirrored back in the mass of bodies you are temporarily merged with. Later, in the international evening news pictures this experience was replicated in the images of other swarming masses, ten million people globally forming one body of compassionate response. Yet, the fascination of this scale of response was immediately overshadowed by the deadening impact of the proclamations of war made by President Bush and Prime Minister Blair, a bitter aftermath to the so-called processes of democracy.

This peace march and some of the other examples are deliberately not taken from art contexts, but social interactions where I have been present either as a member of an audience, a researcher, protestor or within a tourist group. These performances are ordinary enough actions of citizenship, the kind of unthinking experiences where their significance or worth is only arrived at in retrospect, if at all. This kind of participation in seemingly shapeless social forms of watching or reacting are reminders for me that moments of publicly enacted democracy are often disordered and unsatisfying; there are always power relationships being enacted through the choreography of inclusion or exclusion.

Yet, there are aspects of protest events that function as what Nicolas Bourriaud has termed 'interstices, as space-times governed by an economy that goes beyond the prevailing rules for the management of the public' (Bourriaud 2006: 167). The seeming randomness of the constructed encounter only gradually engenders a sense of collective purpose, the symbolic aspects of walking a specific route assist in bringing this cohesion, and in some regards the mediatization of events can bring a retrospective restoration of the worth of the spectacle, which is not always accessible within the moment of participation. Drawing on the research of Abercrombie and Longhurst in 1998, media theoreticians Andrew Hoskins and Ben O'Loughlin have described the interwoven complexity of global perceptions of the changing abilities of citizens as witnesses. They state:

> [T]he West is now made up of 'performative societies'. No event, personal or public, goes unrecorded. Hence those taking part in events come

> to consider potential audiences, creating an imperative to perform. [...] the result of this perpetual acting-for-imagined-others that constitutes daily life is a 'virtual *invisibility*' of performance: it is so ubiquitous we stop noticing. While we have always been aware of ourselves as acting out certain social roles (mother, soldier, friend, student), the proliferation of media makes an unprecedented degree of performance specific to our contemporary new media ecology. Performance is no longer tied to discrete events but has '*leaked out* into the conduct of everyday life'. (Hoskins & O'Loughlin 2010: 81-82)

The repercussions of this media ecology and what it means to our awareness of performing multiple roles, is that everyday life is a subject of continuous record, and we are often captured within the act of validating what we observe and experience. Something in the nature of contemporary performance art is part of this decentring of spectacle framed to become memory, the ordinariness of art actions that alternate on the cusp of visibility raise a question of why for some artists it might seem appropriate or even important to seek to disappear. After all, it is not coincidental that in societies driven by spectacle, the chosen image of anti-capitalist protestors has become the absurdly quasi-smiling mask, concealing anonymous citizens.

In using improvisation as a speculative model to align with other social practices, I am looking for common ground in how trauma is handled in individual and collective circumstances. I make only modest claims for performance art, mainly on the grounds that it is a form that both creates and acknowledges dissonance in structures, ideas and situations. Yet, also performance has a capacity for empathy and healing: both are tools of the emotions, readily transferred from one body across to another, but usually only in instances of trust and concentrated engagement. There are glimmering moments in performance art when there can be a confrontation with the truth of wrong perceptions of another ethnicity, gender or faith, a momentary but precise overturning of privilege and prejudice.

Throughout this study several examples (such as Mary Holland's disturbing statement on her inability to react to the execution of two corporals; Penny Holloway's painfully constrained lecture on the murder of her son; and Boris Nieslony's frenzied demonstration of a body in spasmodic convulsions), this investigation has shown there are reiterations of helplessness in dealing with the memory of traumatic events, and yet the compelling need is to create 'a' language in the place where another has been depleted. This wrenching through the raw edges of expressive gesture may seem far removed and irrelevant to the political sphere. Therefore, for artists the dilemma remains of how to bridge the learning and communication that occurs in the laboratory space, with a wider social adaptation. What can be learnt? And can art be a vehicle for interpreting this seemingly unprocessed and subjective experiential knowledge back into meaningful social interactions? The essential characteristics of suffering, whether the language is primarily verbal or gestural, continue to announce themselves onto all forms of human communication, the question is ongoing of how to turn the vital energy of pain and fear into constructive forces. Art is one of the few 'evidences' that show that this transformation is possible.

EPILOGUE: THE MUSEUM OF AFTERTHOUGHTS

BLUEPRINT FOR A MUSEUM OF AFTERTHOUGHTS, SOME THOUGHTS ON THE COMPLEXITIES OF VALIDATING EXPERIENTIAL OCCURRENCES AS EVIDENCE:

- *The Museum of Afterthoughts stores up numerous specimen spaces, some simulated and approximate, others painstakingly transplanted to this place, pumped full of authentic air.*
- *Visitors navigate through their previous ideas, the 'could have been' or 'should have been' existences. They take shelter in remembering, however, the displays are monitored not to instil 'real' distress, only to invoke previous experiences in dilute quantities.*
- *In general, the visitors who come here are simply invited to prod gently at the corners of their mind, searching for the sanctuary of enigmatic or intractable thoughts, walking into resuscitating emotions, which they then witness themselves experiencing again.*
- *Forgetting has never been more popular or varied, some even come to discharge past happiness that can no longer be accommodated. Walking away from such a room a visitor might observe the glass panelled wall coming down to separate them from what used to concern them, this moment becomes the memento or surface of the scar, beautiful in its economy, infallibly distant from the nervous constellation of attachment.*
- *Visitors report that return visits prove to be experiences akin to a meticulously guided tour beneath the skin of someone else's more excessive, or conflicted self, a curiosity separate from the person they now sense themselves to be.*
- *Tour guides take pains to point out aspects of habitation that once each*

visitor would have known intimately, but now form only an itinerary of anecdotal textures, coded in charts of colour, scale and volume.

– *Nothing can be bought or removed from the museum, although experience has proven that significant gains can be made from such excursions into controlled forgetting.*

The purpose of The Museum of Afterthoughts is to explore ideas of validation, what it entails to prove the authenticity or factuality of events, whether as part of a legal or creative process. This will be attempted essentially through considering the human behavioural and psychological aspects of evidencing incidents, not the empirical evidence of artefacts or location. The background to these ideas is taken from individual experience as a performance artist, working within a personal ethos of valuing actions as representations intended to be captured purely as memory. This rationale developed in reaction to the dominance of media reporting of the Troubles in Northern Ireland, but is also an acknowledgement of the lineage of performance art internationally as an oppositional form of reporting. I propose that this is mainly because the agency of performance art is to locate actions inside the everyday continuum of place, and to create interpretations through embodying observation, rather than rendering images as acts of evidencing. Within this conception, there are further questions of considering the role of memory in acts of what could be termed 'truth-making', the slippages present in the liveness of different forms of social performance, which paradoxically can facilitate an evocation of truthfulness even as it undermines cognitive or technological resources.

Additionally, I wish to reflect on some cultural issues behind the desire to capture and reproduce ephemeral phenomena, and address the frequently predatory nature of these attempts to intercept the multiple forms of live presences. Considering what are the factors in a vast amalgamation of knowledge sources converging that create our impression of memory, including vicarious witnessing that generates memory of unowned experiences. The cultural amalgamation of sources continues to accelerate, but beyond the technologies exists the question of why it is that in a world of expendable information sources we are dependent on possessing the externalised artefacts of our remembering. In writing these observations on the mechanisms of collective memory,[112] I emphasise that they are not constructed from a specialist scientific or theoretical viewpoint, but are reflections that have arisen from a methodology of performance art, where the actions developed are often conceived and transmitted as acts of embodied memory, akin to the act of testimony.

In describing how relationships to mental geography must necessarily alter as environments undergo positive and negative changes, cultural theoreticians Katharine Hodgkin and Susannah Radstone (2003) state that:

> Identity is often located in a specific physical landscape, and through the changes in that landscape, the memory of times when it was different, changes in the self may be perceived and registered. We measure the passage of time in ourselves against the houses that have been built since we walked down a given road as a child, and the children who have already grown to adulthood in those new houses; we return to landscapes known before they were transformed by some tremendous upheaval, and experience the dislocating impossibility of their difference. (Hodgkin & Radstone 2003)

To propose the idea of a museum of afterthoughts is to suggest a scaffolding of perceived individual needs, required to contain the tensions around the continual social reconstruction of collective memory, a reminder that memory, although ostensibly experienced in personal ways, is evolved from numerous cultural sources that continue to merge or dissolve according to broader social changes. Individually we employ diverse means of measuring the self, in an oscillation between past and present most frequently and powerfully evoked in the kinds of spatial dislocation described by Hodgkin and Radstone, or through reliquary objects and oral histories. The issue of identifying what is going on in the constructions of authenticity within collective memory is linked also to the desire to authenticate experiences, especially those which can be considered performative.

---

112 There is an extensive amount of literature available on collective memory such as the works of C.G. Jung, Cathy Caruth, Paul Connerton and Maurice Halbwachs. See for example Jung and Read (1970, 1968). Also, Caruth (1995) and Halbwachs and Coser (1992).

LEGAL CONSTRUCTIONS OF MEMORY, AND THE PRIVILEGING OF LIVENESS AS PRIMARY EVIDENCE

Peggy Phelan has famously stated that the signature values of live performance, and the grounds of its cultural status, lies in its irreproducibility. She argues that: 'Without a copy, live performance plunges into visibility – in a manically charged present – and disappears into memory, into the realm of invisibility and the unconscious where it eludes regulation and control' (Phelan 1993: 148). The emphasis of this formulation is in the capacity of performance to transmit directly to the memory of the viewer, its potency and value is in a connected immediacy which is not shaped by the necessity of repetition, but in fact its disappearance. The uniqueness of (a) given moment retains a mutable ungoverned potential if it is conceived as an act solely of memory, and therefore as unrepeatable it stands outside of cultural commercial concerns.

The issue of the capturability of memory is pivotal to understandings of what can be given in evidence in a legal process, and beyond the performative aspects of memory recall as testimony, further questions exist around how the law has the capacity to police not only the memory but also the subconscious of individuals. Philip Auslander in his book *Liveness* (1999) asks the question why live testimony has persisted as the dominant form of evidence used in legal contexts, despite videotaped trial formats being a more economic and a relatively proven form. The theoretical grounding for this practice is based on the sixth amendment (in the USA), concerning the accused's right to face their accusor. This constitutional right dominates the issue of pre-recorded depositions, (although recordings are sometimes accepted, in certain circumstances and with restrictions). Therefore, in practice, courts continue to utilise and indeed privilege the live presences of witnesses. This is an interesting circumstance considering the widely understood fragility of testimony processes. Although as Auslander points out:

> The legal system has no aversion to incorporating representational technologies into its proceedings, but accepts only incursions of mediatization that do not violate the liveness of the trial. It should be clear that this respect for liveness is ideological and that it is rooted in the unexamined

> belief that live confrontation can somehow give rise to the truth in ways that recorded representations cannot. (Auslander 1999: 144)

The underlying conjecture therefore continues to be that 'liveness equals truth' (Auslander 145) however Auslander discredits this argument which is based on the 'presence' or 'impact' of the live witness, which he contends as being 'intangible and immeasurable'. Auslander also argues that, the legal preference for live testimony has evolved the act of testimony as 'a live performance of memory-retrieval'. [And further, that] 'memory is both policed by law and pressed into service as a mechanism for the enforcement of law' (Auslander 129). The argument is therefore primarily about control of memory, and to what extent as humans we can be monitored and validated through the lucidity of our memory recall. Auslander's viewpoint works as a counter claim to Phelan's conception of performance as eluding regulation because it exists only in memory. Auslander's argument insists that memory is the very substance of testimony. Additionally, the pressures of a 'live' situation strain the faculties of memory, yet still we expect stability, sentience and judgement to be attainable from what is ostensibly an act of both cerebral and sensory reactivation, entailing also the imagination as a tool of reconstructed visualisation.

DOCUMENTING EPHEMERAL PERFORMANCE ACTIONS

Questions of authenticity and memory are especially relevant with regard to forms of live performance. The act of retrieval around gestured forms of communication has a perceived orthodoxy of documentation, usually produced in forms of photography, video, factual written account and spoken testimony. The difficulties of conducting research work on improvisation are linked to problems of providing quantifiable evidence of what the disseminated potential of a performance artwork might be. This innate contradiction in attempting to formalise the value of something intentionally ephemeral, and indeed volatile to documentation, speaks of a commercial and ethical anxiety that underpins all forms of cultural production. Therefore, in research on performance there is a persistent dilemma of representation around events that have happened without recording, or, a deliberate downplaying of the usually negative implications of documentation processes that occur concurrent with the action.

Returning to Phelan's formulation of the ontological characteristics of performance, which she has described as being essentially about qualities of intimacy and disappearance, she observed that, 'Performance honors the idea that a limited number of people in a specific time/space frame can have an experience of value which leaves no visible trace afterwards' (Phelan 1993: 149). This is a question of the integrity attributed to acts of disappearance set apart from commercial concerns, and in this respect the ontology of performance is fought over to retain the unrepeatable qualities of an experience. Central to these issues of evidencing is the thinking around what the role is of the audience at live events, and how their input as unique observers is consistent with any (contested)[113] principles of authentic experiences. I would like to propose the idea that a proportion of live art performances can be understood as actions comparable with that of giving testimony, but one that obstructs the orthodoxy of narrating as being primarily a verbal act. Most performance actions function through gestural rather than verbal language, therefore it is the narration of physicalized memory that is presented. Within this concept therefore, audiences are implicated in the roles of witness or jury. Absorbing or questioning, empathetic or detached, what creates the defining factor between the ways that live events are viewed? Theoretically a jury is supposed to behave neutrally, undirected by emotional content, the environment is structured around facilitating controlled telling, various forms of evidence amassed – including the order of witnesses is stacked in a designated manner, with the objective of ultimately creating consensus among the assembled jury.

When I term the audience for live art as 'unique observers', I am suggesting that the manner in which a performance is viewed is akin to an act of witnessing,[114] because each viewer positions themselves independently

[113] Authenticity is a contested idea within performance studies; the problematic of how to produce credible correspondences of reality through representational forms such as theatre. Contemporary techniques include working methodologies of scripting from verbatim interviews, and utilising factual forms of evidencing events narrated from different perspectives, etc. Equally, authenticity influences technical methods of creative approach, especially the process/style of acting or movement adopted around portrayal or embodiment.

[114] The concept of witnessing is well established within theatre practices, however the

in the space in relation to the performer, they (usually) continue to have autonomy in regard to movement, they may or may not see or hear some parts of the performance, but crucially the etiquette of the collective situation is that they will think individually about what it is they are seeing. Therefore, the 'evidence' invoked by the performer may cause a wide spectrum of reactions in the viewer, and the expectation is not that a consensus will be reached of a unified version of the event, but that in fact the audience will have created fractured and individual perspectives, similar to the act of remembering. This momentum is a strategic unfixing of evidential forms, and is in essence the reason why improvisation in live performance is a reciprocal movement between performer/s and viewers, there is no consensus, only a repeated testing, resisting and opening of physical ideas, with permission passing continually between both groups.

Since the 1960s artists have explored the evidential functions of photography within the tradition of reportage and documentary, by exploring and challenging the capacity and limitations of how a photograph can be used to authenticate an event or performance. David Green and Joanna Lowry have expanded upon the indexical qualities attributed to photography, established by the ideas of C.S. Peirce. They argue that the interpretation of a photograph by the spectator should include performativity, often inferring latent associations that exist beyond the photographic frame,

> [photographs] are not just indexical because light happened to be recorded in an instant on a piece of photosensitive film, but because, first and foremost, they were taken. The very act of photography, as a kind of performative gesture which points to an event in the world, as a form of designation that draws reality into the image field, is thus itself a form of indexicality.[115]

---

testimonial aspect of performance art is overlooked, I would suggest this is because it is largely a non-verbal form that does not cohere to the 'telling' of information. Or, when language is used performers usually adopt non-linear narrative strategies distancing audiences from orthodox understandings of the factual ordering of evidence. Conceivably performance art could more accurately be considered as the inversion of testimony, located in the area of the unspeakable, the behaviour that manifests aspects of the suppressed voice.

[115] Green and Lowry (2002), 'From Presence to the Performative: Rethinking Photographic Indexicality', http://www.skol.ca/files/FromPresenceToThePerformative.pdf. Accessed September 2011.

The truth is not in the image per se as material trace, but in the encounter that pre-empts its capture. Almost invariably in contemporary performance art events, viewers will disregard a performer's formal request for the performance not to be photographed. The fact that the images are taken however, does not negate the artist's counter position, but emphasises something of the innate tension that exists between spectators and performers. We validate, or seek to validate what we perceive as authentic and unrepeatable, and part of the drive to do this is the implication of the spectator's own investment as audience. Live art allows an audience to select significant moments, they self-authenticate what they watch in the moment of its occurrence, and their selection is integrated as a choreography of dramatised looking. The shutter sound of the camera, the rearrangement of the body, separation from the sight lines of other viewers, all designate awareness of the action as predatory and invasive. Therefore, since the act of taking is in itself performative, it produces a breach in contract, not only between the viewer and the artist, but also a glitch in the collective experience. The audience becomes hyper aware of their act of viewing, and in so doing separate momentarily from the actuality of the performance. Inside the vulnerability of live situations, credibility depends on the building of presence, and to differing degrees suspension of disbelief. This matrix of understandings around the temporal moment is a collective act.

Valuing the autonomy of audience, their 'participation' as such (in its most subtle forms), is the give and take of concentration and reciprocal responses. Performance can be a space of contemplation, but also of provoked discomfort, and in both these areas what is offered is oppositional to standard entertainment values. But, it is important also to acknowledge that much of this compulsion around documentation is often instigated by artists themselves; the ethos of ephemeral work which existed for many practitioners in the 1960s and 1970s has almost entirely disappeared from contemporary art practices. This seemingly reflects that the earlier ethos was politically motivated, a signature part of a cultural moment, since replaced by the general acceptance of an immersive multifaceted global environment. Therefore, behind the motivation to capture transitory events is a larger cultural issue of quantifying liveness,questioning what is left of social interactions that can be intentionally preserved beyond the bounds of mediatization. I share Phelan's highlighting of the necessity to protect parts of collective social existence, residing exclusively in the temporal, in order that it can function as critique or opportunity for different perspectives. She succinctly summarises the problem stating that:

> While photography is vulnerable to charges of counterfeiting and copying, performance art is vulnerable to charges of valuelessness and emptiness. Performance indicates the possibility of revaluing that emptiness; this potential revaluation gives performance art its distinctive oppositional edge. (Phelan 1993: 148)

Photographic theory uses the document as the intermediary that can create space for reflection, provocation, etc., and by scrutinising those elements that an image fails to disclose we become aware of the emptiness surrounding the moment of its taking, and the trajectory of time separating outwards towards the viewer. Whereas in performance the intermediary is the performing body, which embodies selective memory vigorously in the present. And, although the artist's body is also to various degrees distanced from the viewer, still it seeks to ingrain its movements on the corporal presence of the viewer, to reprint or implant memory. Crucially, this transaction should not remain attached to the performer, but function instead as an intentional or empathetic transference of content. Accordingly, in order that the idea of memory transfers generatively, the trace of the performer should in fact be erased.

ISSUES OF PRESENCE AND ABSENCE IN CONSTRUCTING EVIDENCE AROUND VIOLENT EVENTS

As discussed earlier one of the fascinations of live work is the transference of subtly defined roles; viewers can be potentially witness, arbitrator, mediator, judge or jury. However, in order that this multiplicity of roles can occur, the situation must be developed around accommodating a bleed of permissions between performer and audience. Significantly, the performer is always in each moment responsible for the images and ideas they produce, and these dynamics are socially ascribed conditions and behaviours. One such example occurred in 2008, when British artist Sohail Khan performed a work titled *Stress Positioning* at New Territories 09 (2009). This performance involved recreating a torture stress position used in various countries for 'softening up' prisoners during interrogation, and referencing in the viewer's mind the infamous Abu Ghraib photographs. In watching this action are we complicit in viewing his torture? One might say categorically, no, the artist's actions are entirely self-directed, however in the moment of viewing there is a sense of moral discomfort provoked, the spectacle raises the actuality of what are otherwise covertly sanctioned barbaric acts perpetrated by governmental agents, and inserts the artist's presence between the viewer and the easily accessible online photographs of torture. Performance is often used in this way to bring audiences into contact with uncomfortable 'truths'. For, despite the transparent staging of the performance, and the ease with which the action is ended by the viewer choosing to walk away, the cumulative effect of proximity, duration and being part of an audience of mute observers brings a disturbing actuality to live performances.

In viewing video documentation of live performance actions, there are also core problems with the emphasis of metronomic running time created by a camera, which distorts the sense of time experienced in watching something live. Equally, as a record of what has happened, video footage spatially flattens and smoothens the traces of human movement, the gaps between video frames exist as an ominous distance segmenting one particle of a gesture from the next; something in these nuances presents a changing alliance within the real. In improvisation tension and skill exists through the performer's ability to transition matter and meaning from the ordinary, into and out of the ritualistic and symbolic. These transitions are not 'facts' of gesture, but gradations, fleeting, sporadic almost incomprehensible, yet they leave behind a diffuse sense of knowledge – something having been stated. This unpalatable loss is exactly the crux of Phelan's emphasis on the disappearances that puncture live experiences, and in so doing register sensations of mortality.

THE MECHANISMS FOR THE RETRIEVAL OF MEMORY: ART AS A TOOL FOR REPRESENTATIONS OF MEMORY, BUT ALSO AS A TOOL FOR ITS RETRIEVAL

Part of the problem of controlling or understanding memory is the intrinsic complexity of what actually triggers memory responses. The links of memory frequently obscure where and how memory is retrieved. This is especially manifest in situations of trauma where victims are often proven from medical and legal perspectives, to have created false memory, an unreality stitched out of fragments that fail to reconstruct (yet these so called flaws and failures still conceal significant information). In creative forms it is this very interplay of the 'agreed' factual and the conceivable fiction, which offers up potential space for reinterpretations that are not bound by preconceptions of truth.

Therefore it is the sensorial activators and the 'failures' of memory that are often used as the material of art invention. In effect, the agitation of tactile memory is a strategy utilised to provoke the attendant sensations attached to situations, as an alternative method of interpretation. In a passage from Samuel Beckett's play *Krapp's Last Tape*, the character Krapp describes the last moments of a vigil waiting outside the house of his dying mother, Beckett utilises the significance of an object, substituting for the experience of not being inside the observed room:

> [Pause.] I was there when – [Krapp switches off, broods, switches on again.] – the blind went down, one of those dirty brown roller affairs, throwing a ball for a little white dog as chance would have it. I happened to look up and there it was. All over and done with, at last. I sat on for a few moments with the ball in my hand and the dog yelping and pawing at me. [Pause.] Moments. Her moments, my moments. [Pause.] The dog's moments. [Pause.] In the end I held it out to him and he took it in his mouth, gently, gently. A small, old, black, hard, solid rubber ball. [Pause.] I shall feel it, in my hand, until my dying day. [Pause.] I might have kept it. [Pause.] But I gave it to the dog. [Pause.] (Beckett 1986: 220)

The transference of the mother's hand for the black rubber ball, the gentle touch of the dog pulling back into the present moment, demanding attention outside of the reverie of grief, the strongest element is the touch of the ball which articulates an intangible emotion. Or is it a conflicted emotion? Aspects of grief are ensnared in a seemingly misplaced sensual exchange, 'his mouth, gently, gently'.

I suggest that artists can contribute to the processes of archiving traumatic events, by working with aspects of sensorial engagement, bringing components of either embodied or disembodied sensory matter to merge with elements of cognitive informing. Ephemeral actions especially can function as a means to reactivate emotional memory. This is particularly potent when artists create or adjust their work in relation to connotations of location. Taking the example of the development of performance art practices in Northern Ireland since the 1970s, the idea emerges that physical presence in itself is a medium of protest. The actuality of positioning oneself in territorial space can be a fitting way to respond to trauma, and in this way revealing that certain things can be unviewable as well as unspeakable.

In this regard, several performance actions made by Scottish artist Alastair MacLennan on the streets of Belfast during the Troubles in the mid 1970s and1980s, are exemplary of an experiential practice that pushed at the boundaries of sectarian exclusion and seclusion. By walking and marking the interfaces of urban divisions, MacLennan's interventions played with the temporality of tolerance, repeatedly addressing the failures of social engagement within a climate of fear. In one sequence of actions – *Target,* August 1977,[116] MacLennan walked each day from his home in East Belfast to his place of work in the city centre, with a dart board attached to his chest and a sheet of polythene plastic weighted down with pieces of cane covering his head and torso (some drawing and arrows were also included). Despite its auspicious provocation and deliberate irrationality as spectacle, many commuters intent on avoiding confrontation or even ambiguous circumstances routinely ignored the actions. The route chosen took MacLennan through the then prevalent security barriers that girded the commercial city centre, where people's belongings and behaviour were routinely searched for irregularity. To literally make oneself a target highlighted the precariousness of the political situation, and by extension the conformity that these circumstances bred into civilian behaviour. MacLennan's Belfast works levered at the edges of permissible behaviour, and the (at that time) increasing invisibility of the population as individuals, since people were

[116] See MacLennan (2011) and MacLennan et al. (1988).

randomly shot for being perceived to be in the wrong place, or became the arbitrary victims of terrorist bombs. A climate of fear makes public space intractable, and these seemingly modest transgressions by MacLennan over several years could be seen as experiments with the parameters of tolerance.

Variations of this kind of integrated social performance action were also developed by artists in the 1970s and 1980s, in geographies of political conflict such as Romania, Brazil and Austria, among others. Often these actions occurred as solitary acts of defiance that created a proof of existence, and generated resistance against margins of state repression. Contemporary social acts such as flash mobbing and other forms of public demonstration stemming from Internet social networking sites, are changing the nature of public protest globally. And, there are many echoes in the tactics of these (often anonymous) collectives, and the solitary actions of artists which continue to evolve. Whether an action is construed as being an art or activist performance, the power of gestures being returned to sites, in alienated and fractured forms, can create a disjunction of time, place and motion opening up underlying narratives. Returning to Hodgkin and Radstone's formulation of the centrality of mental geography to memory discussed earlier, the foundations of identity are mapped outwards from initial knowledge(s) of location. The repositioning of actions within familiar territory is a disturbance of localised memory, yet also a reconnection of dialogue with that past. In 2010 the first Gay Rights March took place in Londonderry/Derry, Northern Ireland. The organisers chose to inaugurate the march by walking a route through the city, synonymous with the historical events and yearly commemorations of the Bloody Sunday shootings that occurred in 1972. This appropriating of the strategy of the original Civil Rights march, and the mirroring of place and gesture, evoked transferences of political thinking and sympathies, creating a request for the civil rights of homosexuals to be acknowledged.-

Such actions operate against the grain of visual representations of the violence committed in Northern Ireland, and the image fatigue that developed around portrayals of victims, perpetrators and locations. Often the features of this type of performance work have been to demolish a perceived affectation of spectacle, to create resistances through small gestures, and to activate the dynamics of location with actions shaped by receptivity to context. Performance of this nature exists as an exquisite handshake;

the relationship can be humble in its openness to the random, often leaving only traces of indefinite emotions. As with the museum of afterthoughts proposed, it creates the capacity to re-enter the briefly lived, to repossess those ambiguities and uncertainties that could not be contained on first exposure. Creative art forms are not categorical gauges of truth, but potent elements in broader social sequences, working towards new understandings about the reality of what has happened in the past. Therefore, the truth exists in a trajectory, and can only be approached and extracted at different points during a society's movement away from violence. Art can function as a watershed of hidden stigmatised subjects slowly unravelling, clearing the space for further inquiry within the bounds of the trauma thresholds of survivors.

MUSEUM OF AFTERTHOUGHTS 2 – SIMULATED ARTEFACTS, EDUCATIONAL MODELS

On visiting the Memorial to the Murdered Jews of Europe in Berlin, a visitor could be forgiven for asking if this self-named 'place of information' is a facility of education or an induction into designed amnesia. The historical realities produced in such museums are moulded to fit the consumer, there are no actual artefacts displayed from the events described, only technological displays. A benign muteness hangs between Plexiglas photographs and sealed in plasma screens. Moving through scripted, synchronised rooms, visitors are guided by the surreptitious running time of video sequences. The oppressive nature of these encounters gradually creates frustration, a covert desire to be finished with scrutinising sediments of digitised information. What is suppressed in this museum is the dramatised sense of moral agency a visitor expects to feel. The cold, highly developed facticity of presentation makes emotion seem somewhat inappropriate, when standing before virtual representations of atrocity. Yet, to be stimulated is the frequency of remembering, and by extension tactility is the probing, jolting disturbance alive within creating knowledge. Moving in synchronised groups, visitors progress in silence sleepwalking through rooms, within which an aura is created around victimhood and the unrepresentable. In these conditions visitors are strategically prohibited from embodying aspects of the lives and deaths described, or by extension, the potential of cultivating em-

pathetic responses. The museum successfully provides a valuable educational schema of evidencing, but without factoring into the equation any purposeful agitation of the agreed-upon narratives. Whereas, a degree of dissonance might in fact induce encounters that are closer to the complexity of an act of witnessing.

In an essay on trauma tourism titled *Never Again and its Discontents* (2011), Laurie Beth Clark proposes that trauma tourism is not determined by visitors who have direct links to the traumas memorialised in specific sites, but that the industry is driven by more casual forms of visitors who utilise these sites as a form of appeasement for broader anxieties about ongoing global conflict. She has suggested that:

> We go to Auschwitz because we don't know how to intervene in Darfur or Guantanamo. However, I am not suggesting that a visit to a clandestine torture centre is a kind of avoidance strategy. Rather, as a repetition compulsion, it is a (re)dramatization of the unresolvable trauma. Furthermore, I believe that we will continue to build memory sites to past atrocities exactly because we still have 'unrepresentable' ongoing violence. (Beth 2011: 68-79)

Clark argues that these sites offer a micro-controlled environment, in which trauma is played out in such a way that the visitor can participate or reject the mantle of guilt, remorse or disquiet. The visit is a performance of social conscience, 'tourists perform their identities and investments for themselves and for other tourists' (Beth 68-79). It is a public performance and therefore the choreography of movement is a crucial element in being socialised within the act of looking and responding. This connectivity is determined by a successful fusing of memory to activity, including the ritual of being in an identifiable group.

The Museum of Afterthoughts I proposed at the beginning of this essay is the realm of intangible evidence, the gaps between fragments of memory. Sensorial exploration is not frequently privileged in art production, but can be a component of de-centring cognitive analysis, and an agitation in the space between what information 'means' and what it evokes. That the evocation is considered a secondary undertaking is a limitation of our ability to attempt constructions of 'truth-making' in art practices. Memory continually undermines assumptions of cerebral and corporeal Cartesian divisions. Although, the visual sense is privileged within the study of memory systems (for example mnemonics), its functioning is strongly attached to spatial awareness, especially the placing of objects in specific visualised rooms. Sensations cross all boundaries of the skin, what can be described as the sensual imagination, where tactile memories have a persistent presence that is non-chronological and non-historical. The exactness of stimulants such as a specific smell can travel with us in time, forming part of the opaque, indecipherable qualities of memory. Perhaps this transference is relayed at its most potent within the decoding of physical movement. As choreographer William Forsyth describes it:

> [Y]ou try to divest your body of movement, as opposed to thinking you are producing movement. So it would not be like pushing forward into space and invading space – it would be like leaving your body in space. Dissolution, letting yourself evaporate. Movement is a factor of the fact that you are actually evaporating.[117]

Forsythe's description of gesture lost inside movement, clarifies the intrinsic complexity of understanding actions, fraught with uncertainties from both external and internal perspectives. Thinking through the body establishes the idea of a corporal eye, reintegrating aspects of the inner body into sight and comprehension. The body moving in space around obstacles and assumptions becomes again innocent, again capable of exploring its own disorientation.

MUSEUM OF AFTERTHOUGHTS 3 – THE SENSUOUS ARCHIVES

Walking towards the last reported scene, the road forward lived sporadically, the eyes the nose the mouth, I repeat, the eyes, the nose, the wail of the mouth enters through the eyes, the mouth expands to the chest, a voice thinned out of existence, passing in seconds, the eyes the nose the mouth compounded together, hold the bones clenched, the eyes the nose the mouth not telling, seeing through the reverse of the eyelid, withdrawn from smell carrying only the scent of the inside, smelling the self withdraw, the scent of blood thickening, passages, a retreat into the roads lived vicari-

117 As cited in Siegmund (2011: 137).

ously through another mind or hand. You have seen what was left behind, after the retreat of the eyes the nose the mouth, a refrain in the ears, a suspicion of carried attachment, the road traversed, eyes looking forwards pull the horizon erect, the eyes the nose the mouth filtering out conditionally all that is scattered at the feet. Travelling out of looking, vision is scorched with the caustic aura of illicit touch, all the debris of vanished emotions that cannot migrate this conspiracy of skin.

Afterthoughts can also constitute the residue of unlived experiences, the proximity of events that cloud consciousness of place in the world, fate, dreams, realities or perceptions of what it is to live within the places we find ourselves. Dangerous forms of knowledge, uncontested inappropriate emotional responses, how we process our predilections for empathy or denial, obedience or rebellion. Carrying a surfeit of undiagnosed remorse, the degrees of separation make our filters unstable, what events seep in, what bile seeps out in the form of hatreds and prejudices. It is not ethics that is in decline but the ability to focus principles and find adequate pragmatic roles for our moral unease. The problems of collective memory, is exactly this crisis over what to respond to within the surplus of conspiring representations. Performance as responsive social act, I have contended, is a practice imbued with a sensibility or aspiration of truth-making, because it exists and erupts from within the temporal, and is primarily interlocked into the actualities of its location and audience. This interdependency means that memory content is placed in tension with the realities of disorder: it can sometimes function as the basis for invention or reconnection, a fragile salvage operation in the directory of tactility. Such acts may be documented and archived in several forms, but they are only fundamentally authenticated, in the originating moment by the proximity and reactions of those who witness. The performer strategically offers upon the viewer, the task of holding the moment in memory against the grain of inevitable loss.

BIBLIOGRAPHY

Achour, Y. B. (2002), 'The Order of Truth and the Order of Society', Enwezor, O. (ed), *Experiments with Truth: Transitional Justice and the Processes of Truth and Reconciliation: Documenta 11, Platform 2*. Ostfildern-Ruit: Hatje Cantz: 123-134.

Adorno, T.W., Ashton, E.B. (1973), *Negative Dialectics*. London: Routledge, Kegan Paul.

Agamben, G. (1999), *Remnants of Auschwitz: The Witness and the Archive*. Cambridge, MA, London: MIT Press.

Agger, I., Soren, J. (1990), 'Testimony as Ritual and Evidence in Psychotherapy for Political Refugees', *Journal of Traumatic Stress*, vol. 3: 115-30.

Akramawy, R. (2011), 'The Scarecrow', http://vimeo.com/29029591. Accessed December 2011.

Alfano Miglietti, F. (2003), *Extreme Bodies: The Use and Abuse of the Body in Art*. Milan, London: Skira, Thames & Hudson.

Alphonso, L. (2000), *Dangerous Emotions*. London, California: University of California Press.

Ando, B. (2011), http://www.bbc.co.uk/news/uk-15234363, BBC news report. Accessed October 2011.

Apel, D. (2002), *Memory Effects: The Holocaust and the Art of Secondary Witnessing*. New Brunswick, N.J., London: Rutgers University Press.

Arendt, H. (1964), *Eichmann in Jerusalem: A Report on the Banality of Evil*. New York: edn, Viking P.

Arns, I., Horn, G., Hartware MedienKunstVerein, Kunst-Werke Berlin (2007), *History Will Repeat Itself: Strategien des Reenactment in der Zeitgenossischen (Medien-) Kunst und Performance = Strategies of Re-enactment in Contemporary (Media) Art and Performance*. Frankfurt am Main: Revolver.

Art as a Public Issue: How Art and its Institutions Reinvent the Public Dimension (2008). Rotterdam: NAi/SKOR.

Auslander, P. (1997), *From Acting to Performance: Essays in Modernism and Postmodernism*. London: Routledge.

Auslander, P. (1999), *Liveness: Performance in a Mediatized Culture*. London: Routledge.

B, F., Johnson, D., Galleria Pack (2006), *Franko B: Blinded by Love*. Bologna: Damiani.

Back, L. (2007), *The Art of Listening*, Oxford: Berg.

Baer, U. (2002), *Spectral Evidence: The Photography of Trauma*. Cambridge, MA, London: MIT Press.

Baudrillard, J., Zurbrugg, N. (1997), *Jean Baudrillard: Art and Artefact*. London, Sage.

Bauman, Z. (2007), *Liquid Times: Living in an Age of Uncertainty*. Cambridge, Malden: Polity Press.

BAVO (2008), 'How Much Politics Can Art Take?', *Art as a Public Issue: How Art and its Institutions Reinvent the Public Dimension*. Rotterdam: NAi/SKOR.

Becker, C. (2002), *Surpassing the Spectacle: Global Transformations and the Changing Politics of Art*. Lanham, Md., Oxford: Rowman & Littlefield.

Beckett, S. (1986), *The Complete Dramatic Works*. London: Faber & Faber.

Beech, D. (2010), 'Uncompensated Trauma: On Art, Technique and Division', Burns, L., Kenny, C. (eds), *The Applied Social Arts: Artur Zmijewski*. Dublin, Ireland: Fire Station Artists Studios: 59-63.

Beecroft, V., Beccaria, M., Castello di Rivoli, Kunsthalle Bielefeld (2003), *Vanessa Beecroft Performances 1993*-2003. Milan: Skira.

Benegas, D. (2011), 'If There's No Justice: Trauma and Identity in Post-Dictatorship Argentina', *Performance Research 16* (1).

Benjamin, W., Arendt, H. (1973, 1968), *Illuminations*. London: Fontana.

Berghuis, T.J. (2006), *Performance Art in China*. Hong Kong: Timezone 8.

Bishop, C. (2006), *Participation*. London: Whitechapel.

Blast Theory (2011), http://www.blasttheory.co.uk. Accessed November 2011.

Boal, A. (1998), *Legislative Theatre: Using Performance to make Politics*. London: Routledge.

Borland, C., De Appel Foundation, Migros Museum fur Gegenwartskunst, Museu de Arte Contemporanea de Serralves (2000), *Christine Borland: The Dead Teach the Living, Selected Works, 1990-1999*. Zurich: Migros Museum.

Bottoms, S.J., Goulish, M. (2007), *Small Acts of Repair: Performance, Ecology, and Goat Island*. London: Routledge.

Bourriaud, N. (2002), *Relational Aesthetics*. Dijon: Presses du reel.

Bourriaud, N. (2006), 'Relational Aesthetics', as cited in Bishop, C. (ed), *Participation*. London: Whitechapel.

Breddels, L., Braak, L.t., van Teeseling, S. (2010), *6(0) Ways – Artistic Practice in Culturally Diverse Times*. Amsterdam, Rotterdam Fonds: BKVB, NAi Publishers.

Brett, G., Institute of International Visual Arts (2004), *Carnival of Perception: Selected Writings on Art*. London: Institute of International Visual Arts.

Bryan, D. (2000), *Orange Parades: The Politics of Ritual, Tradition and Control*. London: Pluto.

Bürger, P. (1984), *Theory of the Avant-garde*. Manchester: Manchester University Press.

Burns, L., Kenny, C. (eds) (2010), *The Applied Social Arts: Artur Zmijewski*. Dublin, Ireland: Fire Station Artists Studios.

Buskirk, M. (2005, 2003), *The Contingent Object of Contemporary Art*. Cambridge, Mass., London: M.I.T. Press.

Butler, J. (2010, 2009), *Frames of War: When is Life Grievable?* London: Verso.

Butler, J.P. (1997), *Excitable Speech: A Politics of the Performative*. New York, London: Routledge.

Cadman, C. (2010), *Pani: Performance Art Northern Ireland.* Belfast: 3rd edn, Bbeyond.

Cage, J. (1966, 1961), *Silence: Lectures and Writings*. Cambridge MA., London: M.I.T. Press.

CAIN (2012), Northern Ireland Conflict Archive, University of Ulster, http://cain.ulst.ac.uk. Accessed February 2012.

Caruth, C. (1995), *Trauma: Explorations in Memory*. Baltimore: Johns Hopkins University Press.

Caruth, C. (1996), *Unclaimed Experience: Trauma, Narrative, and History*. Baltimore, Md., London: Johns Hopkins University Press.

Christie, J., Gough, R., Watt, D.P. (2006), *A Performance Cosmology: Testimony From the Future, Evidence of the Past*. London: Routledge.

Clark, L.B. (2011), 'Never Again and its Discontents', *Performance Research 16* (1).

Cleveland, W. (2008), *Art and Upheaval: Artists on the World's Frontlines*. Oakland, CA: New Village Press.

Clode, George (2010), 'Car Bomb Goes on Display at Imperial War Museum', *Military History Monthly*, http://www.military-history.org/articles/car-bomb-on-display-at-the-imperial-war-museum.htm, Accessed February 2012.

Cohen, S. (2001), *States of Denial: Knowing About Atrocities and Suffering*. Cambridge: Polity.

Cohen-Cruz, J. (1998), *Radical Street Performance: An International Anthology.* Routledge, London.

Coleman, J., Rancière, J., Juncosa, E., Irish Museum of Modern Art (2009), *James Coleman*. Dublin: Irish Museum of Modern Art.

Coley, N., Fruit Market Gallery (2004), *Nathan Coley: There Will Be No Miracles Here*. Edinburgh: Fruitmarket Gallery.

Connerton, P. (1989), *How Societies Remember.* Cambridge: Cambridge University Press.

Crimewatch (2011), http://www.bbc.co.uk/crimewatch/appeals/2011/01/joyeates_latest.shtml. Accessed December 2011.

Cumings, B. (1992), *War and Television*. London: Verso.

Davis, M., Wallbridge, D. (1981), *Boundary and Space: An Introduction to the Work of D.W. Winnicott*. New York: Brunner/Mazel.

Deleuze, G., Guattari, F. (1977), *Anti-Oedipus: Capitalism and Schizophrenia*. New York: Viking Press.

Deleuze, G., Guattari, F. (1986), *Kafka: Toward a Minor Literature*. Minneapolis: University of Minnesota Press.

Deleuze, G., Guattari, F. (1988), *A Thousand Plateaus: Capitalism and Schizophrenia*. London: Athlone.

DeLillo, D. (2008, 2007), *Falling Man: A Novel*. London: Picador.

Dillon, M. (1992), *Stone Cold: The True Story of Michael Stone and the Milltown Massacre*. London: Hutchinson.

Doherty, C., Whitechapel Art Gallery (2009), *Situation*. Cambridge, Mass., London: MIT Press.

Doherty, W., Dziewior, Y., Mühling, M., McKee, F., Kunstverein in Hamburg, Städtische Galerie im Lenbachhaus München (2007), *Willie Doherty: Anthologie zeitbasierter Arbeiten = Anthology of Time-Based Works*. Ostfildern: Hatje Cantz.

Eisenman, S. (2010, 2007), *The Abu Ghraib Effect*. London: Reaktion.

Enwezor, O. (2002), *Experiments with Truth: Transitional Justice and the Processes of Truth and Reconciliation: Documenta 11, Platform 2*. Ostfildern-Ruit: Hatje Cantz.

Flannery, T. (ed) (2009), *Responding to the Ryan Report*. Blackrock, Co. Dublin: The Columba Press.

Fletcher, J., Benjamin, A.E. (1990), *Abjection, Melancholia, and Love: The Work of Julia Kristeva*. London: Routledge.

Frieling, R., San Francisco Museum of Modern Art (2008), *The Art of Participation: 1950 to Now.* London: Thames & Hudson.

Front Line, 'The Tank Man', http://www.pbs.org/wgbh/pages/frontline/tankman. Accessed January 2012.

Green, D., Lowry, J. (2002), 'From Presence to the Performative: Rethinking Photographic Indexicality', http://www.skol.ca/files/FromPresenceToThePerformative.pdf. Accessed September 2011.

Groys, B. (2008), 'Art at War', Kealy, S. (ed), *Signals in the Dark: Art in the Shadow of War*. Blackwood Gallery, Justina M. Barnicke Gallery: 9-16.

Guerin, F., Hallas, R. (2007), *The Image and the Witness: Trauma, Memory and Visual Culture*. London: Wallflower.

Halbwachs, M., Lewis, A.C. (1992), *On Collective Memory*. Chicago, London: University of Chicago Press.

Hamber, B. (2009), *Transforming Societies After Political Violence: Truth, Reconciliation, and Mental Health*. New York, London: Springer.

Harrington, J.P., Mitchell, E., American Conference for Irish Studies (1999), *Poli-*

tics and Performance in Contemporary Northern Ireland. Amherst: University of Massachusetts Press.

Sharon Hayes, Ashley Hunt, Katya Sander, David Thorne, Andrea Geyer (2012), *9 Scripts from a Nation at War* website, http://9scripts.info. Accessed February 2012.

Heathfield, A., Hsieh, T. (2009), *Out of Now: The Lifeworks of Tehching Hsieh*. Cambridge, Mass., London: MIT.

Heathfield, A., Tate Modern, Live Art Development Agency (2003), *Live Culture*. London: Tate Modern, Live Art Development Agency.

Hemispheric Institute (2012), http://hemisphericinstitute.org. Accessed March 2012.

Herman, J. (1992), *Trauma and Recovery*. London: Basic.

Higgins, P. (2012) 'Bombs could be performance art, lecturer tells trial',, http://www.belfasttelegraph.co.uk/news/local-national/bombs-could-be-performance-art--lecturer--tells--stone-trial-13982393.html. Accessed January 2012.

Hirschhorn, T., Bizzarri, T. (eds) (2011), *Establishing a Critical Corpus*. Zurich, Switzerland: JRP/Ringier.

Hodgkin, K., Radstone, S. (2003), *Contested Pasts: The Politics of Memory*. London: Routledge.

Holmes, S., Jermyn, D. (2004), *Understanding Reality Television*. London: Routledge.

Hoskins, A., O'Loughlin, B. (2010), *War and Media: The Emergence of Diffused War*. Cambridge: Polity.

Howell, A. (1998), *The Analysis of Performance Art: A Guide to its Theory and Practice*. Amsterdam: Harwood Academic.

Huyssen, A. (2003), *Present Pasts: Urban Palimpsests and the Politics of Memory*. Stanford, California: Stanford University Press.

Imperial War Museum, http://www.military-history.org/articles/car-bomb-on-display-at-the-imperial-war-museum.html. Accessed February 2012.

Irish Forum for Peace in Sri Lanka, http://ifpsl.org. Accessed February 2012.

Jaar, A. (2005), *The Fire This Time: Public Interventions 1979-2005*. Milano: Charta.

Jackson, S. (2011), *Social Works: Performing Art, Supporting Publics*. New York: Routledge.

Jones, A., Stephenson, A. (1999), *Performing the Body/Performing the Text*. Routledge, London.

Jones, A. (2006), 'Rupture', *Parachute*, no. 123: 15-37.

Jones, A. (2006), *Selfimage: Technology, Representation, and the Contemporary Subject*. London: Routledge.

Jung, C.G., Read, H. (1970, 1968), *The Collected Works of C.G. Jung*. London: Routledge & Kegan Paul.

Junod, T. (2009), 'The Falling Man', www.esquire.com/features/ESQ0903-SEP_FALLINGMAN. Accessed January 2009.

Kafka, F., Scott, D., Waller, C. (1977), *The Trial.* Pan Books, London.

Kantor, T., Kobialka, M. (1993), *A Journey Through Other Spaces: Essays and Manifestos, 1944-1990*. Berkeley, London: University of California Press.

Kealy, S. (2008), 'Maneuvering in the Shadows of Absolute War', Kealy, S. (ed), *Signals in the Dark: Art in the Shadow of War*. Blackwood Gallery, Justina M. Barnicke Gallery.

Kealy, S. (ed) (2008), *Signals In The Dark: Art in the Shadow of War*. Blackwood Gallery, Justina M. Barnicke Gallery.

Keenan, B. (1992), *An Evil Cradling*. London: Hutchinson.

Kester, G.H. (1998), *Art, Activism, and Oppositionality: Essays from Afterimage*. Durham NC: Duke University Press.

Kester, G.H. (2004), *Conversation Pieces: Community and Communication in Modern Art*. Berkeley, Calif., London: University of California Press.

Konig, K., Trummer, T.D., Brohm, A., Prinzing, A. (eds) (2012), *Before The Law*. Cologne: Museum Ludwig; Köln: Verlag Der Buchhandlung Walter König.

Krog, A. (1999, 1998), *Country of My Skull*. London: Vintage.

Kuhn, A., McAllister, K.E. (2006), *Locating Memory: Photographic Acts*. New York: Berghahn Books.

Lanzmann, C. (1995), 'The Obscenity of Understanding: An Evening with Claude Lanzmann', Caruth, C. (ed), *Trauma: Explorations in Memory*. Baltimore: Johns Hopkins University Press.

Lawlor, M. Director of Front Line, The International Foundation for the Protection of Human Rights Defenders, http://www.frontlinedefenders.org. Accessed March 2012.

Lederach, J.P. (1997), *Building Peace: Sustainable Reconciliation in Divided Societies*. Washington, DC: United States Institute of Peace Press.

Lerm Hayes, C-M. (2008), *Post-war Germany and 'Objective Chance': W.G. Sebald, Joseph Beuys and Tacita Dean = Nachkriegsdeutschland und 'Objektiver Zufall': W.G. Sebald, Joseph Beuys und Tacita Dean,* Göttingen: Steidl.

Lerm Hayes, C-M., Walters, V. (eds) (2011), *Beuysian Legacies in Ireland and Beyond: Art, Culture and Politics*. Berlin: LIT.

Levine, E.G., Levine, S.K. (eds) (2011), *Art in Action: Expressive Arts Therapy and Social Change*. London, Philadelphia: Jessica Kingsley Publishers.

Lippard, L.R. (1973), *Six Years: The Dematerialization of the Art Object from 1966 to 1972*. London Studio: Vista.

Lippard, L.R. (1984), *Get the Message?: A Decade of Art for Social Change*. New York: 1st edn, E.P. Dutton.

Macho, T. (2012), 'Case by Case Between Art and Law', König, K., Trummer, T.D., Brohm, A., Prinzing, A. (eds), *Before the Law*. Cologne: Museum Ludwig, Köln: Verlag Der Buchhandlung Walter König.

MacLennan, A. (2011), http://www.vads.ac.uk/collections/maclennan/. Accessed November 2011.

MacLennan, A., Snoddy, S., Arnolfini Gallery (1988), *Is No 1975-1988*. Bristol: Arnolfini.

Madison, D.S. (2010), *Acts of Activism: Human Rights as Radical Performance*. Cambridge: Cambridge University Press.

Massumi, B. (2002), *Parables for the Virtual: Movement, Affect, Sensation*. Durham, NC: Duke University Press.

Matheson, N. (2006), *The Sources of Surrealism*. Aldershot: Lund Humphries.

McIlroy, B. (1998), *Shooting to Kill: Filmmaking and the "Troubles" in Northern Ireland*. Trowbridge: Flicks Books.

McKittrick, D. (2000, 1999), *Lost Lives: The Stories of the Men, Women and Children who Died as a Result of the Northern Ireland Troubles*. Edinburgh: Mainstream.

Steve McQueen (2008), *Hunger*, film, also information at http://en.wikipedia.org/wiki/Hunger_(2008_film). Accessed February 2012

McQueen, S., Storr, R., Institute of Contemporary Arts, Kunsthalle Zurich (1999), *Steve McQueen*. London: Institute of Contemporary Arts.

Mey, K. (2007), *Art and Obscenity*. London: I. B. Tauris.

Mobius, www.mobius.org. Accessed February 2012.

Modern Art Oxford (2004), *Wherever I Am: Yael Bartana, Emily Jacir, Lee Miller*. Oxford: Modern Art Oxford.

Moeller, S.D. (1999), *Compassion Fatigue: How the Media Sell Disease, Famine, War and Death*. New York, London: Routledge.

Morel, G. (2002), 'The "Melancholization" of the Witness: The Impotence of Words, the Power of Images', Enwezor, O. (ed), *Experiments with Truth: Transitional Justice and the Processes of Truth and Reconciliation: Documenta 11, Platform 2*. Ostfildern-Ruit: Hatje Cantz.

Mulvey, L. (2006), *Death 24x a Second: Stillness and the Moving Image*. London: Reaktion.

Munroe, A., Yokohama Museum of Art, Solomon R. Guggenheim Museum, Japan Foundation, San Francisco Museum of Modern Art (1994), *Japanese Art After 1945: Scream Against the Sky*. New York: Harry N. Abrams in association with the Yokohama Museum of Art, the Japan Foundation, the Guggenheim Museum, and San Francisco Museum of Modern Art.

Mytkowska, J., Centre Georges Pompidou (2008), *Les Inquiets: Cinq Artistes Sous La Pression de la Guerre = The Anxious: Five Artists Under the Pressure of War*. Paris: Centre Pompidou.

Nedregard, A. (2012), Mag magazine no. 7, http://www.maagmag.com. Accessed February 2012.

New Lodge Six Inquiry (2002), www.theba2rrack.com. Accessed December 2011.

New Moves International, www.newmoves.co.uk and www.sohailkhan.co.uk. Accessed September 2011.

New Territories 09 (2009), International Festival of Live Art, Scotland, 11th February-21st March 2009, produced by New Moves International, www.newmoves.co.uk and www.sohailkhan.co.uk, Accessed September 2011.

Nielsen, T.O., Goll, M. (2011), *Trampolinhuset*, http://trampolinehouse.dk/about/history. Accessed November 2011.

Novick, P. (2000, 1999), *The Holocaust in American Life*. Boston, Mass Mariner.

O'Neill, P. (Chairperson), New Lodge Six Time For Truth Committee, December (2002), www.theba2rrack.com. Accessed December 2011.

O'Dell, K. (1998), *Contract With the Skin: Masochism, Performance Art and the 1970s*. Minneapolis, London: University of Minnesota Press.

Orlan, McCorquodale, D. (1996), *Orlan: Ceci est mon Corps, Ceci est mon Logiciel: This is my Body, This is my Software*. London: Black Dog.

O'Sullivan, S. (2006), *Art Encounters Deleuze and Guattari: Thought Beyond Representation*. Hampshire, New York: Palgrave Macmillan.

Patt, L., Dillbohner, C., Sebald, W.G., Lerm Hayes, C-M., Cross, D., Institute of Cultural Inquiry (2007), *Searching for Sebald: Photography After W.G. Sebald*. Los Angeles, Calif.: Institute of Cultural Inquiry.

People's Permanent Tribunal (2010), verdict document http://transcurrents.com/tc/2010/01/full_text_verdict_of_the_perma.html. Accessed February 2012.

Peace Women Across the Globe (2012). http://www.1000peacewomen.org/index.php. Accessed March 2012.

Phelan, P. (1993), *Unmarked: The Politics of Performance*. London: Routledge.

Phelan, P. (1997), *Mourning Sex: Performing Public Memories*. London: Routledge.

Pintilie, I. (2002), *Actionism in Romania During the Communist Era*. Cluj: Idea Design Et Print.

Polchin, J. (2007), 'Not Looking at Lynching Photographs', Guerin, F., Hallas, R. (eds), *The Image and the Witness: Trauma, Memory and Visual Culture*. London: Wallflower: 207-222.

Pope.L, W., Bessire, M., Maine College of Art. Institute of Contemporary Art

(2002), *William Pope.L: The Friendliest Black Artist in America*. Cambridge, Mass., London: MIT Press.

Popper, K.R., Eccles, J.C. (1977), *The Self and its Brain*. Berlin, New York: Springer International.

Purbrick, L., Aulich, J., Dawson, G. (2007), *Contested Spaces: Sites, Representations and Histories of Conflict*. New York: Palgrave.

Rancière, J. (2007), *The Future of the Image*. London: Verso.

Rancière, J. (2009), *The Emancipated Spectator*. London: Verso.

Ray, G. (2011), 'Mourning and Cosmopolitics: With and Beyond Beuys', Lerm-Hayes, C-M., Walters, V. (eds), *Beuysian Legacies in Ireland and Beyond: Art, Culture and Politics*. Berlin: LIT.

Ray, G. (2012), 'On the Conditions of Anti-Capitalist Art Radical Cultural Practices and the Capitalist Art System', http://.net/transversal/0806/ray/en. Accessed February 2012.

Retort (Organisation: San Francisco, Calif.), Boal, I.A. (2005), *Afflicted Powers: Capital and Spectacle in a New Age of War*. London: Verso.

Rolston, B., Miller, D. (1996), *War and Words: the Northern Ireland Media Reader*. Belfast: Beyond the Pale Publications.

Rosenthal, S., Foster, S.L., Lepecki, A., Phelan, P. (2010), *Move: Choreographing You*. London: Hayward.

Ross, F.C. (2003), *Bearing Witness: Women and the Truth and Reconciliation Commission in South Africa*. London, Sterling, Va.: Pluto Press.

Ruggles, D.F., Silverman, H. (2009), *Intangible Heritage Embodied*. London: Springer.

Rugoff, R., Stiles, K., Di Pietrantonio, G. (1996), *Paul McCarthy*. London: Phaidon.

Sandford, M.R. (1995), *Happenings and Other Acts*. London: Routledge.

Scarry, E. (1987, 1985), *The Body in Pain: The Making and Unmaking of the World*. New York, Oxford: Oxford University Press.

Schechner, R. (1988), *Performance Theory*. London: Routledge.

Schwartz, F.J. (2005), *Blind Spots: Critical Theory and the History of Art in Twentieth-Century Germany*. New Haven, Conn., London: Yale University Press.

Sebald, W.G. (2002, 1998), *The Rings of Saturn*. London: Vintage.

Sedgwick, E.K. (2003), *Touching Feeling: Affect, Pedagogy, Performativity*. Durham, N.C., London: Duke University Press.

Shevtsova, M. (2007), *Robert Wilson*. London, New York: Routledge.

Sholette, G. (2011), *Dark Matter: Art and Politics in the Age of Enterprise Culture*. London: Pluto.

Siegmund, G. (2011), 'The Space of Memory: William Forsythe's Ballets', Spier,

S. (ed), *William Forsythe and the Practice of Choreography*. London: Routledge.

Sitterle, K.A., Gurwitch, R.H. (1999), 'The Terrorist Bombing in Oklahoma City', Zinner, E.S., Williams, M.B. (eds), *When a Community Weeps: Case Studies in Group Survivorship*. Philadelphia: Taylor & Francis.

Sivan, E. (2002), 'Archive Images: Truth or Memory? The Case of Adolf Eichmann's Trial', Enwezor, O. (ed), *Experiments with Truth: Transitional Justice and the Processes of Truth and Reconciliation: Documenta 11, Platform 2*. Ostfildern-Ruit: Hatje Cantz.

Sooja, Kim (2012) 'A Needle Woman', MOMA PS1, http://momaps1.org/exhibitions/view/24. Accessed February 2012.

Spier, S. (ed) (2011), *William Forsythe and the Practice of Choreography*. London: Routledge.

Steinman, L. (1995), *The Knowing Body: The Artist as Storyteller in Contemporary Performance*. Berkeley, Calif.: 2nd edn, North Atlantic Books.

Stiles, K., Museum of Contemporary Art 1998, *Out of Actions: Between Performance and the Object, 1949-1979*. London: Thames & Hudson.

Stiles, K. (1993), 'Shaved Heads and Marked Bodies: Representations from Cultures of Trauma', http://www.duke.edu/web/art/stiles/shaved_heads.html. Accessed January 2012.

Stitt, A. (2001), *Small Time Life*. London: Black Dog Publishing.

Stitt, A. (2008), *Substance: Residues, Drawings & Partial Objects, 1976-2008*. Exeter: Spacex.

Stoller, P. (1997), *Sensuous Scholarship*. Philadelphia, Pa.: University of Pennsylvania Press.

Stone, M. (2003), *None Shall Divide Us*. London: John Blake.

Sulijevic, A., http://www.1000peacewomen.org. Accessed March 2012.

Tate Gallery Liverpool (2006), *Making History: Art and Documentary in Britain from 1929 to Now*. Liverpool: Tate Liverpool.

Taussig, M. (1987), *Shamanism, Colonialism, and the Wild Man: A Study in Terror and Healing*. London: University of Chicago Press, Ltd.

Taussig, M. (2006), *Walter Benjamin's Grave*. London: University of Chicago Press, Ltd.

Taylor, J. (1998), *Body Horror: Photojournalism, Catastrophe and War*. Manchester: Manchester University Press.

Turner, V. (1987), *The Anthropology of Performance*. New York: PAJ Publications.

Vaara, R., Ferre, S., Amos Anderson Art Museum, Jyva skyla Art Museum (2005), *Ars Fennica 2005*. Helsinki: Henna ja Pertti Niemisto n Kuvataidesa a Tio.

VADS, Live Art Archive, http://www.vads.ac.uk/resources/AMW.html. Accessed November 2011.

Viola, B. (1995), *The Passing*. Amsterdam: Editions à voir. Video.

Virilio, P., Fondation Cartier pour l'art contemporain (2003), *Unknown Quantity*. London Thames & Hudson.

Volkan, V.D. (1997), *Bloodlines: From Ethnic Pride to Ethnic Terrorism*. New York: Farrar, Straus and Giroux.

von Drathen, D. (2004), *Vortex of Silence: Proposition for an Art Criticism Beyond Aesthetic Categories*. Milano: Charta.

von Graevenitz, A., Kolberg, G., Museum Ludwig (2004), *AC: Dispersion Room: Reversal Room*. Köln: Walther König.

Warburg, A., Getty Research Institute for the History of Art and the Humanities (1999), *The Renewal of Pagan Antiquity: Contributions to the Cultural History of the European Renaissance*. Los Angeles, Calif.: Getty Research Institute for the History of Art and the Humanities.

Warr, T., Jones, A. (2000), *The Artist's Body*. London: Phaidon.

Weintraub, L., Danto, A.C., McEvilley, T. (1996), *Art on the Edge and Over: Searching for Art's Meaning in Contemporary Society, 1970s-1990s*. Litchfield, Conn.: Art Insights.

Eyal Weizman (2010), 'Forensic Architecture'. Lecture delivered at the RGS conference at the University of Ulster Belfast. A similar lecture is available at, http://aaschool.ac.uk//video/lecture.php?ID=1245. Accessed March 2012.

Welchman, J.C. (ed) (2006), *Institutional Critique and After*. Letzigraben, Zurich: JRP/Ringier.

Wong, E.L. (2007), 'Haunting Absences: Witnessing Loss in Doris Salcedo's Atrabilarios and Beyond', Guerin, F., Hallas, R. (eds), *The Image and the Witness: Trauma, Memory and Visual Culture*. London: Wallflower.

Young, A. (1995), *The Harmony of Illusions: Inventing Post-Traumatic Stress Disorder*. Princeton, N.J., Chichester: Princeton University Press.

Young, J.E. (1993), *The Texture of Memory: Holocaust Memorials and Meaning*. New Haven, London: Yale University Press.

Zimbardo, P.G. (2009, 2007), *The Lucifer Effect: How Good People Turn Evil*. London: Rider.

Zinner, E.S., Williams, M.B. (eds) (1999), *When a Community Weeps: Case Studies in Group Survivorship*. Philadelphia: Taylor & Francis.

APPENDIX

CUTTINGS 1

The crab pear tree marked itself out in my childhood imagination as a signpost in the centre of invisible pathways. Standing alone in the middle of the backfield, its fruit never ripened beyond embryonic bitter nodules: thick skinned and coarse, the colours on each fruit graduating from insipid green to mottled shades of russet brown. Each year we tentatively tasted the pears yearning for edible fruit. We fought with our fingers, piercing through the lower branches and twisting off the sturdy stems. Persistent in our investigations, we used our childish teeth to scrape away small slithers of the grainy flesh. However, the tree never succumbed to our desires for sweetness, each crop merely swelled into hard kernels before dropping decisively to the ground.

Whoever had planted the tree must have realised that they had left to the land something with a blighted future. It grew in a waterlogged part of the field, surrounded by a bank of nettles and crushed bricks. In among this debris we found old iron horse shoes and a rusted 'Rovers' biscuit tin, which we imagined had, at one time, held an illicit stash of money. However, this was all the treasure that the field offered up, so we grew content to plunder the tree for whatever pleasures it could provide. Whacking nettles with the gnarled fallen branches in some semblance of a 'Star Wars' laser battle, largely achieved through sound effects.

In our house it was never discussed. The carpet was heavily patterned in autumnal shades and I played in front of the coffee table with my back to the TV. In the schoolyard or in the homes of family friends the crisis was picked over and digested in fragmented conversations. Everyone had their hold on what it meant that ten men were slowly and interminably dying. It happened in the full glare of the media, yet without any images of their suffering and with the voices of their representatives masked by lip-synced actors.

It felt as if these deaths were occurring in a distant vacuum far removed from normal experience, and in a sense their deaths have always remained unimaginable. Not a shadow of a doubt was expressed in relation to the manner of their deaths. The politicians calmly spoke away each of the days that were counted out in numbers on the edge of the television screen.

Charles Haughey was elected Irish Taoiseach in December 1979. The election campaign was designed by the London-based advertising company Saatchi & Saatchi. They provided a new image for Haughey, modelled on the one that had brought Margaret Thatcher into power earlier in the same year.

Our parents brought us back swimming suits from America: one each. Mine had a leopard skin print in a silky material, the other one came in a curious silver foil fabric. We immediately named this costume 'Wonder Woman'. My sister and I both held fantasies that wearing it gave you superpowers and the capability of swimming faster than anyone else in the world. No amount of evidence to the contrary dispelled this theory.

David Bowie recorded the song *Jean Genie* in New York on the 6th October 1972. Bowie described it as "a bit of a smorgasbord of imagined Americana". It was Bobby Sands' favourite song and for a while he took to wearing denim in homage.

Our fingers used to handle unwieldy litre bottles of coke. The excitement of pouring and feeling the spasms of the bottle as the liquid exploded from the small plastic mouth. We would hold the bottle at crazy angles: drinking it while rocking backwards and forwards between gulps, enjoying each burst of sweetness. We had competitions swallowing it down, a kind of bravado for the burning aftermath of the bubbles spewing up in the throat and back into the passageway behind the nose and ears. Our eyes sparkling with the effort of giggling and holding down the sugary phlegm stuck in the throat, while tears squeezed out in eruptions of happiness.

Visitors to the wing of Maze prison where the "Hunger Strikers" were hospitalised, reported how, in his final days, Bobby Sands' eyes had turned bright orange.

One night in a storm the tree was blown over, half of its roots were torn out of the ground and left exposed as sharp white limbs stripped of bark. Yet, despite the odds, the tree continued to live on for several more years. The upper half maintained an indignant and resilient crown of greenery, while the leaves on the lower branches withered prematurely, as the branches gradually became imbedded into the earth. White blossoms came and went in quick succession. Shroud-like, the petals spread over the ground. The fruit again made its stubborn appearance, forced on early by the drought in the trunk, then falling and fermenting in the cage of branches left barren beneath. Gradually these dying branches were gnawed away by grazing animals in the height of summer, encased by clouds of tiny flies hovering among the raw animal smells of greasy strands of sheep's wool snagged on the coarse bark.

The last thing that Bobby Sands ever ate was an orange. He said that it tasted bitter.

CUTTINGS 2

Just moments after the Queen Mother died the BBC closed down broadcasting. For several minutes the television became a blank screen. I sat staring at the electronic object, so dense and funereal, vibrating with empty passing scenes.

The ceremonial preparations for her death had been kept waiting on standby. An entire state funeral held in cold storage. All the trappings of the public procession were lined up in rows of antique carriages, harnesses and uniforms. The news cameras scanned around the warehouses of preserved stately relics, waiting to enclose her passing into public memory.

I remember too the nightly watershed. The allure of adult television as the National Anthem pummeled the sitting room walls, floorboards and the wooden sides of the television cabinet. The Queen was sitting up high and immaculate in a uniform of reds and blues, diluted by the watery pixilation of the screen. What colour was the horse? The band kept playing, then the band stopped. The broadcast dissolved into the centre of the screen, dispersing the colours into a halo of grey light, separated beyond the eye's reach. I always found it mysterious to experience this ceremony, the Queen's departure from the room: her presence amongst us so familiar, but always distant and outside of us.

In a dream I am eating death. I devour it as a black liquid syrup from a white bowl. Each spoonful diffuses on the metal of the spoon into an oily brown ink stain. Lying in the dark liquid are images the size of negatives seeped in the juice. I poach them out onto the spoon, one image at a time, not salted, not sweet, slippery to the tongue. Before and between each mouthful I experience a memory of someone, a pause - a forgetting, a pause - a remembering - a likening to and a distancing from each person that forms the taste. Every one of these disappearances yields an indescribable flavor, dense and fetid clinging to the tongue.

Bobby Sands died in the Maze prison on the 5th May 1981. On the 20th July 1982 the IRA carried out two bombing attacks in London in Hyde Park and Regent's Park, which resulted in the deaths of eleven soldiers of the Household Cavalry and seven horses. Consequently, on this day at the end of the main evening news the BBC decided to implement a brief deviation from broadcasting protocol as an act of commemoration. The usual sign off was replaced by the Marine's band performing while a young boy wearing a uniform was shown, in slow motion, laying a wreath at the site of the bombing.

It was the fate of Sefton, one of the Cavalry horses critically injured in the car-mounted nail bomb attack that became the focus of national attention. The horse had been bred in County Waterford in Ireland in 1963 and bought by the British army as a four year old. Sefton's recovery was reported in news stories over several months, charting his gradual return to health, while the British public sent donations, get well cards and mints.

At the Comber cinema we observed the playing of the National Anthem at the end of every film. There was a certain inadvertent humour when the illusory worlds of *Jaws* and *James Bond* were replaced by the images of an ever-youthful Queen. Still, the Queen's horse flickers within my mind, hovering at the epicenter of the image, hooves raised alternately and irreversible. The reality of whether it was walking or trotting has become blurred into inert consciousness. She effortlessly glides across the screen, among a perfectly synchronized choreography of geometry and colours.

Standing for the anthem. There was a certain formality in that unbidden gesture. We learnt to rise up as we watched the same unchanging piece of film, The Queen, the horse, the soldiers on display. In the darkness, we too were on display. No command came to rise to the anthem, but still we learnt to do it. Obeying the invisible order, all of us with our faces hidden in the darkness, standing after the credits among the crackles of crisp packets on the floor and the sounds of coats being pulled on. The Queen rode by, immune to our efforts, never blinking: a displaced person traveling through the unnatural stillness of a mass of men ranked and featureless.

Eyes shut, I believe the horse was white. Polarized, reticent, it floats ghosted across the proceedings.

The night my grandmother died I stood in the bathroom watching for some time a small fruit fly trapped in the room. I watched it flying in circles in front of the mirror, illuminated by a long strip of fluorescent lighting. The insect floated as if on a carousel moving from visibility into invisibility, in and out of the light. All the while the circumference of its flight was never greater than ten centimeters away from the mirror that gently pulled it back magnetically towards the hollow brightness of the glass surface.

On 30th September 2012 police were alerted by a member of the public to the location of a navy Saab car parked in a bridleway. Beside the car, investigators found three mutilated bodies. One of the deceased was Michael Pedersen, a former Sergeant in the Household Cavalry. Pedersen had been the soldier who had ridden Sefton on the day of the Hyde Park bombing. On the ground beside him were the bodies of two of his children, Ben Pedersen, aged seven, and Freya Pedersen, aged six. Pedersen had fatally stabbed the children before taking his own life as an act of revenge on his estranged wife who had filed for divorce.

European Studies in Culture and Policy

edited by Prof. Máiréad Nic Craith (Heriot-Watt University, Edinburgh) and Prof. Ullrich Kockel (Heriot-Watt University, Edinburgh)

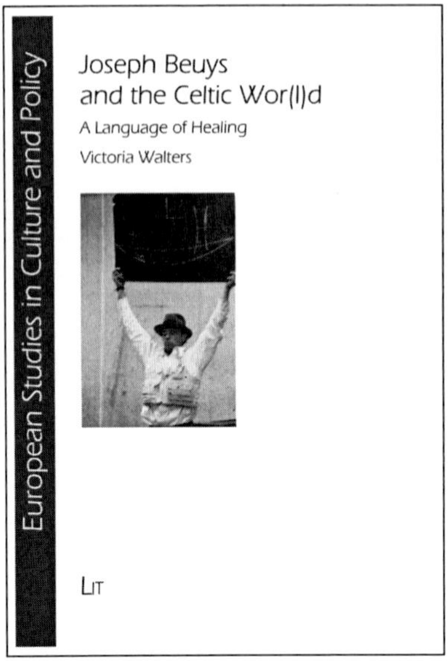

Victoria Walters
Joseph Beuys and the Celtic Wor(l)d
A Language of Healing

During the 1970s, the German sculptor Joseph Beuys made a number of trips to Ireland and Scotland. This interdisciplinary study of the artist's work in the "Celtic world" assesses whether the practice shown or developed during these visits could be seen, in any sense, as a language practice – more specifically as a "language of healing" – and whether Beuys could be said to have interpreted and performed notions of Celticity in these places. The book reflects on the anthropological aspect of Beuys' work and includes interview material with artists who worked with or met him at this time.

Bd. 10, 2012, 416 S., 39,90 €, br.,
ISBN 978-3-643-90105-7

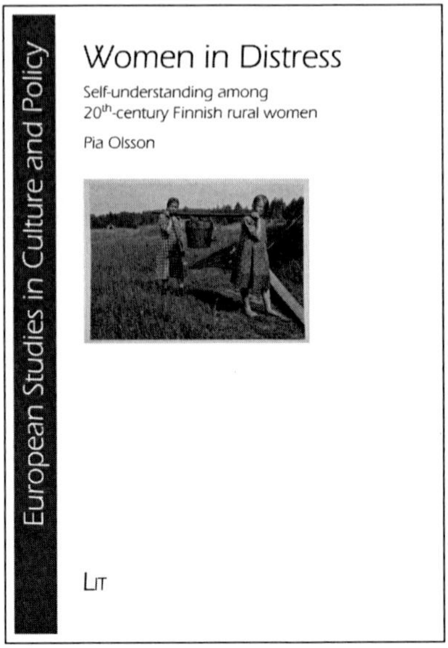

Pia Olsson
Women in Distress
Self-understanding among 20th-century Finnish rural women

Women in Distress presents Finnish women through their reminiscenses. These touching stories provide an idea of the many layered historical and personal elements that have affected rural women's lives during the 20th century. The research focuses on both the way women have experienced their lives and the way they have wanted to depict these experiences. At the societal level, the 20th century can be seen as a time of enormous change for women. However, at the core of these narrations, instances of missed opportunity, gender conflict and mental submission persist, thus challenging the image of the strong Finnish woman.

Bd. 11, 2011, 288 S., 29,90 €, br.,
ISBN 978-3-643-90133-0

LIT Verlag Berlin – Münster – Wien – Zürich – London

Auslieferung Deutschland / Österreich / Schweiz: siehe Impressumsseite